USMC

University of Science Music and Culture
or Uncle Sam's Misguided Children

CHAS ROMEO

PAGE PUBLISHING, INC.
New York, NY

First originally published by Page Publishing, Inc. 2019

ISBN 978-1-64424-902-4 (Paperback)
ISBN 978-1-64424-903-1 (Digital)

Printed in the United States of America

USMC stands for the United States Marine Corps but is sometimes referred to as Uncle Sam's misguided children. Eleanor Roosevelt once said, "The Marines I have seen around the world have the cleanest bodies, the filthiest minds, the highest morale, and the lowest morals of any group of animals I have ever seen. Thank God for the United States Marine Corps!" I prefer to refer to the USMC as the University of Science, Music, and Culture.

This title should tell you something. If you have ever been in the United States Marine Corps, you know exactly what USMC stands for and that is what this book is about. Now just because you've been there, don't throw this down. I think you'll like it. If you have never been in the corps, you are really in for an experience. It is spelled *corps*, but the *s* is silent so it is pronounced like the core of an apple, not pronounced like a dead body (corpse). This word is frequently mispronounced, just listen to our forty-forth president who, incidentally, also doesn't know why we salute each other or much else about the entire military over which he was commander and chief for eight years.

My tour began in June of 1962. I was eighteen years old and, I liked to think, was a typical eighteen-year-old who had just enlisted in the Marine Corps. I had an old Ford, floor shift and all that, a girlfriend, and I was ready for anything. I'm sure I was. I was on what they called the 120-day delay program. Meaning, I wasn't supposed to leave until September of that year. So when they called me in June, I was really wowed. It was a warm day, and I was on the front porch talking with my father when the phone rang. In the sixties, we still sat and talked with our fathers on our front porches and were happy to do it as they were, after all, our heroes.

"Hello," I said.

"Hello. May I speak to Mr. Chas Romeo?"

"This is Chas Romeo."

"Mr. Romeo, this is Staff Sergeant Dumbrowski, the Marine recruiter. Do you remember me?"

I had gone down to the recruiting center a month before I graduated from high school. "Ah yes, I do. What can I do for you?"

"Well, Mr. Romeo, we have had a couple of openings this month made available because our background investigations have turned up a couple of ringers whom we can't accept, and I was wondering if you could possibly make it this month."

Whoa! Rockets, flairs, explosions, and all that other American patriotic stuff. The Marine Corps needs me now! Goodbye, Mom, Dad, and girl.

I said, "Of course, I can make it. Just tell me when and where."

He gave me the information, then he said, "Goodbye and good luck, Marine. Hehehe."

Now you that have already been there, know what the *hehehe* was for, and you that haven't been there, will. Anyhow, it took me about three days to put *hehehe* together, and you'll never know how many times, during the next four months, I heard Sergeant Dumbrowski saying it.

I reported on June 20, 1962, at 9:30 a.m. to the City County Building in Detroit, Michigan, for the swearing-in process, which took about five minutes. They did forty of us at the same time. The oath, in general, says that you will do what you're called on to do by anyone who outranks you for as long as your enlistment lasts. Now just take a minute and let that soak in. Take a moment and give that some serious thought and remember you're going to sign papers and give your word in the form of an oath, the most serious thing there is, like God's covenant.

I went through boot camp in four months. It should have taken at least six months. I understand now that it is only three months, which is a crying shame, and in my eyes, the Marine Corps cannot survive as the greatest fighting organization in the world if they continue to downgrade their training. I really got carried away there, didn't I?

After the oath, we were told to be at Willow Run Airport at 7:00 p.m. to catch flight 333 to San Diego, California. Whoa, movie stars, sunshine, and fine cars. Oh, I almost forgot, beautiful California girls too. Yeah, that's the place for me. I was there on time, and I said goodbye to my father, mother, sister, brother, and my girl. I boarded the plane with the rest of the guys who, I'm sure, felt the same as I did that we were practically Marines already. Well, hell, about the only thing left was to put on the uniform and march away to war for country, family, and sweethearts. Of course, none of us would be killed in the next four years. And our girls would be waiting for us, just like we left them. Now those of you who have been in the corps know whether that last statement is true or not. And those of you who haven't been in the corps also know if that last statement is true or not. I mean, you guys were back home protecting them. Right? There's a real Dumbrowski, hehehe.

We boarded the plane, took our seats, taxied down the runway, and were on our way. There was small talk of this and that among one another, but I really don't think any of us had the vaguest idea what was about to happen. Four and one half hours later, we landed in San Diego. We wandered off the plan and into the terminal. There it was, California. We wandered around in groups of five or six, just looking at this or that, being careful to stay within earshot of the area designated for Marine recruits.

I guess maybe an hour passed before he arrived. He, being the sergeant, assigned to meet us and lead us to the recruit depot. He was such a commanding figure with his erect posture, no-nonsense demeanor, and immaculate uniform. I assumed he was late because he probably had to fight off seven or eight dozen people who wanted his autograph. About five minutes later, I decided he was late because he had to stop and pick up three or four pounds of raw meat, seasoned with gunpowder, to eat on his way over.

He strolled over to our area and asked if we were marine recruits. He got four or five yeses in reply and held a quick roll call and said, "You want to follow me?"

We did, and we did. We followed him through the airport terminal to the outside where it was early evening. There was a large bus with the Marine Corps emblem and *USMC* emblazoned on it. We were asked to file aboard in single file, two people per seat. We took our seats, and the chatter began immediately and lasted about eight seconds before we heard a loud roar. Heaven forbid, it was the friendly sergeant yelling and calling us names—bad names like long-haired civilians, turds, and things like that. He informed us that we were no longer civilians and ordered us to shut up, quit chattering like a bunch of schoolgirls, and sit up straight. Every word was yelled at the top of his lungs with veins popping on his neck and forehead and spittle flying with every word.

It was a quiet, uneventful ride lasting about twenty minutes. We all just kind of sat there looking at one another, stunned. The bus drove through the gates, passed by a few buildings, and stopped outside one large building. We were told that upon departing the bus we would see yellow footprints. We were to place our feet on a pair of them and stand still and shut up until further notice. We left the bus and found our prospective feet. About thirty minutes passed and this little corporal came out. We were all looking around, chatting, and were, quite frankly, happy to see the corporal instead of the grouchy sergeant. Not for long though. The first thing the corporal did was kick the biggest guy he could see right in the shins. The guy yelled, "Hot damn!"

And the corporal yelled, "Shut up and get your feet on the yellow prints. Keep your mouths shut and look straight ahead."

He began to chide us that we weren't in summer camp. We were in boot camp. And we were to follow him in a single line. He turned and walked away, and we followed. The big guy was still pretty upset and had a noticeable limp. We stopped at a doorway and were told that inside the doorway we would find a bucket. Each of us were to pick up a bucket and, in single file, move along a series of shelves that contained personal items such as soap, toothpaste, toothbrushes, etc. As we passed each shelf, we were to take one item per person. This process took about ten minutes, then he led us to a large room with benches and boxes. We were told to fill out an address tag with the address we wanted our personal belongings to go to, then strip our clothes off, place them in the box, seal it, place the address tag on it, and get back in single file as quickly as possible. This took about fifteen minutes. He then led us, single file, to a large shower. We were told to enter and find a shower, and we were instructed on the proper way to shower. "Water on, all wet, water off. Soap up, starting with your head and work down. Hair is dirty. Scrub that hair good, good, good. All soaped up, turn that water on and rinse. Shut water off, step out, and dry off. Now put on the utility trousers, the shower shoes, and the yellow sweatshirt with the big red Marine Corps emblem and follow me."

We followed him to a large squad bay. Upon entering, he told us to deposit our new belongings in the foot locker and stand by our racks. Racks are what our beds were called. They were two high, like bunk beds, with a bunch of springs hooked together and a four- inch cotton-filled mattress on top of the springs. If you had a bad back, it wasn't going to get any better. The locker box was just that—a box, about three foot long, two foot wide, and eighteen inches deep. When you opened the lid, there was a tray about three inches deep. That is where you kept your everyday stuff like soap, cigarettes, money, pictures, etc. The rest of the box, after you removed the tray, held your skivvies and clothes. Fully loaded, these boxes weighed about forty pounds and were one of our basic pieces of workout equipment. We were always carting them around, and they were our chair until we got out of basic training. I don't remember sitting on anything with a back where you could rest your back or abdominal muscles, except in a classroom, until I was out of boot camp.

Let me say here and now, there are many lessons to be learned in this book about how to build a strong body using everyday equipment, no expensive gyms. I almost forgot. Locker boxes had a handle at each end, and you could do curls and lift the box over your head. I cannot begin to imagine how many reverse push-ups I performed on mine. When they weren't being used in one of the aforementioned ways, they were stored under your rack to secure your property—even though none of us had anything of value as we had shipped all our rings, watches, money, change, etc. home the day before. There were no locks on the locker boxes either. Back in the sixties, and I hope even today, you didn't have to worry about one of your brothers stealing from you, and it wasn't because we didn't have thieves in the Marine Corps; it was because of the repercussions that would befall them if they were caught.

I'll never forget that one guy actually brought a radio and slippers to boot camp. He was definitely in the wrong place for those luxuries. The little corporal said, "You're at MCRD, not Annapolis." MCRD stood for Marine Corps Recruit Depot. Annapolis was where naval and marine officers trained. I almost forgot, you should have seen the big guy's shin. That little corporal kicked like a mule. The big guy and this little corporal were just bound to be good friends because the big guy kept smiling every time the corporal looked at him.

Apparently, the little corporal didn't like big guys who smiled at him because when he saw the big guy smiling at him he said, "What are you smiling at, you big shithead?"

And the big guy said, "Oh, nothing, sir. Nothing."

"Then quit smiling."

The big guy couldn't seem to do that, so the little corporal took one of the big guy's shower shoes, folded it in half, and told him to open his mouth. When he opened it, the little corporal jammed the shoe into his mouth. The big guy didn't say "hot damn" this time. In fact, he didn't say anything at all because he was using all the available space in his mouth to try to suck air into his lungs.

We were told that this place was called receiving, and we would be there until more people came. When enough came, we would form a platoon and leave. We were told the little red book in our buckets was called a guidebook, and we were to sit on the locker boxes and read the guidebook. One of the first things the guidebook says is, "The drill instructor (DI) and the recruit will have a father-son relationship." Boy, I can't speak for the big guy, or the rest of us, but I would sure be glad to get away from this corporal and grouchy sergeant and find this fatherly drill instructor because he sounded all right.

Sergeant Dumbrowski said, "Hehehe."

Well, it didn't take long for the rest of the guys to get there. They were coming in all night. Five here, ten there, and by morning, we had enough to leave. After a quick breakfast, we got back on the yellow footprints. This time, the big guy found a pair of footprints all the way in the rear. I guess he was already tired of being a leader. We kind of milled around for ten or fifteen minutes, and once in a while, someone would move the blind on a window in the building we were standing outside of, and we would all quit milling around and stand still. Then two marines came outside. These guys were real Marines. They were both sergeants. One was about six feet three inches, 220 pounds, and looked very fit. The other was about six feet tall and weighed 230 pounds. He wasn't as tall as the other guy, but God, he was enormous. His arms were like tree trunks. He just stood there with his hands on his hips, flexing his tree trunks.

The taller one introduced himself, "My name is Sergeant Erwin. I am your platoon commander. This is Sergeant Mills. He will be one of your drill instructors. We are going to leave here and go to our platoon area. There is a facing movement you will be familiar with in a few weeks. It's called about-face. For now, we'll just say turn around, so, everyone, turn around."

We all turned around. Some better than others, but we all made it eventually. Sergeant Erwin went to the front, and Sergeant Mills stayed behind.

Erwin said, "Let's go, herd."

And we started following him. Guess who was right up front again? Yep, the big guy. Well, fate works in funny ways. At least the little corporal he'd made friends with was staying behind, so hopefully his shins were safe and he wouldn't be tasting shower shoes anymore.

We were still in our shower shoes and having a great deal of trouble keeping up with Sergeant Erwin. He never even looked back, and Sergeant Mills just kept nudging us along. We finally made it to our new home. We were assigned racks and locker boxes and were herded over to supply for our basic clothing issue—boots, trousers, shirts, jackets, socks, skivvies, and more. Then we were herded back home. By the time we finished, we were all ready for a rest, but there was no rest. Sergeant Erwin told us to take our gear, put it on our racks, put on a pair of boots with socks, grab a hat or utility cover, and get back outside. We did. One guy must have known someone who had been in the corps who told him to do exactly what he was told and only what he was told because he was the only guy who didn't have to do extra push-ups.

We were told to take our sweatshirts off and throw them on our racks and return to the street. They wanted us shirtless so they could evaluate our state of physical fitness. A shirt can hide many flaws, but bare chested, they could evaluate us better and see where the real work was needed. Erwin lined us up in two columns, one on each side of the road. He informed us that, from now on, that road would be called the Platoon Street, and when we were told to fall out on the Platoon Street, this is where we would come and how we would stand. He asked us if we understood, and we answered yes. There was one "Yes, sir."

Erwin looked a little mad, disgusted even, and he said, "From now on, you will answer all questions with a loud, 'Sir, yes, sir,' or a loud, 'Sir, no sir.' Do you understand?"

"Sir, yes sir," we all replied, mostly together.

Then he said, "I can't hear you."

And we said, "Sir, yes, sir." Louder and better but it was still not good enough for him because we stood out there for another thirty minutes practicing saying, "Sir, yes, sir" and "Sir, no, sir."

We got good and finally did it all together and loud enough and he said, "Okay, I heard you that time."

Lesson: repetition is a good teacher, but practical application is better. You see, you've learned in these past few pages how to exercise with a wooden box and that repetition and practical application are the best teachers. Oh, me, oh my, there is so much more ahead. We stumbled from our platoon area to the barber shop. We lined up and entered one at a time. It took about sixty seconds per man. Sit down, towel on, clipper on, buzz, buzz, buzz, no more hair, out of the chair and out the door. There was one more thing; they would ask you if you had any moles on your head. If you had any, you were sup-posed to put your index finger on it. If you'd never had your hair cut short enough to know if you had any moles, then when you started bleeding, you would know. Sergeant Mills was waiting, and when we were all looking the same, we went to lunch. We were told we would grab a tray upon entering, line up, and sidestep along the counter. When we saw something, we wanted we would hold our tray out to the person who was serving that item. There were several people in our platoon who were overweight. These people were instructed to yell the word *diet* as they went through the chow line, and they were denied potatoes and all other starchy foods and were given extra high protein foods and salad. There is another lesson on how to lose weight fast. If it's white, it ain't right, do three hours of physical train-ing (PT) a day, and run everywhere you go.

There was also a reason why the heavy person yelled all the way through the chow line that he was on a diet. It embarrassed and humiliated him and motivated him to be like the rest of us and psychologically imprinted in his brain housing unit to stay lean and in shape. Viva la corps! How smart are these people? They have it all figured out. It's not nice, and it's not politically correct, but damn if it didn't work.

We were led to tables with benches arranged in neat, orderly rows. We lined up, elbow to elbow, and we were told to place our trays down in front of us on the table and were given the order, "Ready seats." Nobody did anything except one guy who sat down. When nobody said anything to him, we all started to sit, and we were all told to rise again. The order was explained to us. We were to stand in front of our trays until given the order, "Ready seats." We were then to sit rapidly with our arms folded in front of us.

Mills then said, "Understand?"

"Sir, yes, sir."

"I can't hear you, girls! Understand?"

"Sir, yes, sir." Louder this time.

"All right. Ready seats." And we all clunked down. Not good enough. We were told to stand again and were given the command, "Ready seats." And we clunked down again. Still not good enough, so we ready seated and clunked down for about thirty minutes before we finally made it and were allowed to sit down. God, my tailbone hurt and my food was cold.

We all started to eat, and we almost got the first mouthful in when Erwin yelled, "Oh no, girls, arms folded until the order 'Eat' is given." We practiced that for about five more minutes, and then we were finally able to eat our very cold food. We had about five minutes to eat; then because we had wasted so much time, we had to run back to our platoon area. As a matter of fact, we would run everywhere from now on. Everywhere.

When we almost got to our platoon area, we were stopped outside a building with a name on it. The nameplate read Head. We were told that it was a bathroom and that, from now on, their orders would be repeated by us.

Erwin said, "Head calls are in order for five minutes."

We all repeated, "Sir, head calls are in order for five minutes, sir."

He said, "Make 'em."

And we said, "Sir, make 'em, sir."

And he said, "Now you say, 'Sir, aye, aye, sir' and you do it."

Aye, aye in the corps means "I hear, understand, and will obey." We did as we were told and entered the head. There were about fifteen stools and five urinals where approximately six guys could stand at a time. Those of us who had to relieve ourselves used the facilities.

Exactly five minutes later, Erwin and Mills came in yelling, "Get outside! Your five minutes are up!"

There were some guys who were waiting for a stool and some waiting for a urinal. They were physically thrown outside. The ones still trying to relieve themselves were removed from their thrones and thrown outside. Jesus, these two guys were really strong. Mills grabbed me by the shoulder at the urinal and almost picked me up and threw me outside with one hand, and I weighed about 160 pounds. Christ, we were all tucking in and pulling up, trying to figure where we were and what the hell had happened.

Then we double-timed back to our area, lined up on the Platoon Street, and practiced repeating orders saying, "Sir, yes, sir" and "Sir, no, sir." I only stress this again because the first and last word out of a recruit's mouth when addressing a DI was *sir*.

Up until this time there really hadn't been any rough stuff, and everyone felt it was all right playing these silly games. As we practiced repeating orders that Sergeant Mills was saying, Sergeant Erwin was familiarizing himself with us one at a time. I thought, at first, he was taking neck sizes for uniforms, but I soon found out differently. As he approached me, I kind of looked at him and he looked at me. God, he was angry, but why?

He said, "What's your name?"

I said, "Chas."

He said, "Chas? What kind of a name is that?"

I said, "I don't know. I think it's English for Charles."

He said, "What's your last name?"

I said, "Romeo."

"Romeo? Are you Italian?"

I said, "Yes, I mean, sir, yes, sir."

He said, "I hate Italians." What was I supposed to say to that? Then he said, "Do you like me, Romeo?"

I replied, "Sir, yes, sir."

"Oh, you do, do you?"

"Sir, yes, sir."

"Why do you like me?" No answer from me.

"Are you a queer, Romeo?"

"Sir, no, sir."

"Then how come you like me? I'm a man. Don't I look like a man?"

"Sir, yes, sir, you do."

He said, "Ewe? Ewe? Who are you calling an ewe? Do you know what an ewe is?"

"Sir, no, sir."

"An ewe is a female sheep. Do I look like a female sheep?"

"Sir, no, sir."

"Then don't you ever call me an ewe again. Understand?" he yelled.

"Sir, yes, sir!" I yelled.

POW! He had me, and he was killing me. I know he was. He had placed one hand behind my neck, and with the other hand, he encircled my voice box. He placed his fingers on one side and his thumb on the other side, then pressed in until they were behind my windpipe, then he closed his hand and started asking me questions. I couldn't answer because all I could do was breathe. My eyes immediately began to water. He was right in my face, telling me that from now on the first and last words out of my mouth would be *sir* and he was not an ewe. He was the platoon commander. Did I understand? I tried again but couldn't speak.

He released his iron grip a little, and I said, "Yes, sir."

He squeezed again and said, "Sir, yes, sir. First and last, got it?"

He loosened his grip, and I said, "Sir, yes, sir."

He tightened his grip again and explained that it only took about three pounds of direct pressure to crush my esophagus and that if he did, breathing would become very difficult. I was thinking, *Oh yeah, wow, you've got terrific control.* He let go of me finally and proceeded onto another esophagus. My gus stayed sore for about ten minutes. I just stood there making my old gus practice swallowing. That particular hold, I learned later, was Sergeant Erwin's favorite.

After he finished making his rounds and introducing himself and his favorite hold to five or six of us, he placed himself at the head of his platoon and began instructing us on the proper way to do push-ups, sit-ups, squat thrusts, jumping jacks, pull-ups, not chin-ups, and a number of other bodybuilders. He was really something, but Sergeant Mills was even more. He didn't say much, but when he did, he only had to say it once. As a matter of fact, from that day on, neither one of them had to repeat anything. We did it for them. They had our undivided attention.

That word, *attention*, was one that took a lot of learning. We were taught the position of attention that same day—your heels together, toes spread at a forty-five-degree angle, hands along your sides, thumbs next to the seam in your trousers, stomach in, chest out, head and eyes straight ahead. We were not only told; we were also given time to practice the position, and while we practiced, they helped. They straightened backs, spread toes, closed hands, sucked in tummies, and straightened heads and eyes. When they finally got everyone properly adjusted, they just backed up and watched for about an hour. Every once in a while, you would hear a weird sound, kind of like someone dropping a large soft item from a few feet in the air to the ground. *Splat.* That sound turned out to be a recruit collapsing and hitting the ground. When you're at the position of attention, your head and eyes are looking straight ahead so you only see the back of the head of the recruit in front of you. Also, your chest is out, stomach is in, and your legs are straight, but if you lock your legs in the knees, it cuts the flow of blood to the brain, and after a while, you become that heavy sack making that splat sound as you drop to the ground. I'm sure the DIs had had the phenomenon happen with other platoons, but truly there is nothing like practical application to teach a person a principal. So after about four guys dropped, we were all told not to lock our knees. Keep that part of our bodies relaxed and the rest of our body rigid.

Then it was time for dinner. We were told to enter our huts, which were cement floored, galvanized metal covered, Quonset huts. We were supposed to get one towel and one bar of soap and return to the street quickly.

We said, "Sir, aye, aye, sir" and scrambled off to do so.

Upon returning, we were told we were too slow. We were ordered to return our soap and towel to our locker boxes and come back out. We did. Then we were told to go get them again. We did and, again, too slow. We repeated the process about fifteen times, each time improving our speed, but each time someone would be straggling a little too far behind and we all paid the price. This was the beginning of an established practice. The one who was last was encouraged to increase his speed by Erwin and Mills.

Finally, we did it well enough. I really think we fell out so quickly and organized that last time that they couldn't tell who was last. Just as we were about to leave to wash up for chow, Sergeant Erwin noticed a discrepancy in one of our people. He had forgotten his soap or dropped it or something. When you've got twenty guys trying to get in and out of a doorway at the same time, survival is hard enough, let alone keeping track of your soap. Well, this person was asked to return to get his soap, and the DI's told him to take his time. No hurry. While he was getting his soap, we did push-ups. When he finally came back, we snapped to attention. We double-timed to the wash house and were given five minutes to wash and get back out on the street. We didn't make it. Again and again we were helped out. Eventually we would wash up, make our head calls, and everything else in extremely short amounts of time.

We lined up outside and double-timed to the mess hall. The procedure from lunch was repeated but for only about twenty minutes of standing and sitting this time. We were getting better. After chow, we double-timed to the platoon area and did some more bodybuilding, and we learned from now on that this physical training would be called PT.

At approximately 7:30 p.m., we were told to go into our huts, undress, wrap a towel around us, put our shower shoes on, get a bar of soap, and return to the Platoon Street. We had five minutes to accomplish this. We didn't make it and repeated the process until 8:30 p.m. We were then told to run to the shower house and shave and shower. Let me tell you, I've spent a lot of time in my eighteen years on the planet with shoes on or barefooted. I never owned a pair of shower shoes or flip-flops as they were called in the corps. So the first time I had to run in them, it was a challenging experience for me, as well as most of the other guys.

By the time we arrived at the showers, there were only a few of us who weren't wounded and more than a few of us who would be buying a new pair of those bloody flip-flops. We were given twenty minutes to shave and shower. I was lucky I didn't have to shave every day. I could get away with shaving every two or three days, so all I had to do was find a way to get some of that water on me, soap up, and rinse. I made it but some didn't, and they were removed on precisely the twentieth moment. Some half shaved, some half showered, but all out. We again double-timed back to our platoon area. The distance between these two areas was only one hundred yards. We lined up and were told to go inside, put on some clean trousers and a T-shirt, and return. We did.

Sergeant Erwin told us he realized that some of us probably smoked and that, as a matter of fact, he did too. He told us that, depending on how well we did, our smoking lamp would be lit once, twice, or even three times a day. Wow. I was a smoker, but up until that moment, I had never even thought about a cigarette, but I was thinking about it now. Hell, none of us had any cigarettes because we had sent all our personal effects home.

Sergeant Erwin said, "Smoking lamp is lit."

We repeated, "Sir, smoking lamp is lit, sir."

And he said, "Light 'em," and we said, "Sir, light 'em, sir."

He pulled one out. A Pall Mall, my brand. You'll never guess where he pulled one out from. Okay, I'll tell ya. He pulled up his pant cuff, pulled his sock away from his leg, and pulled the pack of cigarettes out. We all just looked at one another as he lit up and started smoking. We all just breathed in hard and imagined. He told us that tomorrow we would be taken to the PX (post exchange) and be allowed to carry cigarettes and matches but would not be allowed to smoke until we were told to. Anyone caught smoking without permission would be disciplined harshly.

By this time, it was 9:00 p.m. and almost bedtime. We had half an hour to write home or read our guidebooks. Nobody had pen or pencil, so we read our guidebooks aloud and together. Sergeant Mills led us. When he got to the part how the DI and the recruit would have a father-son relationship, Sergeant Erwin cut in and informed us that we would, indeed, have a father-son relationship. He told us how his father had beaten him when he screwed up. Oh boy. Can't wait.

At precisely 9:30 p.m., we were put to bed. I'm going to tell you that there were all kinds of crazy ideas running through my head, like running away, calling my dad, and telling him these big men were mean and I wanted to come home. I probably would have too, but the thought of either one of those guys catching me was enough to change my mind. I decided to try it another day. Sleep came really easily as I was exhausted, and so was everyone else.

At exactly 5:30 a.m., the door to our hut was torn off and thrown inside. Reveille was blowing outside over the loudspeakers, and Sergeant Erwin was blowing on the inside.

"Get up you maggots. Out of those racks. Hit the deck!"

The deck was what marines and sailors called the floor. You already know what a rack is, and right then and there, we were maggots. I remember one guy named Witski. He was a slow waker, and he was mumbling about how he wasn't getting up and wasn't going to school anymore. Erwin walked over to his rack and pulled his blanket down around his legs. Witski yelled at him, called him a son of a bitch, and muttered unintelligibly. We couldn't make out exactly what he was saying because, before he was finished, he was lifted out of his top rack and deposited on the cement floor. He foolishly took a swing at the sergeant and was caught by him in his favorite hold and placed on the floor again. He finally woke up, stood up, and was slapped around for a few minutes. Then we were all told that the only one who would do any swinging would be Sergeants Erwin, Mills, Whaley, or Connors, and if anyone thought they could beat his ass, they were to speak up now and he would meet them in the duty hut right now. There were no takers for that offer.

We were told to dress and fall out for morning chow. About ten minutes later, we were all out on the street. It was still dark. We were told to spread out and get a double-arms distance between one another. This would later come to be known as our PT formation. We began doing PT for approximately half an hour. Then we got soap and towel and double-timed to the washhouse where, once again, we were given five minutes to wash ourselves and brush our teeth. Again, you've got to imagine the pushing and shoving and outright fighting that took place as sixty people fought for sixteen sinks. Everything was hurry, hurry, hurry, and hurry some more. Then they came in. Only this time there were four. Two more sergeants than last time. If you had any thoughts about trying anything, forget it now. We went to chow.

There were three hundred people, all recruits, all waiting to eat. It was time to learn another thing about the corps. You hurried everywhere, and when you got there, you waited. You didn't just stand around; you read your guidebook aloud and together or you did PT together. You did everything together. There was no privacy, no freedom, no choice. You were told when to eat, sleep, wake, shit, smoke, and speak. I began to feel like these people were Communists and I hadn't been flown to California at all but to some prisoner of war camp. We finally got to eat, and eat we did. We were all hungry. Some of us even took more than we could eat, but as we left the chow hall, one of the new sergeants named Connors checked our tray, and if there was anything left on your tray, you were pulled aside and made to eat it. Even if it made you sick. And while you were being made sick, the rest of the people were doing more PT and getting madder and madder at you.

In the beginning, one day ago ("in the beginning"—aren't those the first three words in the Bible?), you were told to take all you wanted but to eat all you took. It didn't take another meal for everyone to learn that lesson. There was no waste in the corps. Everything was done efficiently. The trays we ate off of were made of stainless steel with nice round compartments (one large and three or four smaller ones), so you could compartmentalize your food if you were a picky eater, and the servers would cooperate. Usually you would take some potatoes, meat, and a vegetable, and they all went on the larger area and the fruits would go in the smaller areas. You could manipulate the tray, so most of it went in one of the smaller compartments. If not, it was all going to the same place anyway. Get used to it. After everyone finished eating, each recruit washed their own tray once they were outside of the mess hall. There would be a person from the mess hall standing outside, watching you clean your tray. There were four forty-gallon metal trash cans. The first one was where you turned your tray over and banged it hard enough on the inside of the can to knock all the garbage off. The second can was full of hot soapy water, and the third and fourth cans were filled with hot, clean rinse water. We were told to dip our trays in each of these cans three times, and at the end of the line, you showed your tray to the mess hall guy and stacked it. Then a recruit would grab as big a stack as he could handle and run them around to the back of the mess hall to the scullery man.

The Marine Corps is the most efficient of machines. No muss, no fuss, and no waste. We returned to the platoon area where head calls were in order for five minutes, then back to the Platoon Street. Introductions were in order. The first new sergeant was Sergeant. Connors. He was about five feet eleven inches and 170 pounds. A nervous type. The other sergeant was Sergeant Whaley. He was about five feet nine inches and 150 pounds, and he just looked real mean. He had this way of getting nose to nose with you and yelling in your face as loud as he could. If he yelled loud enough and long enough, he actually started to foam at the mouth and spit all over you. He hated everyone. He would end up being a real problem for me and cause me, for the first and only time, to disobey an order in boot camp. Introductions over, we were lined up and given instructions on how to march—left, right, left, right. We left-righted over to the PX and were allowed to purchase our personal things and one carton of cigarettes, which cost approximately two dollars.

We returned home and put our gear away and fell out on the street. It was just about lunchtime, and there wasn't anything better to do, so we PT'd, washed up, and went to lunch, double-timing all the way, of course, only to stand and wait to eat. We ate and returned to the platoon area where we were allowed to smoke our first cigarette. It was good. We were taught to fieldstrip it when we were done and dispose of what was left. Then we were broken down into squads— four squads, approximately fifteen men per squad. The Marine Corps would place four platoons in a sequenced series, such as one, two, three, and four. Our series consisted of platoons 186, 187, 188, and 189. My platoon was 189. These four platoons never speak to one another. They are stabled within a small area together, but each platoon has its own area and no one from another platoon or series is allowed in another platoon's area or on their street. As I said, we saw the other platoons but never talked. We were in continuous competition. We tried to outyell, outrun, outdrill, and even physically beat one another.

We were told, then, that if any other DI or officer entered our platoon area, we were to subdue that person and bring them to the duty hut, which is where the DIs lived while on duty. We were then instructed to go inside and bring out our locker boxes with both pair of boots. We were all issued two pairs of boots. You would wear one pair for a few days and then the other pair for a few days. It allowed the boots to dry out and extended their life. We were taught how to polish our boots. Then we got our dirty laundry and our bottle of detergent, and we were introduced to the washrack and how to do our laundry. I have to describe the washrack. It was elevated off the ground on a large cement slab. There were faucets about every three feet that drained into a cement trough. You got the water temperature right, soaked your item, and used your scrub brush to scrub it. Then you rinsed your item, wrung it out, carried it to where you hung it up to dry.

Here comes another lesson you civilians never thought of. A fellow can get pretty strong scrubbing fifteen or twenty items of clothing every three or four days. But it isn't the scrubbing that makes you strong; it's the wringing the clothes really good that builds those hands up to where anything you grab you can hold on to. See, everything was about saving money and building a strong machine. The better you wrung your clothes out, the faster they dried. When it was time to collect your laundry, if it wasn't dry, you wore it wet. End of lesson.

The next four months, we did our laundry, and there was an amazing amount of accidents in this seemingly harmless looking place as well as the shower room. After the washing detail was secured, it was time for our evening meal. It was our usual process—hurry up and wait. There was only one thing that was different at this meal. At the end of the chow line, there were little Dixie cups of sherbet ice cream. We were told to take one and eat it all, and we did. We hadn't had any candy for days. The corps doesn't call it candy; they call it pogey bait.

About three months later, I figured out what the ice cream was for. For three months, we weren't allowed any candy or other sweets, but every day at the evening meal we were forced to eat this little ice-cream treat. Why? I couldn't figure it out. About six days before graduation, the ice cream was gone. No one asked why or where, but it was gone. Then about three days before graduation, at about 10:00

p.m., thirty minutes after we were put to bed, I realized what the ice cream was all about. We were all like a band of brothers by that time, and we weren't shy about our bodies or their functions since we'd been doing everything in front of everyone else.

I heard someone say, "Hey, you guys, I've got a hard on."

Someone else yelled, "Bullshit!"

Then someone else said, "Hey, no shit, me too. Hot damn, I'm gonna jack off."

Another voice saying, "Hey, mine's hard too!"

In about twenty minutes, 70 percent of the guys were loping their lamas, beating their rats, choking their chickens, or pounding their pud. Mary Palm and Five-Fingered Lily were worn to a frazzle that night. It appears they had been feeding us a steady diet of salt-peter to keep our bones bent and our minds on the program—their program. Three months we shared our living quarters, and none of us realized our little buddy wasn't there looking up at us every morning like he had been since we were twelve.

After we finished our meal and our ice cream, we filed out and double-timed back to our platoon area for head calls and more PT. At around 8:00 p.m., we were showered and shaved, and by 8:30 p.m. back on the Platoon Street for mail call. Mail call. Hot damn! This isn't half as enthusiastic as we really were. Hell, we lived through everything and anything for the next four months just to make it to mail call. Mostly because it meant the end of the day and about forty-five minutes to write home or talk to one another about back home before bed. We were lined up in two columns, one on each side of the street, and we were instructed on the proper way to receive our mail. When our name was called, we were to answer, "Sir, Private So-and-So, serial number such and such, here, sir."

Then we were to break from the formation, run to the DI holding mail call, stop, slap our hands together over the letter he held out, and return on the double to our place in the formation. Simple, right? Right. That night, only twelve people got their mail. Everyone else blew it and had to wait until tomorrow to try it again. After that first night, there was a lot of practicing going on before taps sounded.

Tomorrow came and was just like the day before, only more things to do, further distances to run, more time to PT, more shots to get, classes to attend, and, finally, the shower and mail call. More of us answered right this night, but still not all of us. Someone was always doing something wrong. In one case, the person who had sent the letter, probably a girl about seventeen, had written on the back of the letter *SWAK*, which stands for "sealed with a kiss." Cute, right? Well, Whaley didn't think so. When Roberts snatched the letter and started to return to formation, he was snatched by the stacking swivel. You guessed it, Erwin's favorite hold. A stacking swivel is located about four to six inches from the end of the barrel on a rifle, just about where your neck is located on your body below your head. It is used to stack two to four rifles together in an upright position, like a tripod, making it easy to access them and keeping them out of the dirt. It was explained to Roberts and the rest of us that for every letter written on the envelope or package you received that wasn't part of the address or return address, you would perform twenty-five push-ups before you received the letter. Roberts knocked off one hundred good ones for SWAK.

We all immediately relayed this message to our loved ones. I said a silent prayer for future mail. I informed my significant other about the new rule because sometimes she wrote more on the envelope than she did in the letter. I could have been doing push-ups until morning chow if she really felt loving. Before she received my message, as it turned out, I did a few hundred extra and so did most of the other guys. It wasn't as bad as the guys who received large boxes of goodies. You know, a whole batch of mom's cookies or a bunch of your favorite candy bars. You know, one of those five-pound packages. These guys were called up first and shown the package, and if there were any cute notes from mom or your girl, such as I know these are your favorite kind, see mom still loves her little man. XXXOOO—that's three kisses and three hugs. They were told to read the notes out loud, then they were forced to eat all the contents themselves and to drink warm water. The results were inevitable—vomit. I suspect the warm water created a foamy, sudsy effect that the stomach rejected.

I told you, the corps is the most proficient, economical corporation on the planet. They know how to do everything and get the results they want without wasting a penny. Some of the guys thought they would find a way around this dilemma by notifying their loved ones not to send little love notes and only enough candy or cookies for one sitting. No big package. Ha ha, got the last laugh that time. So a couple of weeks later, one of the guys got his first special package. It was about one pound of Saunders candy. He was called forward and received his package. Got his warm water and returned to eat his candy. The problem was he had to eat his candy and the little individual wrapper that it came in inside the box. Hehehe. Enter Sergeant Dumbrowski. The crotch wins again.

For the next two weeks, several other recruits learned to eat candy, wrapper and all, until the people at home were finally all notified to forget the goodies. Every once in a while, a girl would try to sneak a piece of gum in a letter. I guess that tinfoil really raises hell with the fillings. After about a month, everyone got their signals straight and mail call was pretty routine for everyone, except me. About every two weeks, my girlfriend would get mad at me because she was sure I was running all over California cavorting with the movie stars. She would write *SWAK* on the envelope or *I love you* just to make sure I got punished. *SWAK* was good for 100 push-ups, and if I wrote her a letter complaining about the *SWAK*, she would get mad and send the next envelope with something like *ZBAYXNMBGTH*. That was good for 275 push-ups. I never could figure out what it meant, but I was sure the last three letters meant go to hell. I felt like I was already there, so I ignored it.

The shots they gave us were really something. They'd line us up single file at one door and we would go in, and there would be one corpsman on each side of us. They stood back a foot or two and kind of threw the syringes at us like a dart at a dartboard. Then they would pull it back out and rub the spot off with alcohol, and we would go out the other door and do push-ups until everyone was through. The push-ups helped get the medicine into our system quickly.

I remember when I was in Vietnam. I was supposed to come home, and I couldn't find my shot card. They couldn't find my medical records, and I had to leave that day. There was no alternative; I had to receive an entire series of shots. I got eleven altogether—five in one arm and six in the other; then I boarded a jet and flew ten thousand or twelve thousand miles home. What a trip. In the sixties, the shotgun, not a real one but a medical one, was just starting to be used, and if you didn't hold perfectly still, it would rip your hide pretty good. I had a miserable flight. Very uncomfortable and pretty painful, but compared to most of the guys I saw and helped load on planes going back home, I was at least alive and sitting up, not lying down with a plastic bag for a blanket.

We were in our fifth day now, and before we were put to bed, we were introduced to another new rule. Around the front and back of each Quonset hut, there was sand. We were told that we would plant grass. We all pretended we had grass seed in our buckets, and we spread it out on the sand and brown dirt. Then we were told to go to the washracks and fill our buckets with water and return. Upon returning, we were shown how to water the grass. You hold your bucket in one hand, away from your body, out in front of you and splash little bits of water on the grass with the other. Be very careful not to sprinkle too heavily in one spot. Spread it out. We repeated that process two or three times every day. We got pretty good at it, but no grass ever grew. I guess that was their way of showing us that it was still fun to pretend. Some ice plant did, however, manage to grow, and you had better not step on it during your comings and goings.

Another lesson: You hold two and one-half gallons of water in one hand in front of you and splash little bits out. It takes you about five minutes and makes you really strong, and it's about the same weight as an ammo box of 30-caliber ammo. You also carry it from the washrack, about one hundred yards away, and when you returned, your bucket had better be damned near full. Finally, it was bedtime, and we all slept like babies.

Reveille is a tune that would play over a loudspeaker in our company area. I'm not musically inclined, but most of you have watched enough movies to know what reveille sounds like. Reveille was at 5:30 a.m. as usual. We went through the regular morning routine:

out of bed, dress, fall out, do PT, wash up, and go to morning chow. By 7:00 a.m., we were ready. Today we were told we were going to learn how to move from one place to another like a marine platoon instead of a herd of cattle. We were herded from the chow hall down two or three side streets until we stood on the edge of a huge open area. It was entirely black topped and flat. Probably about three hundred yards wide and one thousand yards long with buildings on all four sides but nothing on it. Oh yes, there were things on it, I stand corrected, but no permanent structures, only more recruits. They were doing what the corps calls COD, or close order drill. For the next three months, we would spend about 15 percent of our time learning how to perform COD. For now, though, we were instructed to line up along the edge of the asphalt area and observe the other platoons drilling. We were told they were in, at least, their eighth week because their trousers were bloused and recruits weren't allowed to blouse their trousers until after eight weeks. Well, we watched them drill, and it was really something to see. They were so smooth, so fluid, so together. Whoa, let me out there. I'll dance, I'll strut, I'll really show some moves.

After about thirty minutes of observing, we got our chance. What a mess. What a total catastrophe. We literally fell all over ourselves, stepping on one another. One guy actually got punched in the eye by another recruit because he stepped on his heels so much the other guy could hardly walk. This comedy of errors lasted for about an hour. The only reason we were allowed to stop was because our DIs were completely embarrassed. We were told then and there that we wouldn't be allowed on the grinder again until we could do a lot better.

The grinder is what that large area was called, and it was a fitting name. They literally ground us down on it. To be truthful, we were all really disgusted about that. We would learn later to hate, with a passion, that big empty field called the grinder. I'll bet I walked five hundred of my best miles on that hot empty bastard. We ended up standing at the position of attention sometimes for an hour at a time in ninety-degree heat because we didn't do a facing maneuver right.

We ended up taking the streamer for close order drill. You're probably wondering what the hell a streamer is. Well, like I said earlier, there are four platoons per series and for each skill, such as drill, physical fitness, general aptitude tests, and about five other things. The best platoon of the four got a streamer for their platoon's guidon, which was about an eight-foot pole with a flag attached to the top of it, which displayed their platoon's number. The flag was bright red with the platoon's number in bright gold, the Marine Corps's colors. As you won a streamer, it was attached to the top next to the flag. The streamer had whatever the event was written on it in big gold letters, and each streamer, except for the gold letters, was a different color. It was attached so that everyone who saw your platoon could see how sharp, or dull, you were. Actually, I think they were as much for the DIs as for us because, every once in a while, the DIs would almost kill one another to get one for their platoon. Actually, we were the ones who were almost killed every time there was one up for grabs. If we didn't win it, we were really rewarded. If you were the one who messed up, you got beaten up at least three times—once by the DI, then by the guide, and sometimes by four or five others in your platoon at the same time. If that sounds rough, believe me it was, but it was a way of shaping a person up, and we only had three months at MCRD to do that. You'd be amazed how improved that person would be after he healed.

I'm going to tell you now that there was fighting going on all the time. The nicest guy in the world would fight the second nicest guy in the world every other day. This was encouraged by the DIs and even provoked. After all, you don't get to be the greatest fighter in the world by word of mouth, and once you're the greatest, you don't stay on top by shadowboxing. You have to have contact. USMC is a full-contact sport. If you don't believe me, try it for yourself.

We were in our second week now, and almost everyone knew everyone else by name. We started off with sixty-four people, and by the end of the second week, we had lost about four or five for various reasons, such as illness. You know, a guy with pneumonia can't run five or six miles a day and do three hours of PT. For the first week, that is about all we did—run and PT. As I said, just about everyone knew everyone else by name, so this would be the perfect time for introductions. I can't remember them all, so I'll just give you the specs on a few. I'll start with Curtis Frasier. Curtis was made a house mouse. There are two for every platoon. A house mouse is in charge or keeping the duty hut clean and in order. The duty hut is where the DIs live while on duty. A house mouse is kind of like a gopher. He goes for this and goes for that. Curtis was from Michigan. He was about 5 feet 10 inches, 150 pounds, and wore glasses. A really pleasant looking guy of about nineteen. I knew Curtis for four months. We lived together for four months, and he was always pleasant, probably the most pleasant of us all.

Like most people, Curtis had his hang-ups. I found out about them quite by accident after we graduated from boot camp. We were both from Michigan and agreed to meet while on leave. We attended a party at the house of one of his friends. We met at Curtis's house. He introduced me to his mother. His father was dead. His mother was about sixty, small, with white hair. She was really just a perfect little old lady. As we left, she said to be careful and come home early. We went to the party and had a few drinks and a few laughs, and around midnight, we decided to return home.

Curtis was still his pleasant self. We pulled up in front of his house, and he invited me in. The lights were off, and we went around to the side door. Curtis opened it and entered. Just as I began to enter, a scuffle began. It was dark, and I couldn't tell what was happening. I heard some yelling and then a terrific crash and the light came on, and Curtis was not pleasant anymore. He was yelling obscenities and holding a frying pan in his hand. I heard a moan and looked down a flight of basement stairs. There was his mother trying to regain her footing. She had, apparently, slipped and fallen. Curtis was nowhere in sight. Suddenly, he returned, but he didn't have the frying pan anymore; he had a .22 rifle, and he was mad. He was telling his mom that she had about thirty seconds to get out of the house. By this time, she was able to function, and I was trying to steady her on the landing. She was really mad too. She started swearing and rubbing her head and cursing Curtis for hitting her with the frying pan and knocking her down all those steps. Well, old pleasant Curtis wasn't buying any of that bull and started poking her with the gun and telling her she ain't ever going to tell him when to be home again or what to do because he was a marine now and he will kill her. Now get outside, he ordered.

I was just standing there in a daze, and the next thing I know, old pleasant Curtis is pushing his mom outside in the snow, telling her she had until the count of ten to get away. She started running down the driveway to the sidewalk in her nightgown, and he started counting. He got to six, and she ducked behind a tree, and he cut loose with about three rounds right in that tree. He was in the driveway yelling; she was behind a tree, and I was trying to talk some sense into him. All of a sudden, porch lights started going on all up and down both sides of the street. The whole world was lit up. His mother peeked out from around the tree, and Curtis took another shot at her. She was yelling about how cold it was, and he was yelling about killing her because he's a marine.

This goes on for about eight minutes until the police cars came wailing up. One officer got out, walked up to Curtis, and took his gun away. One cop helped his mother into a car, another cop pushed Curtis into a car, and one cop helped me into a car. We all drove down to the station where I showed them my leave orders, and they asked me what happened. I told them as much as I know, and they told me that Curtis and his mom had played this game before. That's what got Curtis into the Marine Corps in the first place. So much for old pleasant Curtis. That was the last time I saw him. I called his home three or four times after that, but no one answered the phone. I figured maybe he and his mom were outside, playing in the snow again.

Everyone wasn't as nice as Curtis. There was one guy named Rod who spent the first two weeks asking everyone he talked to if they had ever done any boxing. When he found out that there wasn't anyone else in the platoon who had ever boxed golden gloves, he went back to the beginning and started punching the eyes out of everyone one at a time. I guess he had won the golden glove title for his weight class that year in New York. He looked like a middle weight. He beat up about six guys. He fought fair and never kicked anyone; he just punched their eyes out. He was really good. Around the end of that second week, at about 11:00 p.m., we were all woken up by a terrific commotion in the duty hut. Pretty soon an ambulance came and took Rod away. We found out the next day he had an asthma attack. Somehow or other, they hadn't noticed his condition when he took his physical. That was the last any of us saw of Private Rod, and believe me when I tell you not one of us was sorry to see him go. Some of us couldn't actually see him go, since he'd punched our eyes closed. I've been waiting to see him on TV talking to Howard Cosell about his next fight, but so far, he hasn't made it.

Then there was Murphy and Roberts. They were both from the same town, went to school together, dated sisters, and even joined the Marine Corps together. Roberts was the leader and Murphy was the follower. Those two spent most of their time trying to get next to each other in formations, at chow, and at drill. They were always jockeying to be together, and they would always get caught. They probably did more PT for being in the wrong place than the rest of us did as part of the PT requirement. Roberts was a real competitor. He practically killed himself at everything he tried. He was a little guy about five feet eight inches and 145 pounds, but he was wiry. As a matter of fact, he led the whole series in PT until two weeks before graduation, and then, one day, he just quit. I mean, he just quit. Now that I think back, he was never the same since that day at the firing range, but I'll save that story for a little later on.

We were all getting pretty military by our third week. We had the position of attention down pat. We were allowed on the grinder, and we didn't always have to run everywhere anymore. Sometimes we marched until we goofed up, then we ran. I remember one day Erwin was marching us somewhere, and he gave a right oblique movement, and we all just kind of stumbled left, right, up, and down until Erwin said, "Whoa, herd." Then he stopped two or three guys who were still stumbling around. Down went his hat; he kicked it, picked it up, and walked away. We all stood there for about an hour waiting, but he never came back.

Whaley came back instead. He marched us to the armory, and we all checked out our rifles. Yeah, real rifles. Hot damn. We were ready now, guns and all. We marched back to the platoon area and were instructed on how to do an exercise called up and on shoulders. After Whaley instructed us, we were given a chance to try it ourselves. Now I believe the M14 rifle only weighs nine pounds. You start this exercise with the rifle in a horizontal position at your chest. Then you raise it above your head and drop it down behind your head until it touches your shoulders. Then up over your head again and back down to your chest. That is one repetition. Nine pounds isn't really heavy, but I can remember doing 500 up and on shoulders, and when Whaley got to 490, he would stop us and ask someone a general order or their serial number until someone answered wrong, then he'd make us start all over again. Believe me, after about 1,500 up and on shoulders, that nine pounds is heavy. It turned out to be Whaley's favorite exercise. He would stand in front and get us started.

We would all repeat aloud, "One, two, three, one, sir. One, two, three, two, sir." And so on until we reached the desired number. Once Whaley got us started, he would leave the front and go around to the back of the formation, where he could see and not be seen.

Every once in a while, he would sneak up behind you, and if you weren't counting, he would say, "Platoon, halt."

He would ask you what number you were on, and if you didn't know, everyone started over again, and boy did they hate you. If Whaley caught you goofing off and skipping a repetition, he'd sneak up behind you and wait until you brought your rifle down behind your head and he'd slap it just as you started up again. The rifle was right at the back of your head, and since you didn't have any hair to protect your head, you always got a super bump and maybe even some bleeding. Whaley loved that, and it only took one day for us all to learn to count the right way and quit cheating. You've got to admit that, regardless of their methods, they got superb results. One, two, three, four, I love the Marine Corps. I don't care how ignorant you are; pain delivered at the right moment and in a precise way will enlighten you and change your life. I remember a guy named Davis. He was doing push-ups one day and had probably done a couple of hundred, not nonstop but twenty or thirty at a time until he could hardly get up anymore. He was a little on the fat side, and the DIs liked to pick on him. He was lying there looking like he was about to die any minute, and Whaley noticed him.

He walked over and said, "Davis, what's wrong, Davis?" Well, Davis was so winded he couldn't even talk. He was huffing and puffing like a bellows with a hole in it.

Whaley said, "Davis, give me ten more for the corps." Davis tried, but he just couldn't make it up again, so Whaley said, "Davis, you're a slob. I'll bet you used to lie around on the couch at home and drink beer while your mother scrubbed floors to feed you." Then he picked up this scrub brush and whacked Davis right in the back of the head with it. Instant blood. Then he helped Davis up and sent him to sick bay, informing him to tell the person filling out the report that he slipped on the washrack or he'll kill him. Whaley was a real animal when you didn't do what he said.

Later that day, after Davis returned, stitched and bandaged, we were having our thirty or forty minutes of free time and he said, "How the hell did Whaley know I used to lie on the couch and drink beer?"

In the next week, we learned all the nomenclature on the M14 rifle—how to take it apart, clean it, put it back together, etc. We could even put it together blindfolded. We cleaned them every day and learned to carry them without dropping them. Every once in a while, someone would drop their rifle, and when they did, they paid for it, usually when it was time to hit the rack. They were escorted to their bed, but before they were allowed to get in, three rifles were placed under the mattress. The mattress wasn't thick and cushy like the ones civilians sleep on; they were only three or four inches thick and filled with cotton. No springs or padding. The rifles were placed across the bed from left to right, widthwise, not lengthwise. Then the recruit was allowed to get in on top of them. I never had the privilege of this little luxury, but everyone I talked to that had the privilege really had a strangle hold on their weapon after that. How smart is the corps? How did they learn all these training procedures? I know, two hundred-plus years of devious minds experimenting on hundreds of thousands of bodies in every conceivable situation and recording and passing along the best ones in order to eliminate costly errors. The end justifies the means—USMC.

Anyone who had a dirty rifle only had a dirty rifle once because they would have to take it apart, take all the parts and a shovel, or an E-tool, and head on over to the sandpit. They were told to dig a hole and dump all the parts in, then fill in the hole. Then everyone ran around all over the area where he buried it. After the sun had dried the area up so that it all looked the same and while we were all enjoying our free time after our evening shower, the one with the dirty rifle was digging around in the sandpit with his entrenching tool, trying to find all the pieces. While we were sleeping, he was digging until all the pieces were found, cleaned, and reassembled. If he got done before reveille, he was allowed to sleep until reveille. If he wasn't, he missed morning chow and dragged his locker box out onto the Platoon Street where he continued to clean and/or reassemble his rifle for all the world to see.

You see, in the contract you sign when you enlist, the Marine Corps only guarantees you one hour of sleep a day and one meal, and that's a fact. Needless to say, but I'll say it anyway, we all became very good rifle cleaners. I guess that rifle was the most important thing we owned. They went everywhere with us and were taken care of better than anyone who hasn't been there will ever realize. We were taught that without it in perfect working order, we were only half a man, but with it, we were an indestructible force for freedom.

As Sergeant Erwin used to say, "The only thing a marine wants to do is take his rifle and kill his country's enemies."

All I wanted to do was go home. I didn't want to kill anyone then. Later on, I'd want to kill everyone. I just wasn't brainwashed enough yet. You see, that is exactly what they do. They take an eighteen- or nineteen-year-old kid fresh out of school who thinks he is really hot shit, and they knock all the hot civilian shit out of him and put their shit back in him and blow it all out of proportion with his own importance as a marine. If you don't adjust to their ways and ideas, they find a way to dispose of you. Understand this: the corps is not a fraternity, it is a brotherhood. You earn your way in with sweat and blood. It has one purpose for its existence, and that purpose is to protect this country from its enemies, not by talking them to death or negotiating with them or believing their promises but by pursuing them wherever they go until you close with them, and then you kill, kill, kill them. Every single one of them. gung ho and *Semper Fi*, do or die. And that's the truth of it, my friend.

Well, we had our rifles now, and we knew how to march around with them and run around with them. We knew how to clean them, how to put them together, and how to take them apart, so how about shooting them? Yeah, boy. We were all ready to start shooting up our enemies. Well, we were ready, but the DIs weren't, and after all, they were running the show and there was no doubt of that in anyone's mind.

The next morning after chow, we took our rifles and marched off to an open area near the obstacle courses. We stacked our weapons and did some PT until a sergeant named Adams arrived. We were called to attention and introduced. He informed us that we were going to learn how to fight with our rifles and fixed bayonets. We were issued bayonets, with scabbards, and shown how to attach them to our rifles. Then we were shown the proper stance for attacking and the proper strokes, such as the horizontal slash, the jab, the vertical butt stroke, the horizontal butt stroke, and the smash. After being shown, we were spread out at a double-arms interval and given an opportunity to practice these different strokes.

Sergeant Adams would yell, "Horizontal butt stroke!" and we would repeat his command and execute the movement at the same time. We practiced in this way for about two hours. He would call the desired command, and we would repeat and execute it. It was fun for the first ten minutes, but the last hour and fifty minutes, it was miserable. Christ the sun was hot as hell, and my arms and legs were tired. I hadn't slept well the night before because the DIs had a poker game in the duty hut, which was right next to the hut where we slept. They kept me up most of the night with their laughing and shit. Besides, about every other time Sergeant Adams would call out another command, I would either get jabbed, slashed, or butted by some really enthusiastic person who was really enjoying all this simulated killing. I guess some people brainwash faster than others.

Finally, the two hours of verbal instruction were over. We were formed up and given the position at ease, and our smoking lamp was lit. That was really weird because it was the first time we were given a smoke break away from our platoon area. Something was really smoking, and it wasn't the cigarettes, but what? Oh well, I enjoyed my Pall Mall, and when I was through I fieldstripped my butt and waited for the next order and was told what I was supposed to do. If you thought about it, life could really be simple in the corps for a private, PFC, or lance corporal. You didn't have to think, just wait and do as you were told. Kind of like Forrest Gump did in the movie. If I'd only thought like that back then, life would have been so much rosier, but I was always trying to figure out everything. I'm going to take a moment here to explain the movements involved in your basic bayonet fight.

Horizontal slash: This move begins with your legs bent at the knee and your feet in a fighting stance. You lunge forward with both hands on the rifle. You raise the rifle and swing from left to right causing the bayonet to cut across the enemy's body in a horizontal direction.

The jab: Same foot position, no swinging, just jab straight ahead with the point of the bayonet aiming for any vulnerable area. Thrust and return.

Horizontal butt stroke: Performed exactly like the horizontal slash, only with the butt of the weapon delivering a blow to the head or body, whichever presents itself.

Vertical butt stroke: This is the one most likely to cause permanent injury to another recruit in training. You are in your defensive/offensive position, like a boxer, rifle at the ready, you close in; hopefully before your opponent's strikes, you strike. The actual stroke is delivered with the butt or stock of the weapon. You lower it and swing it upward toward your enemy's jaw, like an uppercut, or into the groin area, like a dirty fighter would do with a kick. I shouldn't have said dirty fighter; that was the civilian coming out of me. In the corps, when you're at war, look how that rhymes, like they belong together. Hmm, very interesting. However, in the corps, at war, anything and everything is fair. One of Sergeant Connors's favorite move was a good hard bite. Anywhere you could find enough meat to sink your teeth into, and then once you sunk them in, clamp down and shake that head left to right almost exactly like a shark does. He used to say a good bite is as effective as your best Sunday punch.

I found that out for myself how right he was after my tour in the corps was over in a little bar in Riverview, Michigan. Two ladies—and I use the word *ladies* loosely—were having a kind of fight that, until I joined the marines, only girls have. Hair pulling, scratching, kicking, slapping, punching, you name it and they were doing it, and the fur was flying. Everyone was enjoying it except my friend, Jesse, because one of the girls was his wife, Sheila, so he asked me to help break it up. I agreed, but since I didn't know the other girl, I said I'd get Punkin and you get the other one. Punkin was his little nickname for her. I grabbed Punkin around the waist and pulled as hard as I had to separate her from the other body. The problem was, neither Punkin nor her opponent was satisfied that the conflict was over, and they wouldn't let go of each other. By the time Jesse got ahold of the other one, whom I later found out was called Honey Bunny, I was on one knee next to them, and I put Punkin in a side headlock and started to stand up and walk away with her. Well, I got to my feet and took a step or two, and Punkin turned her head and bit me on the side where I feel obliged to tell you the flesh is very sensitive. I never took another step. I immediately released her from the headlock and, as gently as I could, pried her jaws off and moved away rapidly.

Punkin reengaged with Honey Bunny, who somehow had broken free from Jesse. They locked up again in a heap of hair, arms, and legs, and everyone, and I mean everyone, watched until they lay spent in a pile on the floor. Two minutes later, they were scratched and a little bruised; their hair was a mess as were their clothes, and tomorrow and a few days later, they would probably be sore, but believe it or not, in that five seconds I spent in the jaws of Punkin, a.k.a. the Shark, I had more pain and injury than both of them put together. The immediate pain lasted over an hour and cost Jesse two shots of Johnnie Walker Black and a beer, which he paid for. After questioning Punkin about whether her shots were up-to-date, I went home to lick my wounds. I looked at my boo-boo in the mirror. You could have taken a dental impression. Her teeth marks were bleeding, and I got very little sleep that night because when I rolled over on it, in my sleep, it was like the alarm clock was going off. It was ten days before it finished its color display and almost the same amount of time before it quit hindering my life—how I sat, what I wore, don't hug or slap me on the back or side, and absolutely no wrestling around with the guys at work.

The next time I saw Jesse and Sheila, a.k.a. Punkin, a.k.a. Jaws, I asked her a couple of questions. "Why did you bite me so hard?"

She said she didn't know who had grabbed her. She thought it was one of Honey Bunny's friends.

Second question. "Why did you bite me?"

Her uncle said it was a good way to get someone off you in a hurry, and it makes it easy for the police to identify you. Whoa, another lesson learned. I asked her one more question after she told me that, "Was your uncles name Connors?" And she said no.

Back to the corps and bayonet fighting. It wasn't long in coming we were called to attention and marched on the double to another area where there were stacks of football helmets, boxing gloves, and poles with large padded ends. What in the world kind of game do you play with all this different gear? The Marine Corps is kind of a private club that anyone can join as long as he or she is willing to pay the dues. Maybe this was some secret game for club members only. As it turned out, it was called bayonet fighting with pugo sticks. The football helmets, of course, were worn on your head, and the boxing gloves were worn on your hands and the pole was called a pugo stick. It is held in your hands and used in the same way you were just instructed to use your rifle and fixed bayonet. So if you weren't paying attention, while you were supposed to be practicing, you were in real trouble now. We were all ordered to find a helmet to fit our bald head, put it on, do the strap, find a pair of boxing gloves. Oh boy, Rod would have loved this part and grab a pugo stick and get back in formation. We did as we were ordered. Sergeant Mills picked up a pugo stick himself and immediately got our attention. He informed us we were going to put what we had learned into practical application. We were ordered to line up, single file, and stand at ease. In approximately five minutes, another recruit platoon arrived on the scene. They all put on helmets and gloves and grabbed a stick and lined up, single file, about twenty yards away directly across from us.

So there we were, sixty guys on each side, all looking at each other rather puzzled. Sergeant Mills spoke, and the first man in each line was called forward. They were told to assume their fighting stance. When they had, they were told they were to attack each other when the whistle was blown. Sergeant Mills blew the whistle, and they began dancing around, sparring with each other. This lasted about thirty seconds, and Mills blew the whistle and they stopped. Sergeant Mills stood them side by side and demonstrated the proper way to deliver the various blows. Every time he hit one of those two guys, he knocked them right off their feet. This demonstration lasted three or four minutes, and we were then told to be aggressive with whomever we were matched up with or we would be used to demonstrate on. Just imagine being a crash dummy with feelings. The same two guys were put face-to-face again, ten yards or so apart, and the whistle was blown again. They immediately charged straight at each other and collided at full speed. It looked like a couple of rams colliding at mating season. They bounced off each other and landed on their asses. They were dazed but not too dazed to see Sergeant Mills glaring at them. They immediately regained their footing and vigorously attacked each other. There was some grunting and screaming and some pretty good bayonet fighting going on. It lasted about a minute, maybe a minute and a half, and the whistle was blown and they quit.

The next two faced each other and waited for the whistle. The fights lasted a minute or two, sometimes a little longer. Sometimes if the proper horizontal butt stroke was landed on the proper point of the head or body, it would be over sooner, but normally it was a minute or two. We all had three fights and went to chow. As I said, the fights didn't last long, but there was no dancing, no floating like a butterfly or stinging like a bee, just swinging for the fence the whole time. It was exhausting, and there was no weight classes or size limits. A 200-pounder could battle with a 140-pounder. The DIs pretty much stopped it if one guy was really taking it to the other with a little too much enthusiasm. We were all pretty proud of ourselves, especially the guys who were declared winners.

I fought three times that morning, and I did really well. I beat all three guys decisively. I was six feet, 155 pounds, and, I think, in better shape than most guys because I was very active in baseball during the summer months, and because I was a pitcher, I was always made to run more laps and do more exercise than the other players. After the first two fights, which only lasted a minute, but it was one intensive physical minute, I found out I had a special talent for bayonet fighting.

After lunch, we returned to the same place for more of the same stuff. You could tell most of the guys weren't really crazy about doing it again. You could tell that by just looking at their faces. They were scared to death. They knew, however, that if they didn't practically kill or be killed, they had to face Sergeant Mills, which was a worse fate by far. So we all fought our hardest. If you just didn't think about what you were going to do and struck when you saw a vulnerable opening and kept striking faster and harder each time, eventually your opponent disappeared. Personally, I loved it. I can remember some of the guys trying to sneak back to the end of the line to delay their fight or size themselves up to a guy closer to their size. I wasn't saying a word; I just wanted to fight. I found out I had super quick hand-eye coordination, and I rarely got hit hard. Even when that happened, it was good because it got my adrenaline going, and then I would really sock it to my opponent. I remember knocking guys off their feet and moving in to finish them off. Pain motivated me. Hell, Sergeant Mills had to pull me off three of the six guys I fought. Sergeant Erwin was jubilant. He had the best bayonet fighter in the series. Every time he saw someone who had done a good job from the other platoon, he would make sure I got him next. I had seven fights already that afternoon, more than most of the other guys, but I wasn't really tired. I felt like Muhammad Ali must feel before a fight. I was confident, not at all afraid of being hurt because I knew if I got hurt, my adrenaline would start pumping and my mind would respond, and in return, my hands would move faster and with more power.

It was late, and evening chow was about forty minutes away. I was halfway down in the line and knew I wouldn't fight again, so I just rested and watched the other guys do their thing. It was a beautiful sight to behold. The sound of that stick slamming into a shoulder or stomach, the grunts, and the screaming and yelling made you think you were in the coliseum in Rome when the gladiators met, except no one got hurt very much in our coliseum, let alone killed, right? I was standing there enjoying myself and seeing one mistake after another when, all of a sudden, Sergeant Erwin was standing in front of me.

"Romeo."

"Sir, yes, sir."

He said, "I've talked to Sergeant Snell from the other platoon, and I bet him all the beer I could drink tonight at the NCO club that you could beat anyone from his platoon. Now I'm telling you right now that I can't afford to buy him beer all night if you lose. He drinks like an animal and with two fists. So you had better beat the hell out of whoever he picks or get killed out there because I will kill you when you get back if you lose. Understand?"

"Sir, yes, sir."

Then he dragged me by the back of my neck to the front of the line. I put my helmet and gloves on and grabbed a stick. I was ready for war, and it took only one look from Erwin to see that I was going to win or come home in a bag. The guy they matched me with was about my size, but heavier. I'd seen him a few times when he was fighting. He was good, but there was no doubt in my mind that I was better. We were put facing each other with ten yards between us, and the whistle was blown. We collided in the center and began beating each other about the head and shoulders. After a couple of minutes, I could tell I wasn't getting anywhere, and I could feel my blows becoming less effective and his becoming more painful. I was scoring one for every two of his. I had to do something. I decided to work on a different part of his body. I remembered the vertical butt stroke. I dropped down after he hit me in the head to one knee and, at the same time, with all my strength, delivered a vertical butt stroke to his groin area. I heard him groan and saw his feet lift a little off the ground. I rose and continued my attack on his head. Now he was only hitting me once for every two I was giving him. About a minute later, we were pulled apart, and hooowee, was Erwin mad.

He had ahold of my arm and was arguing with Sergeant Snell about how I won and the other man lost. Snell disagreed, saying it was a draw. I was tired. I could hardly stand up, but Erwin and Snell would have a winner, by God. Erwin had already told me that I had better give my heart and soul to God because my ass was his. They decided we would fight again right now and this time no stopping until one of us was down and out. I didn't know what to do. I kept looking at my opponent, trying to see how tired he was. Erwin and Snell were mad, and my opponent looked as tired as I felt, but I knew he had probably been given the same pep talk I had been given, and I figured he valued his ass as much as I did and wasn't looking forward to being killed by his sergeant any more than I was.

One look at Sergeant Erwin and I was ready to go again. Then something happened. Sergeant Snell's man took three steps back and fell onto his side, rolled over onto his face, and went limp. I saw him lying there, and Sergeant Erwin saw him lying there, but Sergeant Snell didn't, so Sergeant Erwin just kind of smiled at me and then at Sergeant Snell and said, "I'll be at the club at 2130. You bring you wallet since your man can't answer the bell." He then turned around, let go of my arm, told me to fall in, and we marched off.

I remember seeing Sergeant Snell roll his man over and yell at him, but he couldn't hear; he was out for the count. Apparently, my vertical butt stroke had taken its toll. I really didn't know what happened to the guy until three days later when Sergeant Connors pulled me aside and told me I'd ruptured the other recruit and he was in the hospital waiting for an operation. I felt so very sorry. I had put a young man in the hospital, so Sergeant Erwin could drink free beer. Never again, I promised myself. Never again.

That promise was in vain because as soon as I said I was sorry that it happened, Sergeant Connors jumped in my shit and said, "A marine never says he's sorry. Never. Being sorry is useless. It never made anyone better. You do what you have to, and you're never sorry for it. By the time you say you're sorry, the damage is done. You are never, but never, to say you're sorry. You sound like a pathetic school-boy, you maggot. Now get out of my sight."

I said, "Sir, yes, sir," took one step to the rear, about-faced, and returned to my platoon. I was completely confused. My emotions ran from sad to glad. I was the best bayonet fighter so far, but at what price?

We were never given time to think or feel anything. We were becoming names, numbers, and objects, not people or individuals; and names, numbers, and objects don't feel or think anything. After our training session, we were allowed to wash up and were marched to evening chow. We spent the remainder of the day in the platoon area, learning general orders and rank structures. Erwin was in good humor and so was Sergeant Mills. I guess he was in on the bet too. Anyway, our smoking lamp was lit two more times, mail call was given, and we had our free time and hit the rack. I tried not think-ing about the pain the other guy was feeling and concentrated my thoughts on home and my girl. Pretty soon, I fell asleep and was back home, ready to renew my relationship with her, when reveille sounded over the loudspeakers and Sergeant Whaley was in our hut, throwing everyone out of their beds.

Hell, I hated mornings, and every morning I promised myself to try it for just one more day before I quit and told these crazy bananas I wasn't going to play their silly games anymore. I was going home. We had morning chow. I really can't knock the chow. They always had a good variety, and there was always enough if you weren't on a diet. I saw guys come in to Marine Corps boot camp weighing 250 pounds, standing about five feet ten inches. Now a guy carrying that much weight at that height is fat. After four months of consci-entious dieting and regimented training program, he was down to 180 pounds. I'm not exaggerating. I'm absolutely serious. Chow to me was enjoyable whenever you had meat. It was as tough as shoe leather. I remember one recruit asking Connors why. We never asked anyone else any questions, just Sergeant Connors because he was the nicest DI. He was the buffer between us and the other three. Sergeant Connors said it was prepared to be especially tough so we would have to really chew it and, in turn, strengthen our jaws and our bite.

The recruit asked why we had to have a strong bite, and Connors said, "A marine uses all his parts in a fight and a good bite on the arm, leg, or whatever, presents itself is as good as any right cross or uppercut." He then grabbed the recruits arm and bit it. The recruit yelled and pulled away in obvious pain. No blood appeared, but a couple of days later, that recruit had a pretty nice bruise right on the spot where he'd been bitten.

I began to put two and two together. What I came up with was ugly, and it was called war. Its face represented crushed bodies, pain, and suffering with no winner, just the survivors and the stinking dead. I did some serious soul-searching for the next few days, and I decided that since I had absolutely no honorable way out of this hell I'd signed myself into, I would be the best at what I was doing. I had, apparently, brainwashed myself.

We spent the next week going to classes on everything from Marine Corps history to swimming and hand-to-hand combat. It was all given to us at an unbelievable pace. We were in each class for one hour. This went on for the entire three months we were at MCRD. In between classes, there were shots to be taken, PT to be done, and, of course, lots of running, running, running. We were gradually leaving all our civilian characteristics behind, and good riddance. I never realized before what a candy ass I'd really been.

Before every evening meal, we were taken to the obstacle course. There were three different ones in the same area. The first one was called the confidence course, the second one, the conditioning course, and the third, the endurance course. See what I mean about my beloved corps? They have, over the years, thought everything out. Not just because they are the smartest bunch in the world. Oh no, their knowledge has come from practical application, the best teacher. The fact that we retained, I'm guessing now, about 90 percent of what we learned just proves the point that practical application is the best teacher. Students only retain about 10 percent of everything they learned unless, and this is for the teachers out there, the student uses it every day like by practically applying it. From this point on, PA will represent practical application because, practically speaking, it takes too long to write it out.

Now you started on the first obstacle course, continued to the second, and ended with the third. We were billeted directly behind the obstacle courses, and anytime we had an extra hour or so, we used them. We were also billeted right next to the San Diego airport, and almost every time we were out on the Platoon Street, there was a jet taking off or landing. I just kept telling myself, one day soon you'll be on one on your way home. I never remember their landing or departing bothering me after taps. I was always too tired to hear. We became very proficient on the obstacle courses because we were so close to them and could use them daily.

I really enjoyed them because we were allowed to run them as individuals, not as one big herd. I loved everything about them. I can remember the start was a climb up staggered telephone poles laid out horizontally, then a straight climb over the top and down, then jumping from one piling to another without touching the ground. Crawling through sewer pipes, climbing walls eight feet high, climbing ropes, swinging on ropes over water, jumping ditches, climbing dry nets, sliding down ropes, and just about everything you could imagine. I was really in love with these courses. Really, I mean it. As I got better and faster, I noticed there were people who couldn't climb those walls and jump those ditches. Two other guys, who were also good on those courses, and I were appointed to be the last to enter the course. We were to help these fatties and weaklings over, around, and through the course. I felt like an eagle with his wings clipped. I should have learned from the bayonet fighting that the better you do, the more you do, but like I said, I was brainwashed and gung ho, which, by the way, I stayed for almost the next three years. Almost. So instead of flying from one obstacle to the next free as a bird, I brought up the end, pushing big butts over walls and through tunnels.

We were given swimming instructions. What a laugh that was. If you could swim, you swam so many lengths of the pool and treaded water for fifteen minutes. If you couldn't swim, you were taught. They asked us all if we could swim. If you could, you were sent to the shallow end. If you couldn't, you stayed at the deep end. You should have seen the look on the nonswimmers' faces when they were left at the deep end, and we were sent to the shallow end. I don't think there is anything more frightening than deep water to a nonswimmer. The corps had its own way about doing everything, usually it is blunt and to the point, like when they told us what to do if we were ever caught in an ambush. They said if you were ever caught in an ambush, you have one of two choices. You can gain fire superiority and break through the weakest point or you can sit down, put your head between your legs, and kiss your ass goodbye. Blunt and to the point.

They also had this little cliché called KISS, which meant "keep it simple, stupid." That is what they did about swimming lessons. They kept it simple. If you could swim, you swam. If you couldn't, you learned quickly. They put one guy at each side of the pool with an eight-foot pole, then they took the nonswimmers, one at a time, and threw them into the center of the pool via the diving board. Then they let them splash around until they either made it to the side of the pool or went down two times. When you came up the second time, they put a pole within your reach and pulled you to the side. This process was repeated several times until the individual nonswimmer was blue or could stay afloat long enough to reach the side of the pool. Once you had qualified, you were done. But until you were qualified, you spent an hour or two once or twice a week at the pool learning. By the end of three months, you were a swimmer. Marines can swim. I don't know what the other branches of the service use for a training program or how they train their people to swim, but during my tour, I met a lot of marines and a lot of sailors, and I didn't ask them all if they could swim, but I can truthfully say I never met a marine who couldn't swim.

Hell, we learned everything in the corps. They even taught us about bad breath. I recall our first inspection. We were to fall out in our laundered utilities with our rifles. We were inspected by the series gunnery sergeant. We all fell out and awaited the gunny. He arrived and began his inspection. Everything seemed to be fine. There were a few dirty weapons, and a couple of guys didn't shave close enough. I believe that was to be expected. After the inspection, we marched back to our platoon area, and the ones with the dirty weapons were put through the standard rifle cleaning drill that I described earlier. The ones who weren't shaved properly dry-shaved for the next two weeks until the series commander's inspection. When you dry-shave, you don't use any shaving cream or water and your face tends to get a little irritated.

They weren't the ones who were in real trouble. The ones who were in real trouble were the ones with bad breath. I believe there were two of them. They were told that there was no excuse for bad breath. They were taken to the head where they were instructed on the proper way to brush their teeth and tongues. That was the key to mouth odor, brushing your tongue. They stood there for about twenty minutes, brushing their tongues. Their tongues got very sore, but their breath was as sweet as sweet could be.

We attended a few classes after the inspection and then went to noon chow. After noon chow, we were given our usual five minutes for head calls and returned to our platoon area. We had been in boot camp for two weeks now, and it was time to clean our hooches where we lived. They were Quonset huts with cement floors. We removed everything—clothes, beds, locker boxes; everything inside went outside, except our buckets. There were approximately twenty people per hut. Ten people were told to fill their buckets with sand, and the other ten were told to fill their buckets with water. When all twenty returned, the ten with the sand were told to throw it on the floor and spread it around. Then the ten with the water were told to throw their water on the sand. This process was repeated three times. I was absolutely sure we were doing it just to make a mess that we would, of course, have to clean up. As usual, I was right and wrong. We were instructed to get our scrub brushes from our laundry bags and move into the hooches and get on our hands and knees and begin scrubbing. We scrubbed for half an hour or so. When we were finished scrubbing, we really had a mess. We were then ordered to take our buckets to the washrack and fill them with water, return to the hut, and proceed to wash out all the sandy water with fresh. This process was repeated until there was nothing on the floor but clean water, which was squeegeed away.

When the floor dried, it looked really great. It was white, clean, shiny, and much, much smoother. The ordeal was repeated every two weeks. The corps has some of the smoothest cement in the world, but this particular cleaning procedure served more than that purpose. It served three other purposes. One, carrying buckets full of sand and water is not easy. They are very heavy, and carrying them built muscles. Two, it was another lesson in doing what you were told, no matter how silly it sounds, without questioning why. This lesson is imperative in a combat situation. Three, the corps, over a long period of time, has saved a heap of money on expensive floor cleaners, and the troops weren't exposed to any harmful chemicals.

By the time we finished putting everything back in, it was time to go to evening chow. Upon returning to our area, we were lined up in the usual two file formation. Sergeant Erwin spoke to us.

"Youse people probably think you've had a hard day and think you did pretty well. Well, let me tell you, maggots, if you think today was hard, wait until you compare it with the next 120. As far as the inspection goes, youse looked like shit and smelled like shit. The next one of youse turds that I catch with a stinking mouth won't ever have to worry about it again because I'll pull your fucking tongue out of your head and bury it. Starting tomorrow we are not going to just take little jogs from one place to the next. From now on, every night before your evening shower, we're going to take a real run. We're going to start off with three miles and work our way up to eight. These runs can take an hour or so, or they can take three or four hours. We'll start together and finish together. Some of youse wormy little slobs won't be able to run that far. Every time one of youse stops, the rest of the platoon will double-time around you until you're ready to continue. After three days, if everyone can't run three miles, the ones who can't will be tied to the ones who can.

Now there is one more thing we have to get out of the way. I'm sure you have all noticed that the other platoons have a guidon. Well, we have one too, and all we need is someone to carry it. The guidon is just that, a long pole with your platoon's series number on a red flag. It's called a guidon because the people to the rear can see it above the heads in front of them and guide on it when the herd turns. It is carried by a marine called the guide. He and the pole, with the flag, lead the herd. This person will be called the guide, and he will lead the platoon and he will be held responsible for their performance. He will also answer to me for all screwups. Sergeant Erwin began walking up and down the two lines, talking. We were all standing at the position of attention, looking straight ahead. He continued speaking of the guide and his various responsibilities and ended his lecture by saying he would like anyone who thought he could handle the job to raise his right hand. There was a slight hesitation, and then three guys raised their hands. One was a heavyset guy from Ohio, the second guy was a tall skinny guy, and the third was the oldest guy in the platoon named McGowan. McGowan was about twenty-four years old, tall, and well-built and was from St. Louis. We all kind of looked up to him because he was so much older and bigger than us, and he knew all the angles. McGowan was slick. He was street-smart. He would turn out to be a very interesting study and one of my better friends by the time the next four months were over.

Sergeant Erwin wasn't very happy that, after his inspiring speech, only three people were willing to be beaten every day for the mistakes other people made. He let us all know, even the brave volunteers, that he was angry by putting us in the front leaning rest position for about fifteen minutes. The front leaning rest position is the up position in a push-up. We just held ourselves in that position until he cooled down.

We were put back at attention in our two columns, and he said, "Only three people are ready and willing to pick up the guidon and carry it. Well, you bunch of turds, since I only have three to pick from and I don't want to hurt anyone's feelings, I'll make my own selection."

All of a sudden, quicker than hot snot runs out of your nose, he is there slapping his big sandwich grabber around the back of my neck and dragging me to the front of the formation where he stops and he turns me around, announcing this will be the guide.

"But once again, since I don't want to hurt these other three people's feelings, I'll give them a chance to be the guide anyway. All any of you have to do is beat Romeo's ass and you can be the guide."

I'm still not quite sure how or what had happened. I was damned sure that I had never raised my hand. Hell, my uncle gave me his best advice he ever gave me when he told me about the corps. He said, never volunteer for anything. Never. Erwin went on to explain that he wanted me to enter the first hut and wait for one of those guys to come in, and when they did, we were to fight until one of us quits or was rendered helpless. When that happens, the other one is supposed to throw the loser outside and wait for the next man to enter and repeat the process. He asked us if we all understood and we answered, "Sir, aye, aye, sir," which means I hear, understand, and will obey.

He sent me to the first hut. Upon entering, I'm thinking to myself, *Lord, whatever am I going to do with McGowan? He's six years older, as tall as me but forty pounds heavier and, I'm sure, a helluva lot stronger.* Then it hit me. All I have to do was lose to the other guy, Hughes. Sure, it was simple if Hughes came in first.

The door opened, and in stepped Hughes, saying to me, "I want to be the guide, Romeo." Just as I was getting ready to tell him how easy I was going to make it for him, the big dummy charged me like a bull, head down, and arms out in front of him, and that blew all my generosity to hell. As he approached, I was going to sidestep him, but instead, I bent over and hit him with my shoulder around the knees and raised up as fast and as hard as I could. He did the most perfect half Gaynor and landed directly on his back on that pristine cement floor. He wasn't even trying to get up. He was just lying there moaning and groaning like a wounded animal.

I bent over him and said, "You all right, Hughes?" He didn't say anything; he just kept moaning. I'm thinking to myself, *Man, that was pretty easy.* I grabbed one of his arms and dragged him outside to the Platoon Street. All the guys were still at attention, looking straight ahead, wondering who had won. Hughes was still moaning. Erwin told two of the guys to help him down to sick bay, and he reminded them that Hughes had slipped on the washrack. Damn, washracks are so dangerous, aren't they?

I used the same move about four years later in a slow pitch softball tournament in Niagara Falls on the Canadian side. I was catching, and we were ahead by two runs. We had two outs; it was the last inning, and a guy on second and the batter hits a ground ball between second and short stop right over the bag. The guy from second rounds third, and I know he wasn't going to slow down, and I was watching him and the outfielder field the ball. The throw came in almost exactly the same time the runner got to home plate. I put the tag on him, but he wasn't sliding; he was standing straight up. I dropped down with my shoulder just below his knee and stood straight up, just like I did with Hughes. As his weight went off of my back, I had time to turn and see him fly about four feet off the ground and hit the back stop and fall to the ground at the same time as the ump called him out. The next team was coming from their last game, and they were going to play their next game against the losers that played on our field, and we were moving to a different field. As I picked up my gear and started walking behind the benches, I saw a face that I'd grown up with in Michigan.

He was a few years older than me and we hadn't seen each other for six or seven years since we'd gotten out of boot camp. Unfortunately, we didn't have time to reminisce as we both had games to play, and I only saw him a couple of times over the next thirty years.

Erwin told me to return to the first hut and wait for McGowan. As I was waiting, the old wheels started turning. I knew McGowan would never be that easy. As slick as he was, he's probably got one of those bayonets from practice hid up his sleeve and he'll kill me. Not that the bastard needed a weapon. He was tough enough even without it. A few minutes passed and I aged three or four years. Then the door opened and my heart skipped a beat or two or three. It wasn't McGowan; it was Erwin.

He stepped in and said, "You okay, Romeo?"

And I said, "Sir, yes, sir."

And he said, "Good."

Seconds later, the door opened, and this time it was McGowan. I swallowed hard and decided I would punch, kick, scratch, and bite until I was out or he quit moving. Ha, fat chance of that.

First thing McGowan did was raise both of his hands in the air and say, "Look here, Romeo. I don't really want to be the guide.

My brother told me all about being the guide. I want to be a squad leader, and I knew by raising my hand he probably wouldn't make me the guide anyhow, but he'd admire my spirit and make me a squad leader. Understand?"

I was thinking that it made sense, but why didn't he want to be the guide? McGowan started walking toward me, explaining that his brother had been in the corps and the guide really had it rough because every time someone screwed up, the guide was called into the duty hut and punished in that person's place. Then he had to punish the person who goofed up to make sure it wouldn't happen again. It all made sense, kind of. I mean, hell, why would McGowan lie to me? He could probably beat me anyhow if he really wanted the job.

So I said, "What are we going to do?"

McGowan put his hands down and started walking toward me while he was explaining his plan. He said, "We'll just tear up a bunch of racks and do a bunch of grunting and groaning for the chumps outside. We'll fake a fight. Maybe even hit each other a couple of times at half throttle, maybe even draw a little blood to make it look and sound good. Then we'll get close to the door, I'll hit him a good one and he'll fall out the door onto the Platoon Street and play unconscious for a minute or two, then I'd be the guide and he'd be the squad leader."

We're standing toe to toe now and I said, "Yeah, McGowan, but I don't want to be the guide either."

And McGowan said, "Yeah, I know, but old Erwin wants you to be."

And I replied, "Yeah, he's used to having things his way, isn't he?"

and McGowan said, "Yeah, he sure is. So let's shake on it and get started before they get suspicious out there."

I was still skeptical about the whole deal. I just couldn't help but feel that any way it turned out, I was getting the shitty end of the stick. McGowan put his hand out, and I started to shake it when I realize he was holding out the wrong hand. As I look down at his left hand, I saw his right hand doubling up and beginning to rise from his side like a hammer. Alarmed, I looked up into his eyes, and I knew I'd been set up and was about to go down for the count. He saw that I saw what was about to happen, and he no longer tried to hide it. I dropped down and came up with the best uppercut you ever saw. It landed just as his hammer bounced off the top of my head. The pain registered like a lightning bolt, but it was not my head that hurt; it was my hand. I felt like I hit a brick wall. As I stepped out of his range, the wall began to fall, only it doesn't really fall; the big gorilla just sat down where he was standing. He just sat there, trying to focus his eyes and shaking his head back and forth. I was really scared now.

In all my eighteen years of life, I had hit my fair share of people but never anyone as hard and solid as I had hit this guy, and he was still conscious. I couldn't think of anything else to do except kick him, but I had never kicked anybody in the head before and wasn't sure what would happen. I couldn't decide if it was fair or not, and I didn't want to kill the guy. I just wanted to prevent him from doing serious bodily harm to me. He was starting to spit up now. A concoction of blood, mucous, and white things that I think were teeth but they didn't look like teeth. They looked like chunks of teeth. They were teeth all right, but they were all stuck together and coming out with big hunks of bloody flesh.

I took one look at this mess and thought, *My God, I've killed him. He's spitting out chunks of his body, and I'm going to burn in hell for this. I've got to get this guy outside.*

I stepped behind him, grabbed him under the arms, and dragged him outside. I looked around for someone to haul me off to jail. Erwin just looked at me. I really believed that he was as shocked as I was, but for different reasons. Priebe was the third person to raise his hand. Erwin acted like he couldn't remember who the third guy was, but being always the ultimate democrat, he asked who the third person was. After seeing Hughes carried off to sick bay looking like he'd been paralyzed and then seeing me drag McGowan out covered in blood and not knowing any more about how they got like that, he must have thought that I had some kind of magic powers. And if Erwin couldn't remember who he was, he would just keep his mouth shut and let this thing blow over. Erwin asked again and received no reply. He began walking up and down on the Platoon Street, and as he approached Priebe, you could see him tense up. Erwin walked past Priebe, and he relaxed. Erwin began talking about how nobody liked a coward and there was no room in his corps for one. He turned back and got nose to nose with Priebe.

He said, "Private Priebe! Cat got your tongue, or have you lost your balls, boy?" Priebe literally shit himself right there. He would have fallen down if old Erwin didn't already have him by the gus. Erwin told me to get back into the hut. As I turned toward the hut, he released Priebe and told him to finish what he started. Priebe immediately began begging off. Well, that was his third and last mistake, or strike—one was volunteering by raising his hand, two was when he denied it, and the third was when he begged off.

Erwin said, "You'll wish you were dead when I finish with you."

And he proceeded to torture Priebe with a series of wrist and arm holds as he threw him again and again to the ground. We all just stood there with our mouths open in amazement how, every time Erwin grabbed Priebe, he seemed to jump up with renewed energy in response to Erwin's touch, only to be slammed once again into the ground. Erwin began describing some kind of martial art he was using on Priebe and how you use the person's own energy against him. Damn, none of us ever knew Priebe had that much energy. I doubt Priebe even knew how much energy he could produce. I'll bet, to this day, if he is still alive, he never wants to produce that much energy again.

Erwin concluded his martial arts demo by saying, "A man lives and dies by the courage of his convictions. A coward dies a thousand deaths. A Marine, only one."

Once again, he had the best, and he had picked me himself. McGowan stood up shakily and finished emptying his mouth into his hand. He took one look at this hand full and chucked it to the ground. For the first time, I realized that they were parts of a denture plate. He had false teeth. Relief flooded my body. I thought for sure I had killed him.

Erwin spoke first, "Now is there anyone else who wants a shot at the new guide?"

I just about shit myself at the thought of another go-around with another tough monkey when I saw Erwin parading McGowan around in front of them. They all stared at him with no teeth in his mouth and blood all over his face and utility jacket, and I knew my fighting was over for another day. What with Hughes in sick bay and McGowan looking like he should be in sick bay too, I was the new King Kong. I really hadn't done much, but it was like a strike in bowling. When you see that X on the sheet, you can't tell whether it was a good hit or a bad one, but it is still a strike. Erwin sent one of the house mice into the duty hut, and he came out with our Platoon's guidon and an armband with the platoon's number on it. He grabbed me, put my arm band on, handed me the guidon, and that was that. I stood there for a moment thinking about all the worrying I had done about what was going to happen, and to be perfectly truthful, I felt good, really good. I decided then and there that, from now on, I wasn't going to get ulcers every time I wasn't sure if I could do something. Instead, I was just going to take all my talent and ability, however much or little, and do my very best.

For the next couple of weeks, remembering that promise to me would make my life just barely bearable. We were given a few minutes to wash up, then we were called out to the Platoon Street. For the first time, we were formed up into a platoon of four squads. There were four official squad leaders picked. I, as the guide, was placed at the head of the platoon. McGowan was made a squad leader, and I never did find out if he really had wanted to be the guide or not. Regardless, he got what he said he wanted. We were ready to march. I was proud. A little confused and a little worried, but mostly proud.

Hughes didn't return from sick bay for three days. I guess he slipped a disc or something. When he did return, he was on light duty for another week. Every time we saw each other, he'd sneer at me and I'd sneer back. He never did step out of line again though. There was a humorous side to this whole incident. It was watching McGowan try to eat with no teeth and a sore mouth. It was more pathetic than funny, but most of us had never seen anyone without teeth, and it did look a bit strange, but no one laughed at McGowan. McGowan didn't look like he would appreciate any laughter. It was hard not to laugh, though, because every time he chewed, his nose would almost touch his chin, making him look fifty years older. The rest of the day was spent on the obstacle course and at the washrack doing our dirty laundry.

That evening, we showered and had mail call. At mail call one of the guys named Pierson screwed up. After mail call, everyone was given forty-five minutes of free time. Everyone, that is, but me. I was called into the duty hut where I was given a thorough ass beating by Sergeants Whaley and Erwin because Pierson blew mail call. I was told to square him away by tomorrow morning, or there would be an instant replay of what just happened.

All I could think about was what McGowan had said about not wanting to be the guide. I figured maybe he had been telling the truth after all. I was really confused now. I left the duty hut and found Pierson. He was on his locker box in the Quonset hut.

I walked in and said, "Pierson, come here."

And he said, "What?"

And I said, "Come here."

He got up from his locker box, walked over to me, and said, "What do you want?"

I still had Erwin's finger marks on my gus, and my face was all red and marked with handprints from where I'd been slapped silly. I said to Pierson, "You know, I just got my ass beaten because you screwed up at mail call."

He said, "Hey, I'm really sorry. I really didn't mean to. I promise I won't do it again. I promise, honest Romeo. Just give me a chance, and I'll get squared away." I had intended to slap him around just like I had gotten slapped around, but after listening to him plead for another chance, I just couldn't bring myself to fire on him.

I said, "Okay, Pierson, just get squared away."

That was my first mistake as guide. There would be many more. The very next night, Pierson screwed up mail call again, and I spent another uncomfortable ten minutes in the duty hut with my two favorite sergeants. I immediately went to see Pierson. This time, I didn't give him a chance to run his sorry act down on me. He was on his locker box again, and this time I walked up behind him and placed my foot on his back and pushed him over on the floor on his face. He turned over with a shocked look on his face, and I reached down and grabbed him, and he kicked me in the shin.

He just laid on his back, and every time I went to grab him, he would scream bloody murder and try to kick me. I said, "Get up, Pierson, you bastard. Get up!" It really hurt getting kicked in the shins with a hard-soled combat boot.

He begged, "Let me alone. Just let me alone, Romeo."

I tried to grab him again, and he kicked and screamed even louder. Every time he kicked, I tried to grab his foot, but I just couldn't get a handle on him. He was really scared. I think he'd have laid on his back on that cement floor all night if necessary. He was screaming so loud that Erwin heard him and came in to see what the problem was. He took one look and called me outside.

"Romeo, you have four squad leaders who will do whatever you tell them to. I suggest you go get one, two, three, or all four of them to help you. If you try beating up everyone in the platoon by yourself, when they screw up, you will never be able to get anything done."

I went out and got all four squad leaders and brought them back to Pierson's hut. He was still on the floor on his back.

I said, "Get up, Pierson."

He whined, "Let me alone, please, let me alone," all the while kicking and screaming as hard as he could.

I said, "Get him up."

And all four squad leaders grabbed a leg and an arm, and he was finally still, but he wasn't quiet. I dropped down next to him and put my hand over his mouth to shut him up, and the bastard bit my hand. When I finally got my hand free, I slapped him as hard as I could. He got this idiotic stunned look on his face, and I told the guys to get him on his feet. They stood him up, and I couldn't think what to do with him. I had never sucker punched anyone, and I'd never beaten anyone up while they were being held. None of this was my style, but I had to do something or he would screw up again. I'd already gotten the shit kicked out of me twice because of him, and I wasn't about to get it again. I decided to kick him right in the shins, like he had kicked me. I kicked him hard right in the shins, and he squealed like a pig headed for slaughter. I kicked him again and told the guys to let him go. They turned him loose, and he took off at a full run. He hit the door, and by the time I got there, he was a good fifty yards down the street, yelling like a scalded dog. I just had to find another way because this routine wasn't getting it.

I went to bed that night with the thought of coming up with a better idea. Ford had a better idea, and now Romeo needed a better idea. It was around midnight before I finally fell asleep. It seemed like I had just gotten to sleep and all of a sudden it was reveille. But it wasn't reveille because the loudspeakers weren't on and neither were the lights, but I was being dragged out of my rack anyway. Just about the time I got my eyes focused and recognized the familiar hold my gus was in, I hit the floor and was immediately jerked up on my feet again. Well, there he was, Jesus Christ, Erwin. I'd already given my heart and soul to God when I was twelve, and I was glad because Erwin had my ass.

He let go of me and said, "Get your locker box out, Romeo."

As I gasped for breath, I got my locker box out, and he stood up on it. It made him about two feet taller. He was normally two inches taller than me, and now he was two feet taller than me. Damn, he looked menacing as hell, towering over me like a Goddamned redwood.

He made me stand at attention right in front of him, then he said, "Romeo, you really taught Pierson a lesson, didn't you? The MPs caught him trying to climb the fence by the airport runway. What the hell did you do to him? He didn't have a mark anywhere."

I said, "Sir, I kicked him in the shins, sir."

Erwin said, "You kicked him in the shins?"

And I said, "Sir, yes, sir."

Then Erwin said, "Hot damn, Romeo, I thought you were an ass kicker, not a shin kicker."

I said, "Well, sir."

And he said, "What's the first and last word out of your mouth, Romeo?"

I started to say "Sir," but I never got it out. He slapped me with one of his big sandwich grabbers and knocked me clean off my feet.

I started to get up when he said, "Get over here, turd."

I walked back over in front of him and stood at attention. My head had cobwebs in it, and I could still feel his fingerprints running from the back of my head round to my nose. He had the biggest hands I ever saw or felt. He said to me, "Did you like that, Romeo?" I was dazed and couldn't think of an answer. He said, "Romeo, did you like that?"

And more, just out of habit, I replied, "Sir, yes, sir."

To this, he raised his hand and gave me another slap on the opposite side of my face. This time I was prepared. He didn't knock me down, but he did move me over a few feet.

I got back in front of him and he said, "Did you like that, Romeo?"

And I said, "Sir, yes, sir."

He said, "Would you like another one, Romeo?"

And I said, "Sir, yes, sir." He gave me another one that put me down again, just to one knee though, but my eyes just wouldn't focus. Every time I opened them, I just got bright flashes and saw spots, but I could hear old Jesus yelling, "Get up, Romeo, get up!"

I tried but could only manage to kneel there. He got off the locker box and said, "Put your locker box away and get in your rack. You've got a hard day ahead of you, Romeo, and you'd better get these people squared away because you and I are going to continue meeting like this until they are."

He walked out the door, and I got up off the floor, put my locker box away, climbed up on my rack, and started racking my brain for a better idea. My head felt like everything inside it was loose and rattling around. What the hell was I going to do? How the hell did I ever get in this mess anyway? C'mon, shithead, try and think. Just then I heard a voice.

"Romeo, hey, Romeo, you all right?" All I could smell was a rotten smell. Whoever it was sure had a case of bad breath.

I said, "You'd better start brushing your tongue or after the next inspection I'll be in the duty hut again."

He said, "Aw hell, I just got up, you prick. What do you expect?"

I recognized the voice now. It was McGowan. Christ, that was all I needed.

I said, "What do you want, Mac?"

To which he replied, "I just want to help you, dummy."

And I said, "How the hell can you help me? Erwin don't want to beat on no one but me. I have to figure a way to punish the guys who screw up so they don't anymore. Or Erwin and I are going to continue to meet like this and I'm not sure I can stand it."

Mac said, "Hell, that's no problem. Just kick their ass. Just walk up and start punching their eyes out."

I said, "I can't, Mac. I have to be mad, hurt, or scared before I can start hurting the other guy. Erwin, Whaley, Mills, or Connors kick my ass, and by the time I get a chance to kick the guy's ass who screwed up, it's two or three hours later and the pain and anger is gone."

He said, "Okay. So you don't like to see what you're doing. When I was in jail and some guy wanted to work another guy over, he'd wait until the other guy was asleep, and he'd get a couple of buddies and a blanket and walk over to where the mark was sleeping. Then he'd throw the blanket over the sleeping guy's head. Someone would grab it on the other side of the rack. They would pull it tight over his head and upper body, and then they would all start punching him until he quit moving around. Then everybody but him would leave and he'd pull the blanket down, wake the guy up, and tell him what the beating was for, then he'd walk away. We called it a blanket party."

I said, "Yeah, that sounds all right."

Mac said, "Well, dummy, get your blanket, and I'll get two more of the squad leaders' and we'll go give Pierson a party."

To avoid damaging our hands, from that party on, we would put a bar of soap in a sock and whip the party boy with that, mostly in the body area, so there were no sore knuckles or teeth marks on our hands. We gave Pierson a party, and he didn't run away this time. When he quit moving, the other guys left, and I woke him up. I told him he'd better get it together or else. Pierson got it together, and I never had any trouble with him again. Thanks, Mac, and please don't forget to brush your tongue.

I went to bed, and reveille sounded. We fell out onto the Platoon Street in our usual two columns. Sergeant Mills was in front of me, and I was in front of them.

He yelled, "Report."

I said, "Squad leaders, report."

And one at a time, they reported that their squads were all present and accounted for. When they all reported, I said, "Sir, platoon 189, all present and accounted for, sir."

He just looked at me and walked up and down, looking the people over. When he got to Pierson, he kind of smiled and said, "What happened to you, Pierson?"

Pierson said, "Sir, I fell out of my rack, sir."

Sergeant Mills asked, "Where the hell was your rack? On top of the Quonset hut?"

Pierson stood there looking dumb and hurt while Mills walked away. We went to chow, then a couple of classes, then to the grinder for some close order drill (COD). We had been practicing our drill for three or four hours a day while coming and going to everywhere we went, and we were getting pretty good at it. Every once in a while, some dummy would mess up, and old Sergeant Erwin and I would have another early-morning meeting. These meetings went on for two weeks, almost every night.

He'd throw me out of my rack, make me get my locker box out, climb up on the locker box, and slap me, usually knocking me down in the process because it was dark in the hut and my eyes weren't focused yet, and I generally didn't see the first one coming. Then he'd ask me if I liked it, and I'd give the standard affirmative answer, and he'd do it again. This process was usually repeated three times, then he'd tell me who it was that screwed up that day and what they'd done and tell me to get them squared away. I'd get McGowan, a blanket, and two more squad leaders, and we'd go have a blanket party with the guy who screwed up.

By the end of the second week as guide, I was a real wreck both physically and mentally. I was only getting a couple hours of sleep a night, what with the pain I was in mentally and physically, and it just wasn't enough to keep up with the platoon, let alone lead them. When we all hit the rack at night, I'd lay there waiting for Erwin to come in and tell me who had fucked up that day, then we'd play his game. Well, I couldn't play anymore. I was going crazy. I felt like I was a prisoner of war in a POW camp. The thought of him hitting me again drove me crazy. My head felt like a mushy rotten tomato inside. Every time I shook it, it hurt. I decided I wasn't going to take any more beatings.

About 1:30 a.m., he came in and pulled me out of the rack. I got the locker box, then he got on it, told me who screwed up, asked if I was mad at the guy, then he hit me. I got up on my feet in front of him and told myself, *If he hits me again, I'm going to fight back.* I knew he'd kill me, but I couldn't go on anymore.

I squared up in front of him, and he said, "Did you like that, Romeo?"

I yelled as loud as I could, "Sir, no, sir."

He said, "What?"

And I said, "Sir, no, sir."

And he said, "Do you want another one, Romeo?"

And I said, "Sir, no sir."

He leaned in, fixed his gaze right on me, and got off the locker box, and I knew he was going to kill me for sure.

He got nose to nose with me and said, "You know what, Romeo? You could have saved yourself a whole lot of beatings if you would have said that two weeks ago, but I'd probably have killed you for being a coward. Now put your locker box away and get some sleep."

I said my prayers and was just about asleep when that familiar smell hit me.

"McGowan, for Christ's sake, turn your head when you talk to me please. Your breath stinks to high heaven."

McGowan said, "Man, I thought he was going to kill you when you said no."

And I said, "Yeah, I thought so too, but I was at the point where I didn't care if he did. Now get some sleep because reveille comes early, and I'm dog-ass tired, and please don't forget to brush that tongue."

That morning, we fell out in our usual way, me in front of them and Erwin in front of me. This morning, instead of saying report, he called one of the recruits up to the front of the formation. His name was Pierson. Old fuckup Pierson. I thought to myself, *Hot damn, what did he do now?* Pierson came up and stood next to me. Erwin reached out, took the guidon from me, grabbed my arm, took my armband, and told me to get in the formation at the rear of the second squad. Then he turned Pierson around, put the armband on him, gave him the guidon, and told us he was the new guide until further notice.

He then said, "Report."

And Pierson blew it, as usual. I was completely lost. I didn't know what was going on. I mean, Pierson? Was he serious? We finally got to morning chow at ten to eight, then we went to a class called hand-to-hand combat where we were basically taught to street fight. We practiced on one another for about two hours. They taught us a few vulnerable areas to attack, how to attack with a knife, and how to defend ourselves against a knife attack. Mostly it gave me a good chance to release some of my anger. My partner was McGowan. While we practiced hurting each other, he explained how they liked to give as many people a chance at being a leader as they could, and that was why Pierson was the guide now. It was nothing personal. He said they would change guides every week now since I had gotten everybody pretty much squared away. He was right as usual. Another lesson well learned.

We finished our class and went to noon chow. After chow, Mac went to get his new teeth. His mouth was all healed up, and he was ready for some good solid chow. He had lost about fifteen pounds in the last few weeks and was looking a little weak. We spent the rest of the day in classes and on the grinder drilling. That evening, we had mail call and free time. I wrote a couple of letters, one to my girlfriend and one to my parents. I didn't bother telling them about what had happened. I just said I was fine and loved them all.

I really felt relieved that night when I hit the rack. Old Erwin would be meeting with someone else from now on, and I could get some good sleep. I closed my eyes and immediately fell into a deep sleep. I was back at home, holding my girlfriend again. God, it felt heavenly. I was just about to renew our relationship when I suddenly felt like I was suffocating. I opened my eyes but couldn't see anything. Then I heard and felt what was going on. It was a blanket party, and I was the honored guest. I started to fight and try to wrestle myself free, but the harder I fought, the harder I got hit and the more it hurt. I realized where I was and what to do. I covered my head as best I could, and the next time I got hit in the head area, I went limp and played possum. I got hit a couple more times but didn't move, and I heard and felt them leaving. As the last one left the hut, I felt the blanket being pulled off me.

I kept my eyes closed, felt my face being slapped, and heard Pierson saying, "Romeo. Romeo."

My nose was bleeding pretty good, and I let him slap me a few more times, then opened my eyes and pretended to be coming to.

He grabbed me by the chin, turned my head toward him, and said, "Listen, you asshole. If you give me any trouble, we'll be back and give you a real party. Do you understand?"

Then he squeezed my jaw, and I said, "Yeah," and gave him a beautiful right cross right on the old horn. His snot locker opened up, and he hit the floor like a ton of hot shit. I pinned his arms down, and he started screaming.

I slapped him and said, "Now you listen, asshole."

Then I explained to him what McGowan had explained to me earlier that day. I told him if he ever screwed with me again, I'd beat him and put him in a dipsty dumpster. He seemed to understand, so I let him up and got back in my rack. He got up, went to the door, and told me he was sorry, but he thought he had to teach me a lesson so I wouldn't give him any trouble.

I said, "I wasn't going to give you any trouble, Pierson. As a matter of fact, I'll do whatever I can to help you because you are going to need all the help you can get."

He started to leave, and I asked him, "Hey, Pierson, tell me one thing. Was McGowan in on this party?"

He said, "No. I asked him, but he said he wouldn't do it."

Pierson left, and I went to sleep feeling like I had at least one real friend in the world. That thought made me feel better, and I fell asleep.

Reveille sounded as usual at 5:30 a.m., but for me, there wasn't the usual enthusiasm, motivation, or anxiety that had been there for the previous weeks. I felt relaxed, free, and easy. I sat up and looked around and watched all the other recruits scurrying around like scared rabbits. I realized I had plenty of time since the only person I had to look after was me. I stretched and casually rolled out of my top rack and began to dress and prepare for the sixteen hours of fun and games that lay ahead.

We were all formed up on the Platoon Street. Instead of being up front wondering how I would make it through the day, I was in the rear of the second squad. The second squad leader's name was Private Lee. He was a pretty good guy. Probably the easiest squad leader of the four. He made his head count, returned to the front of the squad, and made his report.

Morning chow was uneventful. After chow, we returned to our platoon area. We were told to put on our red shorts, yellow sweat-shirts, and tennis shoes. When we were all formed up, we dou-ble-timed over to an area that had been designated as a test area. We were told that this was where we would take our first physical fitness test. We were required to do a series of physical exercises, and we had to do a certain number of each or we failed. If you failed too many, you would be sent to what they called PTU (physical training unit). It was where the weaklings and the fatties were sent and where they stayed until they could pass all the physical tests. The DIs called it the pig farm. Every time we went to the obstacle course, they were working out. That's all they did all day—exercise, exercise, exercise until they were thin enough and strong enough to pass all the phys-ical tests. Sometimes it took a week. Sometimes it took a month. However long it took, you stayed there. When you were ready and could pass, you were put with a platoon that was at the same place the platoon you left was at when you left.

What all this means is that if you got set back, you didn't graduate in three months and go to ITR. All this was explained to us before the testing started. We started with pull-ups, and you had to do at least seven of them. The maximum was fifteen. You got 70 percent for doing the minimum and 100 percent for doing the maximum. At the end of all the events, if you had less than 75 percent for the ten events, you were sent to the pig farm. We all tried very hard, but we all didn't make the 75 percent. I think three people were dropped. The minimum push-ups were forty and the maximum was sixty-five. There was a thirty-foot rope climb and the maximum time was twenty seconds. The minimum time was ten seconds up and down. There was a one hundred-yard dash, and the minimum time to run it was ten seconds; the maximum time was thirteen seconds. Next came the sit-ups. They were timed too. You had three minutes to do at least sixty and as many as a hundred. Squat thrusts were timed. So were the step-ups. We all passed, except the three guys I mentioned earlier.

When we returned to the platoon area, those three guys were told to pack all their gear and report to the duty hut. It was really a sad thing watching them pack to leave. I think we all realized then how cold and unfeeling life was. Boot camp was hard enough when you went through it with the same people you started with. Being taken away just as you were getting used to the routine and people and sent to the pig farm until you were strong enough or thin enough and then sent to another platoon where you were introduced as a pickup was really tough. You had a new routine to get used to and new people to get used to, and they were always harder on pickups because they didn't want you to mess up their platoon.

A pickup was considered an outcast, kind of like a leper who left the colony back in biblical times. Nobody, but nobody, liked you or wanted you around. Now three of our own were condemned to this fate, and I'm sure they felt it was a fate worse than death. Believe it or not, there were some honest to goodness tears shed by and for these three guys.

They left, and we went to noon chow. After noon chow, we went for some shots, then headed to the grinder for some COD. We had a lousy day on the grinder. Most of the guys just weren't with it. Their minds were someplace else. Besides, Sergeant Connors was drilling us and we weren't used to his cadence. Everyone had a different way of calling cadence and giving the movement commands, and we just weren't used to him. Since Sergeant Whaley was with us too, he decided that since we didn't want to drill, we'd do some rifle exercises. He loved doing rifle exercises. Remember, he was the one who taught us how to do up and on shoulders. That was the one he decided we were going to do, and this would turn out to be one of our harder days. I said earlier, if you remember, Sergeant Whaley would cause me to refuse an order and make my life, in general, miserable whenever he had the duty. Well, today was that day.

We started our exercise. It was hot. I'd guess about ninety degrees, and there was no shade because we were on the grinder. We were wearing our green utilities, and they drew the heat and held it. We were all sweating profusely; every time we got to ninety-nine, Whaley would halt us and tell us to start again. We continued for about ninety-nine more repetitions and were stopped again. After about an hour and a half, we were all extremely fatigued. That rifle didn't weigh nine pounds anymore; it felt like it weighed ninety pounds. Whaley would occasionally sneak up behind someone and hit their rifle on the way up, causing them to hit themselves in the back of the head and miss a repetition, and we'd all have to start again.

I was pumping them out, and I had a silly ass smile on my face, and Sergeant Whaley saw it and came over to find out what I was so happy about. He got directly in front of me, and my smile disappeared. He just stood there looking at me, and I continued doing up and on shoulders because no one told me to stop. I could tell he was pissed at me, but I couldn't understand why. He started firing questions at me about why I was so happy, why I was grinning, did I like him, things like that. I wasn't answering the questions correctly, apparently, because he was getting more pissed off by the second.

He called us to a halt and said, "Everybody but Romeo, fall out. The smoking lamp is lit. If you have 'em, smoke 'em."

Everyone fell out, and when they caught their breath, they lit up. Everyone, that is, except me. He told me to continue doing the exercise. He stood there in front of me for a few minutes while I did the exercise and counted cadence.

"One, two, three, one, sir. One, two, three, two, sir. One, two, three, three, sir."

After a few minutes, he walked around behind me and was very quiet. I knew what was going to happen, and I started wishing I had some hair on my head to cushion the blow. It wasn't long in coming. I was on my way up and he slapped my rifle, and I hit myself right in the back of the head, but I kept going.

"One, two, three, one, sir. One, two, three, two, sir. One, two, three, three, sir."

Then he did it again. I hit myself three or four times in the back of the head before he came around in front of me again. He started yelling and calling me vile, disgusting names. He was getting himself all worked up into a lather. He was inches from my face, and he was spitting all over me and foaming at the mouth. It's true. When Whaley got wound up, he foamed at the mouth like a mad dog. He was foaming now, and I was the reason. He kept calling me a smart-ass and telling me how he hated a smart-ass.

Then he said, "Do you understand, smart-ass?"

And I said, "Sir, yes, sir."

That really made him mad, and he told me to stop and I stopped. The rifle was held horizontally in my hands at chest level. He put his hands on my rifle and pulled it away from my chest. He raised it above my head. My hands were still on it because he never told me to let it go. He had a crazy look in his eyes, and he started down with the rifle. It was all too apparent to me where he planned for that rifle to come to a crunching halt. He was going to smash my nose to smithereens with that sucker. I wasn't buying that shit. My hands were still on the rifle, so as he started down, I pulled it into my chest instead of my nose. That totally pissed him off. He still had his hands on the rifle, and so did I.

He said, "Let go of that rifle, smart-ass."

I had a death grip on that baby, and I said, "Sir, no, sir."

He went ape shit. He tried yanking it away, but I wasn't letting go. No way. I held on, and he started throwing me all over the place. Before I knew it, I was on my back and he had a foot on my chest, trying to pull my rifle away from me. He finally gave up and told me to stand up. I got up, and he yelled some more and slapped me a few times. It didn't hurt much, not half as much as a broken nose would have hurt. Hell, Erwin hit three times as hard as he did.

He walked away and told the platoon to fall in. We all fell in and double-timed it back to the platoon area where we washed up and went to evening chow. That night, we went on our usual run. We were up to about five miles by now, and everyone was making it pretty well. After that, we showered up and had mail call. After mail call, we were given some free time to write letters and square our gear away.

I was just about to write a letter when Peters, a house mouse, came running up to me and said, "Romeo, you're wanted in the duty hut."

I put my gear away and reported to the duty hut. As with everything else about the corps, there was a regular routine for entering the duty hut. First, you beat on the right side of the doorway three times as hard as you could, and then someone inside would say, "Who's there?"

And you'd say, "Sir, Private Romeo, platoon 189, serial number 2515190, requests permission to speak, sir."

And then they would say, "What is it?" or "Speak."

One of those two, usually, then you would say, "Sir, Private Romeo requests permission to enter the duty hut."

Whoever was inside would usually say something like, "I can't hear you." And you would have to repeat the process, sometimes seven or eight times until your hand was sore. You didn't just knock like you would at someone's home. You made a fist and pounded the wall three times as hard as you could.

The object of this game was to make the whole wall rattle. But this time, the first time I beat on the hatch and requested permission to speak to the DI, the person inside said, "Get in here."

I entered and the person inside was Sergeant Erwin. I positioned myself directly in front of his desk at the position of attention and said, "Sir, Private Romeo reporting as ordered, sir."

He looked me over, stood up, walked around his desk, and positioned himself directly at my right side and said, "Romeo, I understand you don't follow orders anymore."

I said, "Sir, the private doesn't understand, sir."

He said, "You heard me smart-ass. I heard you don't follow orders anymore."

"Sir, no, sir."

"No what, Romeo?"

"Sir, no, sir, I follow orders, sir."

"You shit, Romeo!"

"Sir?"

"Sergeant Whaley told me you disobeyed a direct order today, you shitbird. Is that right?"

And I said, "Sir, yes, sir." Slap, grab, punch, kick, and I was on the floor looking up.

"You son of a bitch! If you ever disobey a direct order again, I'll take your head off and shit down your neck. Do you understand, Romeo?"

"Sir, yes, sir."

"All right, get out of here before I lose my temper."

"Sir, Private Romeo requests permission to speak to the platoon commander."

"Speak."

"Sir, Private Romeo would like to explain why he disobeyed Sergeant Whaley's order, sir."

"So go ahead, you bastard, but it had better be good or so help me I'll have your ass."

I began to explain exactly what had taken place between Sergeant Whaley and me earlier that day.

When I finished, Sergeant, Erwin looked at me and said, "Romeo, I'm going to check this out, and I'll get back with you. So help me, if you lied to me I'll have you thrown out of my corps. Do you understand?"

"Sir, yes, sir." He dismissed me, and I took one step to the rear, about-faced, made a right turn, and double-timed out the door to my Quonset hut.

It was just about time for taps, so I undressed and got in my rack. The lights were still on, and I lay on my back, staring at them until they shut off. I can't remember what was going through my mind, except what he said about having me thrown out of his Marine Corps. Suddenly, I didn't want to be thrown out of the corps. Suddenly, I didn't want to go home anymore. Suddenly being a marine was the most important thing in my life. Would Whaley lie? Would Erwin really find out the truth?

The next morning, before chow, seven people were called to the duty hut one at a time. They stayed five minutes or so apiece. We went to morning chow, and after chow, I was once again called to the duty hut where I went through the proper procedure and was told to enter on the first try. Erwin was in his chair behind his desk, looking unhappy and angry as usual. He asked me to repeat what had happened between Sergeant Whaley and me the day before. I explained it detail by detail, step by step while he listened.

I finished and he said, "Well, Romeo, regardless of what you thought Sergeant Whaley was going to do, the fact still remains that you did disobey an order when you refused to give Sergeant Whaley your rifle, didn't you?"

"Sir, yes, sir."

"Well, we will have to find some kind of extra duty for you so you won't think you can get away with this again. Do you understand?"

"Sir, yes, sir."

"All right, get back to the platoon. Oh, and, Romeo, I wouldn't cross Sergeant Whaley again if I were you." He stood up, came around behind me, and ran his big sandwich grabber very gently over the back of my skull and gave me a gentle pat and said, "He's not the nicest guy in the world, and I don't think he loves you anymore. Understand?"

"Sir, yes, sir."

"All right, now get out of my sight."

"Sir, aye, aye, sir." I took one step to the rear, about-faced, made a right turn, and returned to the Platoon Street on the double.

The only thing that happened in the duty hut that didn't seem right was when Erwin put his hand over the back of my head and gave me a gentle pat before dismissing me. It was like my father would do when he wanted to show me, without saying it, that he was proud of me or just wanted to touch me because he loved me. But why had Erwin touched me? It was hard to believe he had any love in him for anything but his beloved corps, and I was pretty damn sure if he did have a little love left over it wouldn't be wasted on me, but why the so-called gentleness from him to me? I stood on that Platoon Street until well after the pain and humiliation went away and until we were dismissed to be busied with another chore.

That night, as I lay in my rack, I was still trying to figure out the gentle stroke and the pat. I mean, I'd felt it before, but it came from a man that I knew loved me and would have died for me—my father. I put my hands behind my head and laid my head on my pillow, and as quickly as I did that, my question was answered. I felt three or more decent-size bumps on the back of my melon from where Whaley had slapped my rifle into it the day of my disobedience. Like I said, I'd explained exactly what had happened that day, in detail, to Erwin, and he hadn't forgotten that part. Having had it done to him years before when he was just a boot, he knew those lumps don't go away right away. That's what he was doing, feeling for evidence that I hadn't lied about that part. And I'm sure if I had lied and those bumps weren't there, that little pat on the back of my head would have been a really good slap, just like my father would give me when I screwed up, followed by a swift kick in the pants. Only with Erwin it would have been a severe beatdown like he would have gone medieval on my ass. That's a quasi-popular saying nowadays. The end result would have been a trip, probably by ambulance, to sick bay, and honestly, at that particular stage in my career, it may have broken me.

Thinking back now, and believe me I'm standing in that duty hut as I'm writing this, that little pat after the feel was Sergeant Erwin's way of saying, unconsciously I'm sure, he was pleased and, yes, he did love me. Decades later, as an old man, if he were here, I would tell him to his face that I totally understand it all now how it works and why it has to be done the way it was, and I'd tell him I love him for his courage and convictions and his service to our beloved corps. Thanks to all of you hard ass NCOs of the corps.

I felt better. I was still in Erwin's corps. I wasn't a marine yet, but I was sure I would be one someday. For those of you who have never made a trip to the duty hut, I believe I've made the whole thing sound a little too easy. So let me tell you now that when you were called to the duty hut or when you had to go to the duty hut for a reason of your own, it was terrible and you would rather have had a scheduled fight with Rocky Marciano than to have to go.

I remember a recruit in our platoon named Lawson. Lawson was medium built, medium tempered, and, I think, medium intelligence. I guess you could say Lawson was your basic medium guy. In boot camp, everyone had a nickname, and Lawson's was mad dog. If Lawson was such a medium guy, why did he get a nickname like mad dog? Well, one day, Lawson didn't have to go the bathroom too badly when the five-minute head calls were in order. Besides, there were so many guys and so few commodes; he figured, *Why bother? I'll go later*. Well, later came, and Lawson went to the duty hut to request permission to make an emergency head call. Remember the procedure to enter the duty hut? You hit the right side of the wall three times as hard as you could and say, "Sir, Private so-and-so, serial number such and such, platoon such and such, requests permission to speak to the drill instructor."

Then when he answers, you say, "Sir, Private so-and-so requests permission to enter the duty hut." When he says, "Enter," you enter. There is a specific way to enter also. You walk in the door, stop directly in front of his desk, make a left face, step forward until you are standing exactly six inches from his desk, and you stop. When you stop, you assume the position of attention and look straight ahead with your eyeballs looking directly ahead at a set of eyeballs painted on the wall behind him, and you wait.

After a few minutes, he'll say something like, "Speak" or "What do you want?"

And you say, "Sir, Private so-and-so requests permission to do whatever it is you want to do."

Well, Lawson had to make a head call, so he would say, "Sir, Private Lawson requests permission to make an emergency head call, sir."

Then if you've done all this properly with no mistakes, the DI would say something like, "Granted" or "Make it," and you would take one step to the rear and say, "Sir, aye, aye, sir." Give a hand salute, make an about-face and a right face, and double-time to the head, and that would be it. Don't forget to flush and wash.

That's what happened if you didn't make any mistakes. Lawson went to the duty hut and began to go through the ritual, but today wasn't his day. He knocked and knocked and knocked, and he requested several times permission to speak to the DI, then he requested permission to enter the duty hut several times. He even got inside several times but kept getting thrown outside because he kept blowing it. Remember, he had to shit pretty badly now. He'd forgotten his serial number, platoon number, or to say sir or he didn't knock hard enough. But believe me, he never forgot why he was there as his bowels were screaming for release. He had to shit right now. He had waited until he was really ready before he went to request permission because he knew he would probably only be given a matter of minutes to make the head call. So all these games were really taking up time he didn't have to spare.

Believe me when I tell you that the DIs knew this too, but they loved playing games with people, so the fun continued, and Lawson was thrown out again, and this time they told him to stand at attention until he could get it all right. Lawson kept trying, but he just couldn't get it right. Even if he would have gotten it right, they probably wouldn't have let him go to the head. They had already decided he was going to shit in his pants. So they made Lawson stand at attention until nature took its course. When nature did, nature's little helpers were right there to applaud Her Majesty; they also made sure we all knew what Lawson had done. I wasn't going to put this part in, but it's true, so here we go. They told him to remove his trousers, shake the shit out in the sand, and put the trousers back on. Only this time, put them on over his head and button up the fly. He stood there in the hot California sun, baking for about thirty minutes, marinating in the smell of his own shit. Yeah, fine cars, beaches, movie stars, that's why I went to California.

After that, they made Lawson remove his trousers and take them to the washrack and launder them and himself. Well, you can bet the next time head calls were in order and Lawson thought he had to go, he went. He was like a man possessed of the devil. It didn't make any difference who was occupying the space; Lawson removed them and seated himself, thereby earning the name Mad Dog Lawson. Now if there are any of you that have to go to the bathroom, report to the duty hut and request permission. The drill instructor is in.

They had all kinds of little games and tricks to play on the recruits. There were so many, in fact, I sometimes think there must have been a special guidebook for drill instructors titled *Games You'll Enjoy and They'll Hate*. I remember when the Dionne-Dewey act got caught smoking without permission. We called them the Dionne-Dewey comedy act. Anyhow, they just had to have a cigarette, so when we were given some free time that evening, they decided to try and sneak off and have a smoke. As they were sneaking off, they decided that they couldn't stay out in the open and smoke, so they climbed into a dipsty dumpster, which is a huge trash container, and lit up. Just about the time they got those babies going really well, along comes a brand-new second lieutenant who sees, hears, and smells everything. When he walks past that dipsty dumpster, he smells smoke. Naturally he thinks the damn thing is on fire, so he starts yelling, "Fire! Fire! Fire!"

Along come ten or twelve guys with their water buckets. Just as they arrive, he grabs the top of the dumpster and lifts it and the recruits reach over the side and deposit their water right on the Dionne-Dewey comedy act. They aren't yelling; they are crouched in the corner, hiding from the shavetail lieutenant. Like the hero he knows he is going to be, he jumps onto the dumpster to take a closer look and smell to make sure the inferno is out, and he sees the comedy act soaking wet and cowering in the corner. By this time, Sergeants Whaley and Connors arrive. Dionne and Dewey climb out and are escorted back to the platoon area where they are really given the opportunity to perform for the whole platoon. Center stage baby.

The term *shavetail lieutenant* comes from the cavalry days when there was an ornery horse or mule that would kick at you when you got behind him. They would shave his tail to identify him because being kicked by it could really ruin your life. Second lieutenants who are green behind the ears and really don't know shit could also, in their zeal to prove themselves, do dumb things that could ruin a trooper's life, thus the term *shavetail lieutenants.*

If you have ever seen one of those French dances where the man throws the woman all over the stage, you've got a pretty good idea how their act started out. Whaley and Connors had the male leads, and Dionne and Dewey played the females. Everyone was terrific. The first part of the act, which lasted about five minutes, showed a tremendous amount of stunt work. The second part of the act consisted of a series of physical exercises with the locker boxes and buckets of sand. This lasted for the better part of an hour. Then it was on to the third and final act, the finale, so to speak.

For the finale, they both got one white towel, which was dampened, and they were presented with one cigar each. The damp towels were wrapped around their heads and faces so that there was only a very small hole in front of their mouths where the cigars were placed. Then the cigars were lit, and Dionne and Dewey began puffing away, like mad. Those two were really smoking. They made smoking Joe Frasier look like he was a beginner. There was smoke coming out all over their towels. Pretty soon they started coughing and gagging and they dropped their cigars, but Whaley and Connors stayed right there and, on cue, placed them back in their respective holes. Their act continued until their cigars disappeared into their respective holes. Then the towel began to smolder a little, and the Dionne-Dewey comedy act began getting weak in the knees and folded up. The towels were removed and the act was revived. They were a little green around the gills and they vomited some, but the real problem was their lips. They were really blistered, and eating for the next few days was a pretty touch and go deal. Their smoking lamp was put out for the remainder of boot camp, and I don't remember ever seeing them crawling into or out of the dipsty dumpster for the remaining eight weeks. I haven't heard from either one of them since boot camp, but if either one of you clowns is out there, drop me a line. I'm curious to know if you are smokers or not.

It is imperative to follow orders exactly and immediately. People's lives depend on it. Smoking, especially at night, is visual. Everyone has seen or heard about the sniper. Well, I'll tell you the smoke and smell that comes off the cigarette can be smelled in a pristine environment from a lot farther away than the ember can be seen and you can't hide it.

Things were pretty routine for the next week or two. We went to classes, practiced our drills, cleaned our quarters and gear, and took our fair share of lumps from the drill instructors and each other. We were in our ninth week now, and in a few days, we would finally get a chance to fire all this steel and wood we'd been lugging around for the last couple of months. Christ, I never thought the day would come, and here it finally was. We spent more time cleaning our rifles and learning their nomenclature than anything else now. The day finally came when we were going to leave for the rifle range. We had morning chow, returned to our platoon area, collected our gear, and loaded onto a bus. We drove across the recruit depot and came to the main gate. Sergeant Erwin showed the marine guard our orders, and we pulled out onto the boulevard and headed to the range.

I looked around at some of the other guys, and I could see some of them would have liked nothing better than to walk right off that bus and head for home. Not me though. I was ready for this turkey. I couldn't wait to fire that damn gun. I'd carried it two months everywhere I went; I'd cleaned it up, not good enough sometimes, dug it up piece by piece, and had put that gun back together a hundred other times. I'd been hit with it, built my body with it, and even slept with it. Now I was ready to fire it. I'd gone through all the courting rituals; now I wanted a climax. We drove through San Diego and out to the highway. We saw our first civilians in months, and I had to admit it all looked pretty good. I don't know how long the drive from MCRD to Camp Matthews took. That busload of recruits was all drooling over themselves every time they saw a girl or a fine old car go by. Being among civilians was like being in the middle of the biggest candy store ever, and we were all little kids again.

We traveled for a couple of hours and finally arrived at Camp Matthews. We were told to saddle up, grab our gear, and file off the bus single file and form our platoon. We were standing in front of a large two-story brick building. Sergeant Erwin informed us, in his own inimitable way, that this building, or at least the upper floor, would be our home for the next two weeks. He also informed us that it was a new building and we were, in no way, to deface it. Then he got to the meat and potatoes.

"Youse maggots are here for one reason and one reason only—to learn how to fire this weapon. If any of youse don't learn to fire it proficiently, then do me a favor and learn how to operate it well enough to blow your own lousy heads off because, as far as I'm concerned, any maggot who can't at least qualify with his rifle doesn't deserve to be a marine. And if he's got any sense and he's in my platoon, he's better off killing himself before I get my hands on his raunchy ass. Do I make myself perfectly clear?"

We all replied in unison at the top of our lungs, "Sir, yes, sir."

He said, "From now on, your living area will be referred to as the squad bay. Is that perfectly clear?"

Once again, we replied, "Sir, yes, sir."

"All right, you maggots, saddle up and head to the squad bay, and upon arriving, find a rack, put your gear in the locker box under the rack, and stand at the foot of the rack."

We all replied, "Sir, yes, sir."

To which he yelled, "Do it!"

We grabbed our shit and ran like a Hottdamn bunch of maniacs up the stairs and into the squad bay. Upon arriving, we found that we no longer had double racks. We had single racks, and we all began to choose the rack of our choice. Some guys wanted to be as far away from the windows as possible. This, naturally, caused a great deal of instant hate and discontent among the troops which, naturally, led to the thing we had learned best—fighting.

About 50 percent of the platoon began practicing their latest hand-to-hand combat techniques. The other 50 percent had found racks that no one else seemed to want when Sergeant Erwin walked in. I was standing at the end of my chosen rack and I thought, *Oh my God, he's going to kill those guys.* Instead, he looked at the battle going on like a lion surveying his domain, smiling like the cat that licked the cream, and left the room. The war ensued for about fifteen minutes more before a silent truce was signed and everyone had a rack he was satisfied with or, at least, could defend from any-one else who wanted it. This, by the way, was the first time we were allowed to make a choice by ourselves. I assume Erwin had decided we worked well enough as a group, and it was time to allow our indi-viduality to come out a little.

There was some humor in this whole ordeal with the humor, of course, being supplied by the Dionne-Dewey comedy act. Dionne wanted to be by Dewey, and Dewey wanted to be by Dionne. There was only one problem: there were about five other guys who wanted the two racks they had decided to set up housekeeping in. Just about the time Dewey would beat the people away from his rack, there would be three people attacking Dionne, and Dewey would have to go to the aid of his friend, and by the time they got his rack secured, they would have to go back and recapture Dewey's. This went on for fifteen minutes or so, and they finally ended up next to each other, which, of course, caused them more problems than joy because they would talk to each other all night, and instead of getting six or seven hours of good sleep, they would end up getting only a couple of hours, which definitely affected their performance at the range. These two guys were from Ohio and knew each other since elementary school, practically their whole lives, and going through high school, then joining the corps together. They even dated sisters. They were close buddies.

It was about 12:30 p.m. before Erwin returned. We were all standing at the foot of our racks as we were instructed to do and he said, "Get washed up for chow and fall out in front of the building. You've got five minutes."

Then he left, and we all began to stampede, but to where? Where were the washracks located around here anyhow? Some guys ran out into the hall and downstairs with their soap and towel. Some guys stood and looked at one another with their soap and towel. There were two doorways located in the squad bay; neither door was marked and both were closed. We had no idea what was behind either door.

Mad Dog Lawson opened the first door. He was still hell on wheels about heads and washrooms. A natural born leader, you might say. He threw open the door and charged in, towel flying behind him and a hearty gung ho on his lips. We were all about ready to gung ho in after him when he suddenly came flying back out of the hatch on his back. We all made an abrupt stop and stared at him lying on his back on the floor. In another second, we all knew what had happened to our leader. He had run into a brick wall by the name of Sergeant Mills. Sergeant Mills stepped into the doorway and filled that opening from side to side and top to bottom.

He said, "What are you slimy turds doing?"

One brave trooper in the rear stammered, "Sir, we thought, I mean we were looking for the head, sir."

To which Sergeant Mills replied, "Well, this isn't the head, asshole. This is the new duty hut. The head is through that door." And he pointed to the second door and said, "Now get out of my sight."

We all began our stampede to the second door, right over Private Lawson, a.k.a. Mad Dog. Boy, some leader he turned out to be, taking us right into the enemy's camp.

We washed, returned our gear, and headed for the Platoon Street. As we passed the door that our former leader had so gallantly entered earlier, we saw him standing in front of it, beating on the wall and requesting permission to speak to the DI.

We also heard Sergeant Mills saying, "I can't hear you, Lawson. I can't hear you."

Huh, if he couldn't hear him, how did he know who it was? Strange games these people played. We formed our platoon, and the squad leaders reported their squads all present and accounted for, except Private Lawson.

Erwin asked, "Well, where the hell is he, Deeds?" Deeds was our new guide. He was the fourth one since me. Pierson had only lasted four days as our guide.

Deeds said, "Sir, he's upstairs in the squad bay, beating on the wall and screaming, sir."

Everyone kind of snickered at that, except Erwin and Deeds knew then and there that he had fucked up. Erwin walked over to where he was standing, got him in his favorite hold, and dragged him back upstairs to the squad bay where Lawson was still beating on the wall and screaming. When he saw Lawson, he let go of Deeds and walked over to Lawson. He pushed Lawson out of the way and barged through the doorway. They were both expecting him to come flying out because we all assumed Sergeant Mills would think Erwin was Lawson. What didn't happen surprised both of those guys.

They heard Erwin say, "What the hell are you doing playing games with my time, asshole? I'm trying to get these animals fed so we can get down to work, and you're jacking off up here." Lawson and Deeds looked at each other and wondered who he was talking to, surely not Sergeant Mills.

Then they heard Sergeant Mills's voice saying, "What the hell is wrong with you?"

Then Erwin said, "You, you, Goddamn gorilla. Quit fucking around with my troops."

I believe that was Sergeant Mills's first platoon, and he had never taken a platoon to the range, and I don't think he was aware of the seriousness of these next two weeks.

Erwin said, "We've got a lot of work to do here and no time for playing games." They thought for sure that World War III was going to start, but it didn't.

Sergeant Mills just said, "All right, Sergeant Erwin, whatever you say."

Erwin said, "You're fucking right now. Let's get these assholes to chow."

They came out together, Erwin first, then Mills.

When they looked up and saw Lawson and Deeds standing there, they looked at each other, and Erwin said, "You assholes, get down with your platoon."

Lawson and Deeds about-faced and double-timed down the stairs and returned to formation. We all double-timed to the new chow hall. It was about two miles away. We went through the chow line in our usual way and were given ten minutes to eat. We double-timed back to our squad area and got out rifles and were told to bring them back outside with our cleaning gear. I figured we were going to fire a couple hundred rounds apiece just for effect and familiarization and then clean our weapons, but we didn't. We were told to find a place to sit and listen up. All we listened to was the same thing we'd listened to before. It was another class on the nomenclature of the M14 rifle, semiautomatic, air-cooled, gas-operated shoulder weapon. I was thinking to myself, *For crying out loud, aren't we ever going to shoot this frigging thing?*

Sergeant Connors was giving the class, and Erwin, Mills, and Whaley were walking around, giving extra help and instruction where needed. Whaley wasn't thumping anyone. He hardly ever did when Erwin was around.

He stopped in front of McGowan, grabbed his rifle, and said, "McGowan, you big dummy, what is this?"

Mac looked at him perplexed and said, "Sir, my gun, sir." And Whaley went nuts.

"Your gun? Your gun? You big stupid overgrown pile of human excrement! Your gun? Get on your feet, McGowan, and grab your cock!"

Mac said, "Sir, what, sir?"

Whaley said, "Your cock! Grab it, you big dummy."

Mac looked at him real strange-like, and Whaley gave him a quick slap in the nuts and said, "Grab it, stupid! Don't act like you've never grabbed your cock before. Grab it now." Mac did as he was told with no small amount of embarrassment.

Whaley then said, "Hold on to it real tight and hold your other hand out in front of me."

Mac did, and Whaley placed his rifle in his free hand and said, "Now, Private McGowan, this is your rifle," pointing to his extended arm. "And this"—with another slap on the nuts—"is your gun. This rifle is for shooting, and this, the cock, is for fun." Then he slapped him again and said, "You got that, shitbird?"

Mac said, "Sir, yes, sir."

"Then repeat it, McGowan."

"Um, this is my rifle," and he held it up and kind of grinned. "And this is my gun" and looked down at his crotch. "This is for shooting and this is for fun. How's that, sir?"

Whaley just looked at him and said, "Good. Good, McGowan. Real good. But you'll get better. I want you to come out here on the sidewalk, and I want you to keep holding what you have where you have it, and I want you to run up and down the sidewalk, repeating what I told you until I tell you to stop. Do you understand, Private McGowan?"

"Sir, yes, sir."

"Then do it. Do it."

"Sir, aye, aye, sir."

McGowan began running back and forth, holding what he was holding and repeating, "This is my rifle and this is my gun. This is for shooting and this is for fun."

He did it until we went to evening chow three hours later. His voice got hoarse, and you could hardly hear what he was saying, and every once in a while, he'd stumble and fall and have to let go of his gun to catch himself, but he never let go of his rifle, and he always got back up and started again.

We all felt bad for him, and we all hated Sergeant Whaley in the worst way, but we all knew what the M14 was. It was a rifle. Around 5:00 p.m., we secured our weapons and gear and washed up for chow. After returning from chow, we fell back outside and were taken for a four-mile run over to what they called the snap in area, and then we returned to the squad bay. McGowan really enjoyed the run. It was just what Dr. Whaley would have ordered for him.

In the squad bay, we were told to shower, write letters, and do what we wanted until taps sounded at 9:30. This was really strange because we were always given ten minutes for this and ten minutes for that, and now we had two hours to shower and do what we wanted. Of course, we had to stay inside the squad bay, but still, this was a first. Some guys started undressing, and others just sat down and shot the bull with one another. The place took on a college-dorm atmosphere.

About ten minutes later, Sergeant Erwin came out of his office and living quarters, and someone yelled, "Attention on deck." We all snapped to attention.

Erwin said, "There are about ten number ten cans in my office filled with sand. I want you"—and he grabbed a turd by the shoulder—"to go in and bring them out here and place them around the squad bay." The turd was released and went into the office and began distributing the cans.

Erwin said, "These cans are called butt kits. They are for discarding cigarette butts. They will be cleaned and emptied every morning, or the smoking lamp will be put out for good." We all looked at him in amazement.

Up until then, we were only given one or two cigarettes a day, usually after a meal or before taps at night, so we didn't understand when he said, "From now on, when you're in the squad bay, the smoking lamp will be lit." Then he turned and walked away. We all looked at each other and, almost at once, started scrambling for our cigarettes and lighters. All of us, that is, except Dionne and Dewey. This was more like it. We were in our ninth week now, and we were finally going to be treated like people, or at least like humans. Most of us spent the next hour or so writing home to whomever was most important to us or talking to one another or taking a leisurely shower for the first time in two months.

I took my shower first. There were about twenty showerheads and only ten or so being used. It was a real strange sight. One of the other guys in the shower with me was Lawson. He was on the other side of the room, and I could see he wasn't enjoying the shower much. He had this crazy look in his eyes like, at any minute, fifty more guys were going to come charging in, and he'd have to fight for his place, as usual. It never happened, but it wouldn't have made any difference; he only took about three minutes, and he was gone. I stayed in that shower about a half an hour until I realized I was giving up my free time. I charged out, dried off, put on some skivvies, and began my ritual. First, I opened my locker box and withdrew my picture of her, then my letter writing gear, then my cigarettes, then I closed my locker box. I sat on one half of it and used the other half for my desk. I spent the next part of the hour writing, dreaming, and smoking.

At 9:00 p.m., we were told we had half an hour before taps, and when the lights went out, so did the smoking lamp. We were told to get some sleep because tomorrow was going to be a busy day.

I put my gear away and was just about ready to crawl into my rack when Lawson said, "Hey, Romeo, how come you think Mills let Erwin talk to him like that?"

I said, "What are you talking about?" and he explained what he had heard when Erwin came up looking for him before we went to chow.

After he told me, I replied, "I don't know. I can't imagine Sergeant Mills being afraid of anyone, can you?"

"No, but he must be because he sure took it."

Just then Sergeant Mills came to the door of the office and said, "Deeds and Lawson report to the duty hut."

When we were first given our free time after evening chow, Lawson had told me what he'd witnessed between Erwin and Mills. Lawson's heart sank like the *Titanic*, wondering what was in store for him now. They both stood up and ran to the door.

Lawson was just about to start knocking when he heard Erwin say, "Get in here." They entered and stood at attention.

Erwin told them, "Stand at ease. I'm only going to say this once. If either one of you repeat what you heard earlier today, you'll have me to answer to, understand?"

They said, "Sir, aye, aye, sir."

"Sergeant Mills and I are both sergeants, but I have more time in grade, so legally I outrank him. That's why I'm the platoon com-mander and he's a drill instructor. He isn't afraid of me, and I'm not afraid of him. A good marine isn't afraid of anyone because there isn't anyone who can kick his ass until they've done it, but when someone outranks you, you respect him and you don't question his decisions or test his authority. Understand?"

"Sir, yes, sir."

Then he asked Sergeant Mills, "Do you have anything to say?"

Sergeant Mills replied, "No, Sergeant Erwin, you've said it all."

Erwin said, "All right, you two, get out of here"

They about-faced and left. Lawson came over to me and told me what Erwin had told him.

"Well, that answered that question, didn't it?"

He said, "Yeah, but I wonder who's really tougher."

And then Lawson said, "I don't know, but I guess I'm not a marine yet because I know both of them could whip me and ain't neither one of them done it yet."

I just laughed and Lawson said, "Before I go home, I will be a marine, and then my older brothers better get the fuck out of my way."

Lights went off, taps played, and we all slept like baldheaded babies.

The next morning, before reveille sounded and before I could get out of my rack, McGowan was kneeling next to it and complaining to me about how sore his dick was. He said he couldn't hardly touch the sonofabitch because he'd rubbed it raw running up and down for two and a half hours. Reveille sounded at 5:30 a.m. as usual; it was still dark out as usual, and we all rolled out, washed up, and fell out as usual.

We ran to morning chow, ate, and were taken to the distribution center where we were issued some new gear. The new gear consisted of two items—a small notebook to keep our shooting information in and a shooting jacket complete with patches on the sleeve and a pad on the shoulder. It looked mighty fine, and I was proud. Now if they would just give me some ammunition and point me in the right direction, I would go out and destroy my country's enemies. That's just how I felt—proud, cocky, and ready to take on the world. We all put our shooting notebooks in the pocket of our jackets and put our jackets on our backs and looked at one another. Cool, real cool.

You could see we were all thinking the same thing—which way to Vietnam.

We formed up and double-timed off into the rising sun, but we weren't going to Vietnam, no sir, but we were going to war. We would be spending a lot of time over the next seven days going to where we were yesterday before we returned to our squad bay. Going to the snapping in range and we didn't even have any ammunition.

"For crying out loud, what's the big deal?"

I have to break in here and tell you that I had never fired a rifle in my entire life, only a shotgun. It was a single shot 16-gauge Winchester, and I used it to hunt birds and rabbits. I also have to tell you that I wasn't a bit afraid to fire this rifle. I was dying to fire it, in fact, but there were some guys who were afraid. I'd say probably 30 percent of the people in my platoon had never fired a weapon of any kind. We got to the snapping in range and were introduced to our professional marksmanship instructor (PMI). His name was Corporal Peschke. He was about 6 feet 1 inch, 190 pounds, and good-looking, and he spoke like a Southern gentleman. He walked with an easy natural gate that reminded me of a country boy walking through a field with no shoes on. I was impressed with him. He introduced himself to us, and our original leaders, Erwin, Mills, Whaley, and Connors stepped to the rear and remained silent. Corporal Peschke told us to stand at ease, make ourselves comfortable, and smoke if we liked. Now we all liked him. He began to tell us that there were a lot of things we had to learn and not very much time to learn them, so we had better listen up to everything he said and if there was anything we didn't understand, we should ask questions and to be sure before we did anything or someone could get killed.

Then he lowered the boom on me by saying, "Does anyone have any ammunition?" Of course, no one said anything because no one had any yet. Then he said, "Good, because you are not supposed to have any yet." Then he lowered the boom and said, "And you won't have any until next week."

I was shattered. It seemed to me that I would never get a chance to chamber a round and see what I could do with this rifle. What I didn't realize at that particular time in my illustrious Marine Corps career was that the Marine Corps got the leftovers. They were the redheaded stepchild of the military, and they were at war, and they didn't have five thousand rounds for each of us marine recruits to waste shooting at a cardboard target.

We were told to stack our rifles and follow him. He took us to a large open area and told us to sit down. He proceeded to show us the four shooting positions. The first one was called offhand. You stood sideways, facing your target, feet spread shoulder width apart. The second position was sitting. You sat flat on your butt facing your target, sidewise, knees bent, feet touching or crossed at the ankle. The third position was kneeling. You tucked one foot under your butt and placed the other one out in front of you, half bent, and leaned your weight forward onto it. The fourth position is called the prone position—lying flat on your stomach, arms in front and off to the side, feet spread out behind you. He assumed all these positions for us, and then we were placed, one at a time, in each position for about five minutes. Then we went and got our rifles. For the next few hours, we practiced one position—the offhand. We learned to steady our holding arm with the sling of the rifle.

All this time I thought the sling was just for carrying the sucker. After a while, the sling would cut off your circulation and you really were steady. We were taken to chow on the double, and we returned on the double and learned another position. We spent the entire day there learning one position after another. The only time we weren't practicing a position was when we were double-timing to and from the chow hall, and believe it or not, when one of our DIs would call us into a formation and yell, "Double time," we were happy because getting into all those torturous shooting positions with that sling all wrapped around you was painful as hell. That was all we did for about twelve hours a day.

Every once in a while, someone would come along and punch the end of your rifle, and if you fell over backward, you were in trouble. By the end of the day, our legs were sore, our backs were sore, our shoulders were sore from being punched on our patch by hitting the end of the barrel and driving the stock into our shoulder. Our arms were black-and-blue from the damn sling being wrapped so tightly around them. I never would have dreamed that shooting without ammunition could be so painful.

We were told to do whatever we wanted until taps. Everyone charged for their cigarettes and the showers. Taps sounded, and we all retired for the night. People were waking up moaning and groaning all night from the cramps in their legs, backs, and arms. It was really funny until you got one yourself, then, oh boy, you were moaning and groaning with the best of them. I got mine in the upper thigh of my left leg. I called for Lawson, who slept next to me. My whole leg was in pain, and I couldn't move it. He came over and started rubbing the back of my leg. I felt like a candy-ass fool, but it worked and the cramp went away. I believe I finally fell asleep in the prone position, or was it lying down offhand? I really don't remember. I just know as long as I was awake, I didn't even try to move my left leg again.

Reveille sounded, and we went through our normal morning procedure and returned to the snapping in range for another day of yoga. Today, on top of the yoga, we had another thing to learn—the dos and don'ts of the rifle range. These procedures included things like, you never, but never, point your weapon anywhere but down-range. You only load a bullet when given the order to load and lock, meaning insert your magazine, chamber a round, and put your safety on. You never have your safety off until the order is given to commence firing. There are a hundred more dos and don'ts, such as if you have a stoppage while you were firing, you would point your weapon down range, raise your hand, and wait for someone to come and help you clear your weapon. There were so many things to learn and remember, so very many things, and every day we were given more, instructed more, until we thought we were going to burst with knowledge about the M14 rifle, and I felt the week would never end. Never.

After the first day, they started bringing our lunch out to us in trucks so we wouldn't have to run back to the chow hall for it. Before this week, we would all mumble under our breath when we were told to fall out for a run. Now we had come to look forward to the run as a break in the routine and a way to stretch the kinks out of our muscles that were produced by the body-bending rifle positions. The days now dragged by ever so slowly, and our heads hurt as bad as our bodies had before from all the things we had to learn. After the sixth day of snapping in, we were given a day of rest. Well, not really rest, but we didn't have to return to the snapping in range. Instead, we double-timed about three miles over to another range. As we double-timed, we sang or chanted. Sergeant Erwin was running us, and he chanted the best of all our instructors.

We'd be running along, and he would say, "Platoon 189."

And we would repeat, in loud voices, in unison, "Platoon 189."

Then he'd say, "Stand by."

And we'd say, "Sir, stand by, sir."

And then we all knew we were going to chant, and the chanting always made the running easier. Sergeant Erwin would sing out something like, "I got a girl in New Orleans." And the whole platoon would repeat it.

"She kisses sailors and blows marines." And we'd repeat that.

Some of our favorite chants went like this: "I got a girl in Paris, France. She's got a gold mine in her pants."

"I got a girl who lives on a hill. She won't do it, but her sister will."

"Give me glasses tinted green. I'm a Hollywood marine."

At that time in the corps, marines went to boot camp on the West Coast in San Diego, California, and on the East Coast at Parris Island, South Carolina, so we were out in California and were called the Hollywood marines. I honestly, to this day, don't know what East Coast marines were called, but for some reason, in the back of my mind, I always felt that they had it harder than we did, maybe because it is so much more humid in South Carolina than in California.

Anyhow, you get the idea. The chanting always perked us up and made us feel better, and it made the running almost fun. We had run about two miles, and the chanting stopped. We could hear sounds, rumbling sounds, like thunder. It was a beautiful day without a cloud in the sky. We continued to run, and the farther we ran, the louder the sound became. Finally, we turned a bend in the road and were halted by a large guardrail with two marine sentries.

Sergeant Erwin talked with them; they raised the guardrail, and we double-timed through. We ran for another ten minutes and halted in what appeared to be a large parking lot. We were told that we were at the qualifying range where we would spend all of next week. We were here today to watch so that we would have an idea of what we were supposed to do. We were lined up, single file, and given a "face right" command, and Sergeant Erwin said, "Forward, march."

We marched to the edge of the asphalt and were halted. There it was; the ground dropped about ten feet and stretched out about 700 yards, that's seven football fields, but it was actually 700 meters. There were different firing lines about every hundred meters. On the first firing line there was a platoon of marines. From where we were standing, they looked like toy soldiers about three inches tall. They were sitting down on boxes, and on a given command, they stood, took aim, and began firing. As they fired, you would see their bodies jerk and see a puff of smoke and then hear the report of the rifle.

We were told they were firing in the offhand position, and they were given ten minutes to fire ten rounds. The distance was 100 meters, or 100 yards. A distance of 100 meters is equivalent to 110 yards. In front of them, targets were being raised and lowered as each individual would fire a round. The target would go down, be marked, and then come back up, and the shooter would be shown his score by means of a large metal disk on a pole. One side was white. If he hit in the one ring, at nine o'clock, the disk would be placed in the left-hand bottom corner of the target using the target as a clock face. It was to show the shooter where, in the ring, he had hit so he could figure his windage and elevation. A two was the right-hand corner, a three, top left, a four ring, top right. There was no five ring; it was the bull's-eye. When you hit the bull's-eye, they ran the white disk straight up to the bull's-eye, which was in the center of the target. They held it there, then moved it up, down, left, or right, depending on where in the bull's-eye you had hit. Now comes the kicker; there are two sides to every coin, or should I have said disk?

The opposite side of this disk was painted bright red, and it was only used when you missed the target. When that happened, they would turn the red side toward you and swing it from the left-hand corner across the face of the target to the right-hand corner and then back again. That meant you missed everything, you big dummy. It also meant you could expect a visit from Corporal Peschke or one of the other DIs or PMIs. This particular disk sign was called, affectionately, Maggie's drawers. I don't know where the saying came from or who made it up, but I imagine some juggie, back in the beginning of time, was qualifying and just as he was about to squeeze that last round off he thought about the previous night's liberty and the fancy drawers that girl he was with was wearing and he missed the target. Then when the PMIs asked him what the hell had happened and what was he thinking about, he told them and that girl's name was probably Maggie, hence Maggie's drawers. Anyhow, Maggie's drawers were definitely something you did not want to see, at least not at the rifle range. The target was about four feet across and probably five feet long. The bull's-eyes area was eighteen inches across up and down, and that is where you wanted to be, not in Maggie's drawer's country.

We stood and watched them shooting, and our smoking lamp was lit. The platoon that was firing, at the 150- meter line, finished, then assembled and moved back to the 200-meter line. We were told that they would fire ten more rounds from there, from the sitting position, and at rapid fire. The platoon assumed their positions on the firing line. Some commands were given, their weapons brought to the ready, aim, fire position, but there were no targets in view. Suddenly the targets appeared, and all hell broke loose. There were thirty marines firing ten rounds apiece in about fifteen seconds.

The effect on me was like a bomb exploding under my feet, and here I was about 500 yards away. I could just imagine what it was like on the firing line. By now, I was excited. I felt like racing down there and firing ten thousand rounds myself. God, tomorrow would never come. Never. We'd been standing around for half an hour, and we were all absolutely google-eyed at what we had just seen when, suddenly, we were called to attention and formed up to return to our squad bay. The remainder of that day passed unbearably slow. We ate and snapped in, ate and snapped in. Then we were given two hours to write home and shower up before taps. I spent my time writing home and showering up. Taps sounds and Whaley said, "Get plenty of sleep tonight, girls. You'll need it tomorrow."

I lay there thinking about what I'd seen earlier that day, and for the life of me, I couldn't even get to feeling drowsy.

Probably an hour passed when Lawson said, "Hey, Romeo, are you awake?"

"No, but go ahead anyway."

"Are you scared?"

"Scared of what, Mad Dog?"

"Firing your rifle tomorrow."

"Hell no, man, I can't wait. How about you?" There was a hesitation and I said, "Lawson, are you still with me?"

"No, I mean, yeah. I mean, I ain't never fired a gun before."

"A gun? You'd better hope Whaley didn't hear that."

"Oh, you know what I mean."

"Look, Mad Dog, I never fired a rifle either, but you watched thirty guys do it today for half an hour, and they are all just one week ahead of us in training. Hell, man, don't worry. By tomorrow evening, you'll be standing tall and looking good at the five-hundred-meter line, knocking the shit out of that old bull. Don't worry. Look how rotten you were in the head when we first got here nine weeks ago. Now you're the baddest mother in the head."

He gave a little snort and said, "Aw, c'mon, Romeo." And I rolled over and went to sleep.

Reveille sounded, as always, and we all scampered around like maniacs and fell out for chow. We double-timed out to the range. The sun was just coming up, and Erwin told us to fall out and to practice snapping in until our PMIs arrived. By this time, I was so comfortable in the kneeling position that I could almost fall asleep, and I damn near did. I hadn't slept too well after listening to Lawson. I began wondering if I would be scared. Then I remembered to just do the best I could with what I had, and in my mind, I fired about two thousand rounds, everyone in the bull's-eye, of course.

Corporal Peschke arrived about twenty minutes after we did. He looked refreshed and cheerful and said, "Good morning, people. Are we all ready to become dingers?"

We were all so shocked at being called people instead of turds or maggots that we didn't reply. Erwin did. He said, "I hate a sonofabitch who is happy in the morning. Let's get this ass-kicking ceremony on the road, Peschke." I think Sergeant Erwin spent the better part of his evening at the NCO club, which could explain his lack of sociability.

Corporal Peschke just smiled real big and said, "Okay. Fall them in and bring them to the 150-firing line."

"Fall in, you maggots, and don't forget who you are and where you are. If I get shot today, I'll find the turd that pulled the trigger and tear his head off."

We all marched down to the 150-firing line and were placed beside a shooting box. We stood at ease, and the PMIs and DIs distributed the ammunition. They deposited ten rounds in each box and said, "Don't touch anything until you are told to." The look on their faces said, "Or I'll break all your fingers, toes, arms, legs, and anything else I can break." In other words, they were serious. Corporal Peschke took over from there.

He had a bullhorn, and he said, "Gentleman"—then he smiled and looked at Erwin who was frowning, as usual—"we're going to fire one round at a time from the offhand position. You won't need your magazine. You will put one round in the chamber at a time because two won't fit. Then you will let the slide go home and when you put the round in, make sure the pointed end is forward and safety is on."

Just then, I heard a slide go forward and so did Corporal Peschke. He dropped the bullhorn and leaped about five yards in one jump. As he did, the recruit that had let his slide go forward turned with a startled look on his face. Before he knew it, Peschke had jerked the weapon from his hands and slammed him in the gut with a beautiful horizontal butt stroke. The recruit fell over backward, gripping his stomach.

As quickly as he'd done all that, he ejected the round and threw the rifle to Whaley, who was standing by, and he said, "You'd better have a private talk with this young man." Whaley grabbed the recruit and dragged him off. Peschke resumed his instructions. We all reached for a round and placed it in the firing chamber. As soon as I touched that shiny projectile, I fell in love, and it's been the longest lasting relationship of my life so far. So small and compact and shiny I couldn't imagine it hurting a flea.

Peschke came over the bullhorn and said, "You never, but never, do anything while you're on this range until you are told to and then you do only what you are told to do. No more, no less. Now keeping your muzzle pointed downrange, check your safeties and make sure they are on, take one round, place it in the chamber, and let the slide go forward. The sound was wonderful, all metallic and clicky; it was music to my ears.

Peschke said, "We're going to fire this round. I want everyone to bring their weapon to their shoulder and adjust their feet so they have good body alignment on the target. Your rifle should fall on your target naturally when your body alignment is right. Be sure you're on the right target, and when your position is right, without moving your feet, sit down on the box." We all did that very well.

Then he said, "Now when I tell you to commence firing, you stand up, take aim on your target, take your safety off, and squeeze the round off. Remember everything you've been taught in the last week, and probably nobody will get killed. Once you've fired, put your safety on, and sit back down." Oh boy, it was almost time to fire this baby and I felt like you'd feel just before a fight or just before intercourse, anticipating like the feeling you get when you are about to climax.

The order was given, "Commence fire."

I stood up, brought my sweet baby to my shoulder, closed my left eye, laid my cheek on the stock, lined my front sight up with my rear sight, got a nice sight picture, took the safety off, and squeezed her off ever so gently, and all hell broke loose. My head snapped back when the stock slipped off of my shoulder and careened off my cheekbone, giving me the sensation of being punched. My body turned to the right, and my right arm almost went limp. For a second, I thought I had been shot. My shoulder was hurting, and my head was spinning. I sat down, put my safety on, rested my rifle on my lap, keeping the barrel pointed down range, and began feeling where the pain was. My shoulder hurt a little, my eye hurt worse. I could feel it starting to swell. I looked up and Erwin was standing in front of me, looking anything but pleased.

He said, "Get on your feet."

I stood up, forgetting all about my rifle, and as I stood, it slipped off of my lap. It would have fallen to the ground, except the sling was still secured around my arm.

Erwin immediately tore into me, "You, dumbass, you're not firing a BB gun. You're firing a real rifle. You have to hold it firmly, not like a fucking loaf of bread. Put your weapon on your shoulder like you were about to fire." I did as I was told, and as I lay my cheek on the stock, I felt my cheekbone again. It was throbbing like hell.

He said, "Now pull it into your shoulder and hold it firm."

And I did. Then he reached up and slapped the other side of my stock, slamming it into my cheekbone again and sending waves of pain shooting through my head. I never moved or flinched or anything, I just held on to that steel and wood for dear life and inwardly groaned as he hammered my stock two or three more times.

"Don't forget, dummy. Now sit down and listen up."

I sat down and looked down at that sonofabitch rifle and thought, *You, bastard, as nice as I've treated you and you try to beat the hell out of me. I'll never call you sweetie again. You're a bastard from this day on.* But the truth of the matter is, when you are shooting a high-powered rifle, you have to make sure it is fitted snugly into your shoulder so that the recoil is absorbed by your whole body. It's like being punched and the person's fist is right on your shoulder. It will push you a bit. If the fist is farther away, the punch comes in harder. I was focused so much on my sight picture and trigger squeeze as we had been snapping in for an entire week, but when we pulled the trigger then, there was no recoil.

I quit talking to that bastard when I heard Peschke on the bullhorn, "Did everyone's weapon discharge? If your weapon failed to discharge, put your safety on, and raise your hand." No one raised their hand, so he went on, "Now if you've moved your feet, stand up and get your body alignment again. Your targets are being marked now, so watch the butts, and the targets will be coming up and your marks will be given." We all sat there watching the empty area in front of us. A few more seconds passed, and suddenly, from out of the ground, all the targets appeared. A second later, signs started appearing. It was like New Year's Eve and the Fourth of July. There were red signs waving from left to right all up and down the firing line.

I heard Erwin, who was standing right behind me, say, "Wonderful, just fucking wonderful."

My sign appeared; it was white and came up from the bottom of the target and stopped directly over the bull's-eye and went directly down again.

He looked at me and said, "Is that your target?"

I just shook my head in bewilderment, and he grabbed the phone and said, "Remark number 23."

Again, the white disk came slowly up to the center, stayed a second, and disappeared down.

He yelled into the phone, "Where at on the bull? Numbers 12, 9, 6? Where?"

A second passed and he hung up and he looked at me and said, "You lucked out, Romeo. You were in the V-ring on the bull, probably for the last time this week." Then he walked away. Corporal Peschke came back on the bullhorn. He asked us how much elevation we had on our weapons. Nobody said anything; we'd forgotten all about the elevation and the windage.

He said, "Zero your elevation and your windage. Now at this distance, you should have approximately six clicks of elevation, and if you'll look off to the side of the targets about halfway down the firing range, you'll see a flag hanging on each side. It doesn't look like there is much or any wind blowing at the moment, so leave your windage at zero. Is everybody done?" A couple of hands came up here and there because some of the troops have never messed with their elevation or windage knobs and weren't sure what to do so a DI or PMI would go over and instruct them.

After everybody was squared away, Peschke said, "All right, take another round, sit back down, reload." As we were getting ready to fire again, all the instructors were busy squaring away one recruit after another, telling this one to do this and that one to do that.

Then Corporal Peschke gave us the order to commence fire when our targets appeared.

I prepared myself for shock. I was holding on to my bastard for dear life this time. I lined up my sights, waited until I saw black on the end of my front sight blade, and began to squeeze. As I took up my trigger slack and squeezed, I remembered what happened the previous time. Just as I felt in my mind that the round was about to go off, I jerked the trigger and it exploded. The pain returned to my cheek, not as badly as before, and my shoulder didn't hurt at all.

As I sat down I thought, *Hmm, not too bad when you hang on tight.* Then I wondered where the round went. The targets appeared and Erwin came strolling over.

"Well, where'd that one go, dummy?"

I said, "Sir, what was that, sir?"

"Where'd you hit on the target, turd?"

"Sir, I couldn't say, sir." I sat and he stood, and we both waited for the targets to reappear. They came up and were marked. My disk was white again, but not at the bull's-eye. It went to the lower left-hand corner and then all the way to the top of the target. I'd hit in the zero ring, or non-scoring ring, at twelve o'clock—from good to poor but still not a Maggie's drawer.

I looked at Erwin, and he said, "I watched you. You jerked the round off. You anticipated it going off, and you jerked the trigger instead of squeezing it," and he walked away. We were given the order to lock and load again, and we did. The order to commence fire was given, and we did. I'd like to say, here and now, the reason you locked and loaded was because, occasionally, a military rifle, or any rifle, I imagine, will do what they call slam fire. When you let the bolt go forward, it twists and locks the bullet in the chamber, and occasionally, if a primer on that bullet isn't set just right or if there is a malfunction with the bolt or firing pin, that weapon will fire, but not with the safety on.

One other thing, back in the sixties, we didn't wear earplugs or shooting glasses, and I can't recall one eye injury or anyone mentioning hearing loss. Don't all men get hard of hearing when they get old? That's why they learn to read and write when they are young, isn't it?

Back to the real world. I won't go over shot by shot what happened, but I got one Maggie's drawers and two more bull's-eyes, and the other five shots were somewhere from the zero ring to the four which, compared to some of the other guys, was really good. We had a couple of guys who did really well. One of them was Kowalski. He got about six bull's-eyes, and everything else was inside the three ring. It seemed strange to me because he hardly ever did anything else right. He messed up on drills sometimes and on the runs every time, and I was always getting slapped around because of him. I'd have to have a talk with him tonight and find out what the deal was. We were told to clear and lock all weapons and retire to the two-hundred-meter line. We all waited for someone to give the order to fall in, but no one did.

Then Corporal Peschke came over the bullhorn, "Well, people, let's go. We've got a lot to do."

Then Erwin said, "There will be no formations going from line to line. Just straggle back and don't take all day."

Hmm, the range was sure different from the weeks preceding it. We all started walking back to the two-hundred-meter line in twos and threes. I saw the guy who'd let his slide go forward ahead of time and asked what Whaley did to him. He turned around and held up his index finger on his right hand. It was a little bloody, and the nail was broken.

I said, "What the hell did he do to it?" thinking maybe he'd chewed on it for a while.

He said, "I'll tell you later. I think I'm going to be sick." He walked away and relieved himself of breakfast. We proceeded to the next firing line. When I got there, I looked back and saw Whaley standing over him, yelling. Then he made him come to attention, and he just walked away, leaving him standing there. When we all arrived and were seated, Corporal Peschke asked Sergeant Whaley what he was doing.

Whaley said, "What do you mean? I'm standing here looking at you."

Peschke said, "I mean, what are you making the recruit stand out there for?"

"Recruit? I don't see any recruit out there, just a shitbird. Go ahead and commence fire."

Peschke looked at Whaley and then at Sergeant Erwin and said, "C'mon, we've got a job to do."

Erwin yelled, "Murphy, get up here on the double and take your place." We were all ready for the two-hundred-meter line. I looked down the firing line and caught Mad Dog Lawson's eye. He was smiling from ear to ear and gave me the old A-OK sign. I smiled and returned the sign.

Corporal Peschke said, "We'll fire ten more rounds from this range, only it won't be slow fire. It will be timed fire from the sitting position. Take ten rounds from your box and put them into your magazine. Hold the mag in your left hand and your rifle in your right. Rifle right, mag left. There's an old shooter saying that best explains how to fire timed or rapid. It's called BRASS. BRASS means breathe, relax (blow about half your breath out), aim (take up the trigger), slack, and squeeze. If you'll all do that before you start firing, you'll do much better. Now insert your magazine and lock your weapon. Now assume the sitting position."

My sitting position wasn't my best, but I felt it would do.

Peschke said, "We have moved back fifty meters, so I want everyone to add one click of elevation to their rear sight." We all made the adjustment.

"When you hear the command lock and load, you'll chamber your first round, and when you hear the command, commence fire, aim in, and, when your targets appear, take your safety's off and begin firing. If there are any malfunctions during the firing time, put your safety on and raise your hand and someone will help you. Are there any questions? All right, you may commence firing when you see your targets."

I believe we had thirty seconds to fire ten rounds. We were all aiming in on nothing because the targets were in the down position and we couldn't see them. Just as my right eye began to water and blur up, the targets came into view and everything exploded around me. I lifted my head away from my stock and rubbed my eye, trying to clear my vision. Just as I got it fixed and zeroed in on my target, the targets disappeared. I didn't know what to do. They had come and gone, and I'd never even fired.

Corporal Peschke said, "Clear and lock all weapons. Anyone with any rounds left or who had a malfunction, raise your hand."

About ten of the thirty or so people raised their hands and instructors came to help them. Sergeant Connors came to help me. I unslung my rifle and handed it to him and dropped my head. He released the mag and cleared the chamber, then he took out nine rounds from the mag and said, "Not even one round, Romeo? Did you have the safety on? Jesus, are you afraid to fire or what?" I started to answer, but the bullhorn cut me off.

"Stand by. Your scores are coming up."

And up came the targets and the disks. I watched mine and saw there were seven hits and three Maggie's drawers. I turned and looked at Connors, and he shook his head and said, "Jesus! Jesus!"

Hell, I hadn't even fired and I had seven hits on my target.

Connors turned to Pierson on my right and said, "How many hits do you have on your target, Pierson?"

"Sir, only two, sir."

Connors went crazy. "Jesus, Jesus, Jesus!"

Then Erwin came over. "What's wrong?"

"Romeo never got a shot off and he's got seven hits on his target, and old Pierson fires ten times and only hits his target twice. The dumb shit shot the wrong target seven times and his own twice, and he missed both fucking targets with the tenth round. He's a real dinger. And Romeo? He's quick, quick, quick. I quit already."

And he walked away. Before Erwin could get us, Corporal Peschke came on the bullhorn, thank God.

"Anyone who has fired all ten rounds may have a seat on the benches to the rear of the firing line and mark their score books. Anyone who did not successfully fire all ten rounds, reload what you have left, and when your targets appear, commence firing." Well, by God, I loaded my ten rounds, and this time, I just put my rifle to my shoulder and held my head away from the stock with my eyes closed until my target appeared.

When it appeared, I dropped my cheekbone on my stock, then the thought occurred to me, *What target do I shoot? Mine or Pierson's?* I was lined up on mine. All of a sudden, everything started booming on both sides of me. Erwin had apparently been standing behind me and saw I hadn't fired anything, so he waved his hands at Peschke, who told everyone to clear and lock their weapons and, if there were any alibis, to hold up their hand. I held up my hand again.

Erwin simply looked at me, shook his head, and said, "What's wrong with you?"

"Sir, the private doesn't know which target to shoot at, sir."

"Good question, but it doesn't really matter since we're not keeping score for qualification. He said I'll have them pull your target now and tape it up, and when it appears again, please shoot the gun."

I looked at him, and he said, "What's the matter?"

"Sir, I'm not holding my gun, sir."

And he said, "You smart-ass fuck, I mean your rifle."

He turned and told Peschke what to do with my target. Peschke called the butts, and I waited for my target to appear. When it did, I took a breath, relaxed, aimed, took up the trigger slack, and squeezed. *Boom, boom, boom!* And all the rounds were gone. I clicked the trigger again to be sure, checked my chamber, and locked my weapon. We were all told to retire to the rear and await our scores. A few minutes later, they came up. I got six threes at five o'clock, three twos at twelve o'clock, and a one at twelve o'clock. Corporal Peschke came over, looked at my book, and told me to add a click of elevation and two clicks of left windage, and he said I'd be all right. I added my windage and elevation, and as soon as we moved back to the three-hundred-meter line, I would find out if I was all right. My cheekbone didn't seem to bother me at all the last time I fired, probably because I was thinking about Sergeant Erwin and what he'd do if I didn't get all my rounds off and in the target. With a guy like Erwin hovering over you, you're capable of doing almost anything.

We moved to three-hundred-meter line and took our places behind our targets. Corporal Peschke came over the bullhorn and said, "You are going to fire ten rounds from this yard line in slow fire and assume the sitting position. Once you are in your sitting position and your targets appear, commence fire. Are there any questions? No questions? Do not rush your shooting. Just focus on the black dot on the end of your front-sight blade, and as long as it is covered in black and you squeeze the trigger, the bullet will be in the scoring ring. Make any adjustments necessary, and once again, there is no hurry. Are there any questions? No questions? All right, everyone, get your proper body alignment, and when your target appears, you may commence firing."

The targets appeared and the firing began. My target appeared, and I put my rifle to my shoulder, released the safety, and began remembering the 150 things you had to do to be a good shooter. I got my front-sight blade lined up perfectly horizontally and vertically with my rear sight, and I breathed and relaxed and aimed and took up my trigger slack and then squeezed, and my weapon went off. I rocked slightly backward and came to rest in my original position. My target went down, and I made sure my body alignment was still on the proper target. It's hard to describe what it is like to fire your weapon with people on two sides of you all firing theirs at different intervals. I'll just say that the first couple of days it did unnerve me a bit, but by the third day, I felt more relaxed.

I got used to the person beside me squeezing off his rounds and then saying, "Sonofabitch!"

Because he knew he'd fired a Maggie's drawers. I also realized, I think, for the first time nobody was firing back yet. Just as I began to squeeze off my round, I became oblivious to everything around me. Only your weapon and your target were important. My target appeared, then the disk. It was white, a three at four o'clock. I marked my book, put my weapon to my shoulder, got my sight alignment, and touched off another round. The target went down, came up, and was marked, another three at three o'clock. We were told to line our front-sight blade up with our rear sight and squeeze the round off when we saw black on our front-sight blade. I prepared to fire again, and this time I would be sure I saw black before touching it off. I saw black and fired. My target went down and came up, and it was a bull's-eye at two o'clock. I placed my weapon into my shoulder and was just about to squeeze my fourth round off when I felt someone touch my hand. I looked up and saw Sergeant Mills. He was holding my trigger finger.

He said, "Put your safety on, and let's have a look at your book."

I put the safety on and handed him my book.

He looked at it and said, "Romeo, I believe you're milking the stock."

I said, "Sir, what's that, sir?"

"You're putting too much finger on the trigger, and you're dragging wood. They call it milking the stock. Use only half of the first notch of your trigger finger. That will leave a space between your stock and finger when you squeeze the trigger. Try another round, Romeo."

I took my safety off, put my weapon to my shoulder, inserted half of the first notch of my finger, aimed, and squeezed off another round. The target went down, came up, and was marked. This time, it was a bull's-eye at four o'clock. I looked up and smiled at Sergeant Mills.

He didn't smile back; instead he said, "Now add another click or two of left windage and mark your book." He threw my book on the ground and walked away. These people were hard to figure out. They tell you something that really helps you and you try to thank them and they get mad. Oh well, what the hell. I fired the next five or six rounds, got two more bulls, a couple of threes and a four, and still had two minutes left out of my original ten minutes. I stayed where I was and watched some of the other guys who were still shooting. Pierson was beside me, and I heard his rifle go off and turned to see what he had gotten on his target. It came up, and he was given a big pair of drawers.

I looked at him and he said, "That's the third time I missed the target, Romeo. I'm not going to make it."

"How many times have you fired?"

"Three times."

"Three times and you missed all three? Christ, I guess you ain't going to make it. Fire another round, and I'll see if I can see what you're doing wrong."

Pierson put his rifle to his shoulder, dropped his cheek on his stock, and began to squeeze. The end of his barrel was moving all over the place—his arms were shaking, his hands were trembling, and he took forever to fire. The longer it took, the more the barrel moved and his hands shook. Finally, he jerked his head back. I assumed he was going to take a break and try it again, but just as he jerked his head back, his weapon went off. He rocked back and then settled forward. I figured his weapon discharged accidentally.

He looked at me and said, "Well, did you see anything wrong?"

And I thought to myself, *Good Lord, did I see anything right? Where do I start? This guy was going to be a real problem.*

He was scared to death, and I decided I probably couldn't help him, so I said, "No, man, I didn't see you doing anything wrong. I did see a round hit the butts in front of the target. Maybe you got a bad rifle or something."

He said, "Yeah, that's probably it. I'll tell Sergeant Connors. He'll help me. They'll probably give me a brand-new rifle, then look out, I will be dinger, Pierson."

Back in the '60s we didn't use any ear or eye protection. I believe it was because the corps was trying to simulate actual combat conditions, and I don't think they realized back then how much damage could be caused from not wearing ear and eye protection. Pierson stood up and signaled for Sergeant Connors.

He came over, and Pierson said, "Sir, this rifle ain't no good, sir. Romeo watched me fire a round and said he couldn't see me doing nothing wrong, and I still never hit the target. It's probably got a bent barrel. I need a new one."

Sergeant Connors said, "Well, you've dropped it enough and slept on it enough. I wouldn't doubt it. Just sit down, fire another round, and I'll see if you're doing anything wrong."

Pierson sat down and prepared to jerk another round off. I stood up and retired to the benches to the rear and did my best to disappear. I had really fixed myself up good this time. Connor was already disgusted with me for my rapid-fire exhibition, and now old shaky ass Pierson tells him I said he wasn't doing anything wrong. Pierson adjusted his sling, put his rifle to his shoulder, dropped his head, and began to move and shake all over. As much as he moved around, about the only thing he could have hit the target with would have been a claymore mine, and it fires 150 pellets in a 50-foot arc about two and one half feet off the ground, depending on how you have it tilted. Sergeant Connors just stood there, waiting for him to fire. Thirty seconds passed, forty seconds passed, and Connors was just about to reach down and grab the rifle when Pierson jerked his head up and pulled the trigger.

Connors jumped back, threw his Smokey the Bear hat at Pierson, kicked him in the leg, and screamed, "Jesus, Jesus!"

"Sir, what'd I do wrong?"

Connors just looked at him and called for Corporal Peschke. Corporal Peschke came over, and Connors said, "I want you to see a real dinger."

Just as he said it, Pierson's target came up and was marked with the biggest bull's-eye you ever saw. Pierson looked at it and smiled broadly. Peschke looked at it, then at Sergeant Connors.

Connors looked at it and said, "Remark number 22."

They did bull's-eye. Connors just shook his head, muttered another "Jesus," then said, "Fire another round for Corporal Peschke to watch." Then he walked away. Pierson smiled and prepared to fire again.

Sergeant Connors took about four paces and stopped; he turned toward me and said, "Romeo, did you tell him his barrel was bent?"

I said, "Sir, no, sir."

Connors walked away shaking his head. I sighed a huge sigh of relief, and Peschke waited for Pierson to fire. Pierson began his ritual—the shaking, the barrel weaving back and forth, then the big head jerk just as he pulled the trigger. Corporal Peschke was truly a cool Southern customer and a true professional. Besides a quick look over at Sergeant Connors, he never registered any emotion, except to tell Pierson to clear his weapon and follow him.

Then he said, "We're not wasting any more ammo today, maybe not tomorrow either."

For the next couple of days, Corporal Peschke worked with Pierson continuously to no avail. Pierson would never qualify, not in a million years. He may stay at the range until he has his twenty years in the corps and would continue to tell anyone who would listen, "My barrel is bent." We finished our slow fire at the three hundred and broke for lunch. We were led to a large parking area where a portable chow line was set up. We grabbed a couple of sandwiches and milk, sat down in small groups, ate, and talked. I made it a point to find Kowalski. I wanted to know why he was such a good shooter. He was sitting by himself, as usual. Like I said earlier, he was always screwing things up, and no one wanted to be around him. I sat down right next to him. He looked at me funny but didn't say anything.

I ate one sandwich, drank some milk, then said, "Hey, Ski, how's it going?"

"Okay, Romeo. How you doing?"

"All right, I guess. I've only been roughed up once so far. How about you?"

"Nobody has bothered me so far. Not even Whaley."

"No shit! Whaley always spent a lot of time with you before we came here, didn't he?"

"Yeah, I was his pet project." I guess he was because Whaley was always thumping Ski. He had him covered like a blanket, like stink on shit.

"I wonder why he's leaving you alone."

"Probably because I'm doing so well."

"How come you're doing so well?

"Because I'm a good shooter."

"How come?"

"Because I like shooting. I always have."

"You mean, you were a shooter before you came into the corps?"

"Yeah."

"For how long?"

"Since I was twelve years old."

"You're kidding?"

"No, I belonged to three rifle teams last year. I can hit a ten-inch target at seven hundred yards about nine out of ten times from the prone position with a bolt-action rifle."

"You're shitting me?"

"Nope."

"How come you didn't tell me that from the start?"

"You didn't ask."

He really pissed me off with that. Everything else he did he screwed up. Hardly anybody even talked to him because he was such a shitbird and now he was being a smart-ass because he was a dinger. I stood up and started to walk away, but I couldn't.

I turned around and said, "Hey, Ski, did you hear about the Pollack who broke his arm raking leaves?"

"No."

"Yeah, he fell out of the tree." Then I turned and walked away.

We finished lunch and returned to the three-hundred-meter line. We were to fire ten rounds in twenty seconds. It kind of frightened me. Corporal Peschke came over the bullhorn and explained the procedure. Ten rounds, rapid fire. I didn't know how shaky Pierson was before, but now I did and I thought of him being next to me shaking all over the place, and it was a little too much for me to bear. We assumed our positions, loaded and locked, and waited for our targets to appear.

I heard Pierson mumbling, "Damn bent barrel. Maybe if I point it that way I can hit the target."

Oh boy, I could feel those rounds ripping through me. Targets appeared, and we all commenced firing. Just that quick they disappeared, were marked, and reappeared, and our scores and marks were given. I'd done pretty well—three bulls, three fours, two threes, two ones, all between the two and five on the target. Pierson did pretty well too. Three rounds on the target, seven rounds in the butts.

Peschke said, "Pierson, do you realize if we all shot like you, we would have to carry a thousand rounds of ammunition apiece? Hell, boy, you're terrible. What the hell are you scared of? Those targets can't shoot back."

A couple of years later, I would find myself in Vietnam, and I remember hearing a statistic; for every confirmed kill from small arms fire, hundreds of rounds were fired. Now bullets back then only cost thirteen cents apiece. I hope everybody in the service has become a better shot because I'm pretty sure that same bullet is well over a dollar now. But let's get back to Pierson.

"Sir, I think my barrel's bent, sir. Romeo said he even thought so too."

"Oh shit, give me that sucker."

Peschke had them pull Pierson's target down, paste it up, and pull it back up. He loaded Pierson's rifle with ten rounds, sat down, adjusted the sling on his arm, put the rifle to his shoulder, and fired ten rounds about as fast as it took you to blink your eyes four or five times. I'd say it took all of five seconds.

He picked up the phone and said, "Mark number 22."

Pierson was standing there with his mouth open. We all were. The target went down and came back up. We counted the bulls first; there were nine of them and one three at two o'clock.

Peschke looked at Pierson and said, "Bent barrel my ass" and handed him the rifle and walked away. We all laughed and wandered back to our positions. I saw Ski ahead of me and caught up with him.

I said, "Now that's a dinger, Ski."

He said, "Yeah, he did all right, but if he had hesitated a little and not fired so fast, he'd have gotten ten out of ten. Now that's a dinger."

"Well, let' see you get ten out of ten dinger."

"Okay, nothing to it, that's my favorite position."

"Nobody likes a smart-ass, Ski."

"I'm not being a smart-ass, Romeo. I'm being serious we moved back to the 500-meter line."

We all got behind our proper targets and adjusted our sights, added some new windage and elevation, and waited until all the targets were in the up position. As I looked out over the firing line at my target, I shook my head, blinked my eyes, and looked again. I couldn't believe it. They expected us to hit that bull's-eye from here? Good Lord. It was no more than a speck on the front-sight blade. This is too much. I knew for sure now that I wasn't going to do very well.

Corporal Peschke came over the bullhorn and in a very assuring voice said, "Now listen up, people. I know you're all thinking that this is impossible that there is no way you are ever going to hit that target, but believe me when I tell you this will be the easiest part of the whole range if you'll just do what you've been taught. Remember to adjust your sling so it holds your arm in the proper place, spread your feet so your position is stationary, line your front sight up evenly with the rear sight, breathe, relax, aim, take up your trigger slack, and squeeze when you see black on your front-sight blade. Your targets will go down, and when they come back up, you may commence firing. You have ten minutes to fire ten rounds. Don't rush your shooting and mark your books after each shot. Be sure you have the proper dope on your weapon for the five-hundred-meter line. There is no real wind, so your windage should be all right from the three hundred line. Now this is important. Be sure you're on the proper target, Pierson, and don't kill anyone. I've already cleared all aircraft within ten miles from here, so as long as you point your bent barrel downrange, we should all be safe. Commence firing when your targets appear."

Our targets went down, and I said a silent prayer. When they came up, we all began firing. I did everything I could think of and waited to see black on my front-sight blade. It would appear and disappear. The slightest movement could take you completely off the target. I tried to hold steady. I focused my eyes again and again until my vision began to blur. I pulled my rifle from my shoulder in disgust and rubbed my eye. Then I looked at the ground directly in front of me until my eyes focused clearly. I kept my eyes focused, then put my rifle to my shoulder, raised my head, and lined up my sights, and at the first sign of grayish black, I squeezed the trigger quickly. I barely had time to lift my head away from the stock and my target had disappeared. I couldn't believe the bullet traveled so fast. It was like magic, but the real magic would be if I hit the target. A few seconds passed and my target appeared.

Up came the disk; it went to the nine o'clock position and to the three ring using the target like the face of a clock. I was shocked, marked my book, put my rifle to my shoulder, lined everything up, and waited for black. The harder I looked, the less I saw. I left the rifle on my shoulder, turned my head from the target, and looked at the ground directly in front of me until my eyes focused on it, then I raised my head, rested my cheek on the stock, lined my sights up, and waited until I saw black. When I did, I squeezed the round off. My target went down. Magic. It came up, and I had a four at eight o'clock. That was real magic. I fired my remaining rounds and got threes and fours and two bulls. I was really happy. I stood up and walked back to the benches at the rear of the firing line. Ski was back there smiling. I thought, *There is no way he'd gotten ten out of ten, is there?*

I said, "How many dinger?"

He smiled, "Only eight, Romeo. Only eight."

"Well, what happened?"

"It took me two rounds to get the proper windage and elevation."

Corporal Peschke said our windage was all right from the three hundred yard line."

"I know, but if you're a real dinger, you can always zero it in better. Besides, I line up my sights at six o'clock on the bull, not when I see black."

"How the hell can you line up at six o'clock on a speck?"

"It's easy once you learn a few tricks. I'll show you tonight if you're interested."

"Okay. I'll see you tonight."

After ten more rounds of rapid fire, we secured after everyone had finished and were double-timed back to our area. We were given a few minutes to put our gear away and wash up for evening chow. After chow, we returned and were given a pep talk by Sergeant Erwin. He got out a locker box, stood up on it, and began by telling us that any marine that couldn't qualify with his rifle wasn't a marine. He ended the pep talk with the statement, "All a marine wants to do is take his rifle and kill his country's enemies." He would periodically call one recruit after another and make fun of a particular thing the recruit had done that day. It was funny until you got called up front. I mean, I'd forgotten all about my sore cheekbone until he called me up and thumped me on it with his big Marine Corps ring a few times. I guess the funniest thing was when he called Pierson up front.

He said, "Pierson, what happened out there to you, son?"

"Sir, well, sir, not much, sir."

"Well, that's the truth. Come closer, son."

Pierson stepped closer, and Erwin put his hand on Pierson's shoulder and told him to relax and stand at ease.

Then he said, "Now, boy, tell us all what's wrong. Why couldn't you hit that target, son?"

Pierson looked at him, then at us, then back at him and said, "Sir, I believe my barrel is bent, sir." We all roared.

Pierson said, "Honest, it really is, sir. I'm doing everything right. Ask Romeo. He watched me and said so."

Everyone roared again, except Pierson and me.

Erwin said, "Well, how come Corporal Peschke did so well with your rifle, Pierson?"

"Well, sir, I believe he just got lucky, sir. I believe he was holding it just right that one time."

We all laughed, and Erwin said, "Yes, Private, I believe that's right. He holds it right and you don't. But mark my words, you'll be holding it right on prequal day or I'll have to send you to the showers. I'm going to take this rifle range streamer, and the only way I can get it is to have 100 percent qualification. Believe me, anyone who doesn't qualify on prequal day won't be around on qualification day. Remember, anyone who can't qualify with this rifle isn't a marine. It's eight o'clock. You have until nine thirty to get those weapons cleaned, and if there is any time left, you can do what you want. From this point on, you can sleep as much or as little as you want while we're here. If you feel you need more snapping in to steady your shooting position, you can use the shower area after taps. Do whatever you have to before prequal day, but on prequal day, you had better qualify or you'll never see qualification day. Dismissed."

We all broke up into small groups and began discussing our individual problems. In the corps, you have three days of regular firing and the fourth day is what they call prequal day. You go through the entire course of fire just like you were qualifying. On the fifth day, it's for real. That's what Erwin was talking about. Anyone who didn't qualify on the fourth day wouldn't be around to mess up on the fifth day. I didn't know exactly what he meant by sending them to the showers, but I was sure it wouldn't be as pleasant as it sounded. I located Ski. It wasn't hard. Half the platoon was gathered around him, begging for help from the master. I stood there listening and watching. We were finally taken to the shower room where Ski pasted small black dots on one wall.

He paced off a certain amount of distance from the spots and said, "This line will simulate the five-hundred-meter firing line. Those small spots will be the bull's-eye on the target. Get your rifles, and I'll take you to school."

About fifteen of us returned with our rifles and the master began his class. The first thing he said, "From now on, you will all refer to me as the master. If you don't, I won't teach you. Now who am I, Romeo?"

"What?"

"Who am I, Romeo?"

"You're the master, Ski."

I felt like barfing all over myself, but if this turkey could teach me something that would keep me from being sent to the showers by Erwin, I'd play his game.

He said, "Romeo, you can drop the Ski. Just master will do."

He went down the line, making everyone call him the master, one at a time, until his ego was properly inflated, then he began his instruction. He seemed to know what he was doing, so I stayed up with him until midnight. I was tired, and that hard concrete floor was wearing on me.

I stood up and said, "Thanks" and informed him I was too tired to practice anymore. I started out of the shower room for my rack.

I was clearing the doorway when he said, "Wait a minute, Romeo. You don't just walk out on the master. You get back in here, you maggot."

I stopped where I was because, for a second, I forgot who he was. He sounded just like a drill instructor, then I realized where I was and who he was. I turned around and smiled. He was standing there in his boxer shorts with a T-shirt and looking like anything but a DI. He wasn't smiling, and I knew I'd have to eat crow or tell him to get fucked.

I said, "Get fucked, Ski."

I lay in my rack, letting all the events of the day and night run through my head until I fell asleep.

Reveille sounded promptly at 5:30 a.m. Sergeant Mills had the duty, and he came in our squad bay and informed us of the day's activities. When he finished, we all charged the washroom to clean up before morning chow. I secured a sink and mirror and began to shave when I noticed Murphy next to me. He didn't have the sink next to me; Priebe did, and Murphy was just standing halfway between the two of us, looking lost.

I asked, "What's your problem, Murphy?"

He just held up his hand and showed me his finger and said, "I can't use this hand too well. Can I share this sink with you?"

I had forgotten what had happened the day before between him and Whaley. He hadn't though because his finger was all swollen and the nail was just barely hanging on.

I said, "Sure, Murphy" and moved over a little to make room for him. We both went about cleaning up without saying anything. Pretty soon the other guys began to file out of the squad bay in groups of twos and threes until only he and I were left.

He looked at me and said, "You know, Romeo, something has to be done about Whaley. He's going to kill someone one of these days."

I said, "Yeah, looks like he already killed your finger. What the hell did he do, chew on it?"

"No, the bastard made me do it."

"Made you do what? Chew on your own finger?"

"No, but he made me fuck it all up though."

"How? It looks like he put it through a meat grinder or some friggin' thing."

"He made me lock my slide to the rear, then I had to insert my finger into the receiver and then release the slide so that the bolt went forward and smashed my finger between it and the chamber."

I shook my head in pity and said, "Christ, Murphy, that must have really felt great."

"Yeah, it hurt like hell the first time."

"How many times did he make you do it?"

"Four times and each time it hurt worse. The last time he didn't let me take it out."

"What do you mean he wouldn't let you take it out?"

"Just what the fuck I said. He made me leave my finger in the receiver, trapped between the bolt and chamber, then he made me let go of my rifle with the other hand so that it hung at my side from my finger, and we walked back to the firing line. When we were in sight of the other people, he stopped me and let me remove my finger. He told me if I told anybody what happened, the next time it wouldn't be my finger, it would be my dick."

It wasn't hard for me to believe that Murphy was telling the truth. I remembered only too vividly my own run in with Sergeant Whaley. Murphy was right. Something needed to be done about Whaley before he killed someone, but I doubted very seriously if anything would be done.

Murphy said, "Romeo, did you hear me?"

"Hear what?"

"I'm going to kill Whaley before we leave the range."

"You're what?"

"I mean it. I'm going to kill the bastard, you wait and see."

Murphy grabbed his towel and walked out. We dressed, formed up, and went to chow. After chow, we got our gear and double-timed to the range. Sergeant Mills and Sergeant Connors were always in better moods than Erwin and Whaley in the morning. Hell, at any time they were in better moods. As we double-timed, we chanted. Sergeant Mills had a really deep booming voice, and hearing him say the verse of the chant before we repeated it really inspired us.

We were running, and every once in a while, we'd hear him say in a deep commanding voice, "Left, right."

It was to keep us in step. Then he'd start his chant.

"Give me glasses tinted green."

Then we'd all repeat, "Give me glasses tinted green."

Then he'd say, "I'm a Hollywood marine."

And we'd all repeat that. I'm going to take a few minutes here to try to make you understand how exciting it was to be in a marine platoon double-timing through the canyons and foothills of Pendleton, California, in the early morning when the sun was rising or later evening when the shadows of the evening were falling. A marine platoon on the double has an unmistakable sound. Once you've been a part of that wonderful green machine and participated in platoon runs and heard the beautiful rhythmic sound of sixty or more boots hitting the ground together and sixty or more pant legs brushing together and making a rhythmic whooshing sound all at the same time, you'll know what I mean. If you never have, I'm sorry for you. You've truly been cheated out of a wonderful uplifting experience.

"One, two, three, four, I love the Marine Corps."

Today was a beautiful California day, and it was about 6:30 a.m. We were on a deserted stretch of road in the California foothills, and the sun was just coming up. Everything was fresh and new, and we had our two favorite DIs leading us on an early-morning run.

There was one particular chant that went like this. Sergeant Mills would be chanting, "Left, right. Left, right, Left, right." Then he'd stop.

After a ten- or fifteen-second pause, he'd say, "Give me your left foot," and as soon as he finished saying it and just as we were about to put our left foot down again, we would stomp it down extra hard, making a booming sound that would echo off the canyon walls along the side of the road.

A few seconds later, he would say, "Give me your right foot," and we would do the same thing with our right foot, then came the killer, he'd say, "Give me your left right left," and we'd really stomp them down hard, left, right left, boom, boom, boom.

You could hear it a mile away. I know for those of you who have never participated, this must sound pretty silly, but to us, at the time, and hell even for me writing it now, it was a real thrill. I wish I had fifty or sixty good friends who would double-time with me every morning in the little town I live in now. We'd wake all you late sleepers up with our foot stomping and our chanting.

I remember on an R & R (rest and relaxation) in Japan, I'd gone home with a bar girl and I was enjoying the luxury of sleeping in that morning when I heard the school kids marching through the streets chanting, and I couldn't help but admire the Japanese discipline.

Back to California. It was exactly 7:00 a.m. when we arrived in the big parking area overlooking the firing lines. No one was there but our platoon. We were told to fall out and practice our worst shooting position. As we did, the two DIs went around helping one recruit after another until Corporal Peschke arrived. He was his usual self, smiling and happy.

He said, "Good morning, troops. Shall we begin? This is your second day of live fire. You'll only have one more left before prequal day. We'll go over the entire course twice today and tomorrow—once in the morning and once in the afternoon. There will be two other PMIs with us from now on. Anyone having difficulty, feel free to call on any of us for help because we have a long way to go and a short time to get there. I want you all to remember this: recruits have been qualifying here for a long time. It has been done in the past, and it will be done in the future. Keep that thought in mind and apply yourself 100 percent, and on Friday, you will be proud people. Now let's get down to work."

That day, and from that day until qualification day, all four of our DIs were also there. I asked myself the same question every other recruit was asking themselves at that moment, "Why wasn't Corporal Peschke our drill instructor, and would I be proud of myself that Friday?"

We went to the 150-meter line and were given the same instructions as the day before. I had trouble concentrating. I kept remembering what Murphy had said about killing Whaley. Here we were, with real rifles and real ammunition, and he was very likely to do it. The look on his face said he'd do it. I kind of liked Murphy, and I'd sure hate to see him spend the rest of his life in a Marine Corps brig for killing Whaley.

We all loaded and locked and waited for our targets to appear. They came up, and we lined up and prepared to squeeze our first shots off. When that first round went off, it exploded and broke the quiet morning silence with such suddenness it was shocking. It seemed to wake everyone up. I touched my first shot off and rocked back a little bit. There was no pain like the first round from the day before. I remembered to do all the right things. I couldn't really tell where I'd hit on the target, but I was pretty sure I was on the target somewhere. It went down and came up. My mark was in the four ring at nine o'clock. I was satisfied. I marked my book and loaded another round and prepared to fire. I was on my sixth round when I realized that all but one of my shots was on the left side of my target. I decided to add some right windage. As I was making my adjustment, Sergeant Connors came over and asked to see my book. I showed him and he asked what I was doing to correct it. I explained about adding right windage. He asked where I was squeezing my round off on the target. I told him that it seemed to be going off just before I touched the black of the bull on the left side.

He said, "Well, that's where you're hitting, dummy. Take the windage off and wait until you're in the black before you touch it off."

I removed my right windage and zeroed in. When I was in the black, I fired. My target went down and came up. The disk appeared and went to the center of the bull, stayed there, and then disappeared. Bull's-eye, mutha! I looked at Connor's, but I didn't smile. They didn't like smilers because a recruit didn't have anything to be happy about. I started to look away from him, and he smiled at me. I really didn't know what to do. I just looked at him.

His smile got broader, and he said, "I think you'll be all right, Romeo, if Pierson doesn't shoot you with his bent barrel."

I looked over to my left, and there was Pierson scratching his head and mumbling. The rest of the morning went by okay. Every once in a while, I noticed Ski checking out my score on the big board. The big board was behind the firing line where the benches were, and after you fired your ten rounds at that firing line, you would write your score next to your name on the big board. He looked at it, then at me, and he'd smile his cockiest smile and walk away. I'd walk over to the big board and check his score. At every yard line, his score was far better than mine and his smile got bigger and cockier. I got a little disgusted, but then I reasoned with myself and thought, *What the hell, you couldn't expect a person who had never fired a rifle before to be as good as someone who had been shooting them for ten years.*

We finished at the five hundred around 9:30 a.m., and then it was our turn in the butts. The other half of the platoon finished up around noon, and we all retired to the parking lot for lunch, but there was no lunch today. Someone had screwed up.

We stood around looking at one another and Sergeant Mills said, "Where's the chow, Sergeant Connors?"

And Sergeant Connors said, "Where's the chow, Sergeant Mills?"

And Mills said, "Well, I'll be fucked," and he walked away.

Connors watched him, then turned to us and said, "There ain't going to be no chow for lunch. Fall out and relax for a while. The smoking lamp is lit."

We were all sitting around talking when Sergeant Mills came back. Ski had ten or twenty guys around him, and he was complaining about not having anything to eat when Sergeant Mills came up behind him. The rest of the guys saw Mills coming and started walking away from where Ski was sitting. By the time Ski realized what was happening, it was too late. While he was grousing about how it wasn't fair for all of them to be punished because the sergeants screwed up, Sergeant Mills was listening, and Ski heard him stop behind him. He turned around and looked up at the mighty oak hovering over him. Ski knew he'd had the cock and so did everyone else. Maybe no one had messed with Ski since we'd gotten to the range, but someone was about to now.

Sergeant Mills put his hands on his hips and looked down at Ski and said, "What are you bitching about, boy?"

Ski stuttered and stammered and finally managed to spit out, "Sir, nothing, sir."

Mills said, "Get on your feet, maggot, and stand at attention when you speak to me."

Ski got to his feet, and Mills got nose to nose with him and said, "I heard what you said, you slimy little cunt, crying about missing one stinking meal while there are people all over the world starving to death. You ain't shit. I've got a fourteen-year-old brother who could kick your ass on his worst day. You wouldn't make a pimple on a marine's ass. So you're hungry, are you? Well, let me tell you something, asshole. Do you remember that contract you signed before you came here? Well, turd, in the fine print it says the Marine Corps would guarantee you one hour sleep each twenty-four hours and one meal each twenty-four hours, just one of each every twenty-four hours. Now if you've got a bitch, you write your congressman. Don't try to entice my troops. Are you still hungry, Private?"

"Sir, no, sir."

"I'll tell you what, you grab your shit and you hit the road. If you remember where's the chow hall is, you go there and you eat. When you get through eating, you double-time back here. Now git."

"Sir, Private Kowalski requests permission to speak to the drill instructor."

"Fuck you, Private. Eat and return here on the double."

"Sir, aye, aye, sir."

Ski grabbed his rifle and hit the road. We all watched him disappear down the road. It was a thirty-minute run back to our squad bay and another twenty to the chow line. Ski would be gone about two hours altogether. We didn't sit around picking our noses while he was gone. No, sir. We did PT. A couple hundred push-ups, sit-ups, knee bends, and squat thrusts, and then we low crawled around the parking lot for about fifteen minutes.

Lunch was over. We didn't have to worry about brushing our teeth or picking our teeth or doing anything except gritting our teeth when our scores appeared. Half the platoon went to the butts to pull targets and the other half assumed their positions on the firing line. We started our second relay for the day a little after 12:30 p.m. About an hour after we started, Ski came running around the bend and saw all of us. While he requested permission to speak and rejoin the platoon, we stopped firing. Sergeant Mills said we should all thank Ski for the exercise.

We yelled in unison as loud as we could, "Thank you, Private Kowalski, for the exercise!"

He stood there looking lost and alone, very unlike what he looked like when he was the master. He was told to rejoin the platoon, and we all began our routine again.

I didn't notice Ski checking the big board, and when I checked to see how he was doing, I was surprised because I was doing better than him. I guess he was a little worried about the way some of the guys were looking at him. There was no special session with the master in the shower room that night, but there was one in the master's bed after taps. I guess about ten guys gave old Ski a blanket party. I didn't participate because, to be truthful, I think we were all upset about not getting our lunch. We were used to three squares a day for the last two months, and Ski hadn't been the only one bitching about it; he was only the one who'd gotten caught, and he had gotten caught because he had become a leader since we had reached the range. Being a leader has its good points and its bad points. The blanket party was one of the latter. Come to think of it, in boot camp being a leader had about forty-one bad things for every good point.

I said earlier that Ski was always messing up, and he was. This wasn't his first blanket party. It was probably his tenth, but you would have thought it was his first the way he fought back and carried on.

They worked him over for about three minutes before he finally lay still. I talked to him the next morning and asked, "How come you didn't play dead after a few good hits?"

And he said, "I didn't do anything wrong, and I wasn't going to take an ass kicking lying still. I figured if I fought back I could get in a few good licks on someone."

I asked, "Well, did you get in a few good licks?"

"Hell no, they throw that blanket over your head and upper body and you can't see shit. You know that."

"Yeah, I know that and you should too. You've had about nine more parties than me. It looks like some of your guests got a few good licks in."

"Yeah, it was that fucker McGowan. He had a hold of my head."

"How do you know that?"

"Like you said, I've had a lot of parties and McGowan always holds the blanket over the guy's head, and when you try to get up, he punches you on the top of the head with his free hand and you go back down. Besides, I could smell his breath. He popped me about six times, maybe seven. How many lumps have I got on top of my head?" He bent down, and I counted about five good bumps and a couple of possible lumps.

I told him, "Looks like six, maybe seven. It's hard to tell because some of the groups are pretty close, if you know what I mean, master."

Ski raised his head and smiled, and everything was back to normal. I knew that yesterday afternoon would be the last I'd outshoot him. That was the way it was in the corps back then. If you screwed up, you paid the price, and once you paid the price, everything went back to normal. Just like it's supposed to be like when you serve your time in prison.

Today would be our last day of so-called free shooting. Tomorrow was prequal day, and Friday was qualification day. D-day, the World Series, and the Super Bowl all rolled into one. Everyone knew it and almost everyone dreaded it. I know I was dreading it, and I wasn't hitting the target too badly at all.

I had my elevation for each firing line written down, and it was working. All I had to do was make the proper adjustment on my windage and squeeze them off. My groups were especially tight in rapid fire. A lot of the guys were all over the target on rapid fire. I enjoyed rapid fire more than slow fire. I think because I just couldn't imagine slow firing in a combat situation. Can you see yourself with three thousand of your enemy charging you at the same time and you inserting one round at a time and taking five or ten minutes to fire five or ten rounds?

Rapid fire brought the target to life for me, but then the target was stationary. Could you imagine a man standing still while you put ten 7.62 × 51 mm rounds through his chest cavity? In the sixties, the Marine Corps needed a better way to qualify and train people. Today, I believe, they have it. They fire at silhouette targets that appear for a few seconds, then disappear while others come up from different positions and go down when they are hit. In this regard, I believe they have improved the training. They are not using the M14 rifle anymore. It fired 170 grain 308 bullet that wasn't easily deflected by a piece of elephant grass. Now it's about a 70-grain bullet, you figure it out. I know some of the why they got rid of the M14. It weighed in at nine pounds versus seven for the M16. The bullets weighed half as much, almost, so you can carry a lot more ammo with the M16.

We had chow and double-timed to the range. We were early, as usual, and we snapped in while we waited for our PMIs to arrive. When they did, we were taken to the firing line, and our morning began. Today we had Sergeant Erwin and Sergeant Whaley with us. They were both their usual cheerful selves. Erwin hated a happy person in the morning, and Whaley hated everybody all the time. First thing Whaley did was call Private Murphy over to where he was standing. Then he asked Corporal Peschke if he had any trouble with this little shitbird.

Corporal Peschke said, "I never have any real trouble with my people. I know how to handle them."

And he walked away. Whaley did a slow burn, and we all knew he'd be hell for the rest of the day. He didn't say anything to Peschke. He put his hand on the back of Murphy's neck and gave him a hard shove forward. Murphy was standing at attention and wasn't prepared. He stumbled forward and fell. He tried to catch himself with his free hand, the one that had the smashed finger, because his rifle was in the other hand, and he didn't want to take the chance of screwing up his sights by hitting them on the ground. When his hand hit the ground, his finger literally burst open, and blood and pus squirted everywhere. When he saw that and felt that, he jumped to his feet, reeled around, and aimed his rifle at Whaley and pulled the trigger. Whaley just stood there with a shocked look on his face until he heard the metallic click and realized there was no round in the chamber.

Then he smiled and said, "You still have the rifle, boy. C'mon, let's see how bad you are."

Murphy was furious. He swung the weapon from a firing position to a bayonet fighting position and stepped forward. All of a sudden, from nowhere, Erwin appeared in front of him.

He didn't say anything to Murphy; he just put one big dick skinner on Murphy's rifle and said, "Give it to me, son."

Murphy released the weapon, dropped his hands to his side, and looked down at his feet. Erwin turned to Whaley, handed him the rifle, and said, "Let's see how bad you are, boy."

Whaley stood there and ate shit. Then Erwin told Whaley to return to the platoon area and have sick bay send an ambulance to pick up Private Murphy. Whaley turned and started to walk away.

Erwin grabbed the rifle and handed it to Murphy and said, "How do you feel, son?"

Murphy said, "Fine, sir. I mean, sir, fine, sir."

Erwin told him to have a seat until the ambulance arrived. Corporal Peschke came over the bullhorn, and we all went back to the business at hand. When the ambulance arrived, Murphy left and didn't return until after lunch. When he did return, Whaley was with him. He came over to where we were all seated. Erwin told Murphy to rejoin the platoon. He and Whaley talked for a few minutes, and Whaley walked back to the ambulance, and they pulled away. Murphy had a splint on his finger. The doctor told him it was badly infected. He asked him how it happened, and he told him he fell.

The doctor said, "Into what, a bear trap?"

Then he told him to come to sick bay every day and have the dressing changed or he could lose the finger and he may never have full use of it again. Murphy was noticeably disturbed. He had to qualify in two days, and he didn't want to be a nonqual, and he didn't want to be dropped from the platoon and set back. We all did our best to cheer him up. His shooting that afternoon wasn't good, but it wasn't that bad either once he took the splint off. He had a lot of trouble with the rapid fire, but the slow fire was all right. We finished the afternoon off and returned to our platoon area. After evening chow, we were given free time. We cleaned our weapons, washed out some laundry, showered, shaved, and sat around in groups, talking. Mad Dog, McGowan, and I were shooting the shit about Murphy and Whaley. I think most of the guys were talking about it. Mad Dog couldn't get over how Murphy turned on Whaley.

"You know, if his gun would have been loaded, there wouldn't be no more Sergeant Whaley."

McGowan cut in and said, "You mean rifle. This is a gun," and he tapped Mad Dog in his junk.

Mad Dog said, "Yeah, rifle."

"You should know the difference better than any of us, McGowan. Even after that, he was ready to fight him with just the empty rifle."

Mac smiled and said, "Lawson, Whaley ain't shit. I'd take him on without anything. Now Erwin and Mills, I'd have to think about taking one of them on. Even with a loaded rifle."

I said, "Mac, the way you shoot by the time you got your eye patch in place and your sling adjusted properly and your sight picture, it would be dark out."

He laughed and said, "I'll qualify, Romeo."

And I said, "With your rifle or your gun?"

And we all laughed at that. McGowan really looked comical on the range. He had to wear an eye patch because he couldn't keep his left eye closed without closing his right eye. His shooting jacket was too small, and he was afraid to ask for a bigger one. He took forever getting into his shooting positions.

Before they ordered the targets up, they would always say, "All ready on the left, all ready on the right, all ready on the firing line. Watch for your targets. When they appear, commence firing."

As soon as they finished saying it, the targets would appear, so as soon as they said it, Mac would raise his hand and say, "Sir, could you wait a minute, sir? I'm not ready yet, sir."

Then little Sergeant Connors would usually hurry over and start pushing a leg down here, pulling an arm in and out there, and tightening his sling for him. After he had McGowan all adjusted, he'd push him two or three times to see how steady his position was. It was funny because McGowan was so big and Connors was so small and nervous. Connors would be pushing something down and something else would pop up.

He'd say, "Jesus, McGowan, help me, you big ape."

And Mac would say, "Sir, I can't, sir."

Connors would be shouting, "Tuck that arm under, pull that knee up, sit up straight, do this, and do that. No, don't do that, you dummy."

After a couple of minutes, he'd have him just right and he'd pull back and push on him to see how steady he was, and McGowan would topple over backward.

Connors would throw his hat down and start yelling, "Jesus, Jesus, Jesus, McGowan!"

And Corporal Peschke would say, "I'll clear all planes with the air traffic controller."

When they finally got everything together and Mac was steady, Connors would jump back really fast and shout to Corporal Peschke, "Now hurry, hurry!"

And Peschke would say, "All ready on the firing line? Commence shooting when your targets appear."

One time, when Mac was firing from the sitting position, he fell over backward and didn't get all his rounds off.

When Connors asked why, he said, "I fell over, sir."

Connors said, "Were you ever dropped when you were young?"

Mac looked at him and said, "I don't know, sir. I'll write my mother and ask, sir."

Connors walked away, shaking his head.

There was another activity at the range that I've neglected to mention. There were only thirty people firing at a time, half of the platoon. The other thirty people were pulling targets and marking them in the butts. It was kind of like playing blind fish. That's a game we used to play at school carnivals. They had little fishing poles with a plastic hook and a couple feet of string attached to them. You would put the hook and the string down through a hole on the top of the counter. You paid a quarter and you would let the hook down, and you would usually get hooked onto one of several little gifts that were down there. You couldn't see what your hook was catching on until you pulled your line up. I always seemed to hook into the cheapest prize.

Anyway, we spent half the morning shooting and half pulling butts and half the afternoon shooting and half the afternoon pulling butts. It may sound sexy pulling butts, but it wasn't. It was downright dangerous. I never saw anyone get hurt, but the way some of those guys shot made pulling butts an exercise in combat action. Not every one of these guys could hit the target. When the bullet went through and hit bunker hill twenty yards away, it was absorbed. You stood directly below the target on a small platform, and there was a cement wall that went up to where the target appeared above ground. The target holder was made of wood and angle iron. Occasionally, a round would hit the holder and wood splinters would fly. If the shooter hit in front of the target, dirt and gravel would fall down on you.

They had little sayings like, "Pull 'em down and paste 'em up," "Pull 'em up and mark 'em." Sometimes during the rapid fire, they'd say, "Pull 'em down and paste 'em up."

You'd start pulling the target down, and the guy shooting would be trying to get his last few rounds off, and a round would hit the top of the target holder and wood and lead would fly, and it would scare the hell out of you. The poor guys who got stuck marking Old Bent Barrel Pierson's target would run his target up and run down two or three targets because Pierson fired too many rounds into the butts. Generally, working in the butts was fun. You got to where you could guess or just about guess where the next round would be. You never knew whose target you were marking until the end of the day.

We'd be sitting around talking and someone would say, "Hey, who was marking number 20?"

And the guy who marked it would say, "Me, why?"

"Are you sure I didn't hit the target on my third shot in the offhand position?"

"Yeah, I'm sure you got a Maggie's drawers, didn't you?"

"Yeah, but I was sure I was in the black at three o'clock when I squeezed it off."

"Well, you weren't or I would have given you a bull at three."

Then the guy would say, "Aw, you never liked me anyhow, you bastard"

And they'd say, "Hey, I didn't know who was firing on the target until now."

"Oh yeah, that's right. I forgot. You know, with Pierson out there shooting, I'm not about to stick my head above the butts to look around at the shooters."

If Pierson heard you talking, he'd say, "Screw you, assholes. My barrel's bent."

That was pretty much when the discussion ended. Every once in a while, there would be a fight. We were pretty far into our training by now. In fact, we only had two more weeks and two days of training before we graduated from MCRD and went to Camp Pendleton for our last four weeks of infantry training regiment (ITR). When we went there, we would leave our present DIs and get new ones. We finished our afternoon firing and returned to our living area. Sergeant Erwin told us to have a seat on our locker boxes and listen up.

"You guys are in your tenth week now, and you have gone through a lot together. Some people who started with us haven't made it this far, but those of you who are listening have. Tomorrow is prequal day, and Friday is qualification day. Everyone will qualify Friday, I'm sure. Now in order to continually better our training, we ask every platoon at this point to fill out what we call a bitch sheet. We would like each and every one of you to write down what you like about your training so far and what you think should be changed. In other words, should something be made easier or harder? Should we change something because it is too hard, or should we make something harder because it's too easy? You don't have to sign these bitch sheets. Just tell us what you liked and what you didn't like and how you feel we could improve our training program. No one will read these except us and you can feel free to say anything you want. There will be no disciplinary action taken against anybody. When you are all through, have one recruit collect them and bring them to the duty office. You have twenty minutes before we go to chow."

We all got a piece of paper and pencil and tried to think of one thing we liked about the training. It was hard, but when you thought about it, it had to be hard.

I said, "I think the obstacle courses should be made harder. I feel they were too easy."

Then I thought about Whaley and what he'd done to Private Murphy's finger and what he had tried to do to my face and I said, "I could understand why they sometimes had to slap a recruit around and rough him up, but I felt they should stop short of doing permanent damage and that Sergeant Whaley was not qualified to be a DI because he had little or no control over himself once he lost his temper."

I didn't sign it, and I turned mine in with all the rest. It was funny to watch Priebe as he collected them. He'd hold out the stack he'd already collected, and the guy who was turning his in would lift up a few and put his under them. I think everyone said something they didn't want read when he returned with them to the duty office, and Erwin and Mills took us to chow. When we returned from chow we were given free time. Sergeants Erwin and Mills went to the duty office and the door closed.

We all started screwing around with one another when, all of a sudden, someone yelled, "Attention on deck!"

We all snapped to attention and saw our series lieutenant walk out of the duty office with a bunch of papers under his arm. As he left the squad bay he said, "Stand at ease." And we all returned to our own business.

Pierson said, "Where'd he come from?"

Someone else said, "He took his bars off and marched in with us."

We laughed and forgot about it. It was about eight thirty when Sergeant Erwin came to the door of the duty office and said, "Privates Romeo and Ramsey, report to the duty office on the double."

Everyone was quiet. We looked at each other and headed for the duty office. We didn't have a chance to knock because we were called in as soon as we appeared. I'd never been inside the duty office before. It was a small room, about twelve by fifteen. There were two single racks, a desk, and a small head with a sink, toilet, and stand-up shower. The head only had about four feet of floor space. It was really small and compact. Sergeant Erwin was standing by the head door, and Mills was standing by the desk.

He said, "Which of you, assholes, wrote this?" as he held up one of the bitch sheets. It looked a little like my writing, but it wasn't what I'd said. I wrote with a distinctive backward slant, like a left-hander, even though I was a right-hander.

Erwin said, "Well, did you, Romeo?"

And I said, "Sir, no, sir"

"Then it was you, Ramsey." Ramsey, as you would recall, was Murphy's best friend. They were the Dionne-Dewey comedy act.

He said, "Sir, no, sir."

Mills said, "One of you is lying. Are you left-handed, Romeo?"

"Sir, right, sir."

"And you, Ramsey?"

"Sir, left, sir."

"Well, we've checked your handwriting, and you both write like this. One of youse wrote this."

He handed me the paper; it was one paragraph and it said, "Drill instructors were sadistic animals and that Sergeant Whaley should be shot for the way he screwed up Private Murphy's hand."

It wasn't signed, of course, but I hadn't written in. A person can tell his own handwriting, even a recruit. I handed it to Ramsey. He looked at it and shook his head. Sergeant Erwin called us both over to where he was standing.

He said, "One of you motherfuckers wrote this, and I'm going to find out which one."

He grabbed me by the esophagus in an old but familiar hold and dragged me into the little head. He didn't bother shutting the door. He threw me up against the wall and started slapping me back and forth until I was sliding down the wall. Then he stopped and asked me if it was me. I couldn't answer because he had my esophagus held too tight, so I just shook my head no. He yelled and screamed in my face. Called me a lousy liar, then he started slapping me again. When he stopped, I could see Ramsey standing in the doorway, and he looked absolutely terrified. Erwin continued slapping me some more, and when he finished the last round, I was sitting on the floor and he was kneeling beside me, breathing hard. He stood up and told me to get out. I didn't even try standing. I just crawled through the doorway and collapsed outside the duty office.

Ramsey moved out of my way just as Sergeant Erwin reached out and grabbed him. He said, "Come here, you slimy little shit. Did you write that fucking letter? Do you think I'm a sadistic animal?"

Ramsey started babbling at about one hundred miles per hour saying, "Sir, no, no, no." Then Erwin started in at two hundred miles per hour, slapping him over and over again. There was a mixture of saliva and blood coming from Ramsey's mouth, and he slumped to the floor. Erwin tried to raise him back up, but he was completely limp. I thought he was dead. Erwin grabbed a cup of water and splashed him. He began mumbling, and Erwin started trying to get him to stand up. He opened his eyes and immediately started chattering and crying.

"Please don't hit me anymore. You promised we wouldn't get into any trouble for what we wrote. You promised."

Erwin really tore into him this time. He started calling him all kinds of names, like sniveling crybaby bastard puke, just about everything but a marine. I wanted to scream that they had promised. They had told us to write what we thought. They said there would be no disciplinary action taken and we had believed them.

Sergeant Mills came up behind me and dragged me out of the doorway. I stood up and walked away, and the door shut behind me. My head was still spinning. I walked over to where my rack was and sat down and put my head in my hands. I wanted to cry. I wanted to be alone so I could cry like a baby, but you were never alone in the corps. Never. Some of the guys came over and wanted to know what happened. I didn't answer. I just sat there holding my face in my hands until they walked away and left me alone. To this day, I can remember exactly how badly my face hurt, like it was on fire, and how swollen my lips were and how the cracks in my lips hurt for days; but most of all, I remember how absolutely insane it makes me to this very day when someone slaps me in the face. Ramsey stayed in the duty office for what seemed an eternity, but it was actually closer to ten minutes.

I have no idea what happened to him besides what I saw and heard, but when he came out, he was a changed person. As I have said before, he was wiry. He used to lead us all in PT. He was always getting into trouble with Murphy, and from that day on, he was different. There was no more life or spirit left in him. The fire had gone out. He qualified at the range, and he returned to MCRD with us, but three days later, during the physical fitness test, while he was doing pull-ups, he'd only done about four or five and he could always do fifteen or more, but he completed his fourth and started up on his fifth when he stopped halfway up, let go of the bar, and fell to the ground. He sat up and never said a word. The DI's tried to get him up. They prodded him, talked to him, coaxed him, and threatened him, but he never moved and he never said a word. He just sat there staring off into space. Finally, they called Murphy over to talk to him.

Murphy asked him what was wrong and Ramsey said, "I quit."

Murphy tried to get him to stand up, but he wouldn't. He never said another word to any of us. They called an ambulance and took him away. He never returned to our platoon, and two weeks later, when we graduated, without Ramsey, the Dionne-Dewey comedy act was dissolved.

I really don't know what happened to him, but I know where and when it happened to him. It happened in the duty office that day ten minutes after I left. I never told anyone what happened in there, and I don't know what they did to him, but I do know why they did what they did to us. After Priebe turned in all the bitch sheets, the recruits and the DIs went to chow. The bitch sheets were left on the desk, and while we were gone, the lieutenant pulled an unscheduled inspection of our squad bay. After he looked around, he went to the duty office and had a seat to await our return. While he sat there, he apparently noticed the sheets and, being a bit nosy, stumbled across the one about the sadistic drill instructor. I imagine he found quite a few he didn't like, and when our DIs returned, he was pretty angry about what he had read. He probably read them the riot act and said he was going to get to the bottom of this as he didn't condone physical abuse. The DI's told him they hadn't even read them yet and wanted to know what he was talking about. That's probably when he threw them the one Ramsey and I had read.

At that particular time in the corps, there were a lot of Whaleys. They were frustrated marines because they had never been in combat, and there was a war going on and they were missing it. Although being a DI is strictly a voluntary thing, it is a two-year tour of duty, and once you volunteer and are accepted, there is no way of backing out until your two years are up. These guys thought the war would be over before their tour as DIs was over and war is what the Marine Corps is all about. There is nothing worse in the world for a career marine than to be stuck stateside when there is a war going on. There were a lot of Whaleys doing a lot of distasteful things to privates, like Whaley had done to Murphy. Some people were writing their congressman about their little Joey, and the congressmen were writing the commandant of the Marine Corps and he was writing the commanding general at MCRD, and he was sending out memos to the battalion commanders, and they were doing the same to their subordinate people right on down to the DIs.

The DIs were on very thin ice because they were at the bottom of the hill, and shit rolls downhill. So although they were the ones who had to take all of us chicken shit civilians and turn us into good marines in a matter of twelve weeks, they were expected to do it with kid gloves. And believe me, with some of the recruits they received, that was impossible. And in their minds, they were missing a wonderful opportunity to make rank and receive medals and accommodations because during a military conflict is when the lifetime marines receive their reward for doing what only they can do.

During this time frame, a DI at Parris Island came back from the EM Club, probably a little liquored up, and formed his platoon up at about 3:00 a.m. and took them on a forced march into a swamp and a few of them died. It got a great deal of publicity and put the Marine Corps and their methods under closer scrutiny, so after that, everyone was on pins and needles. Ramsey and I had received our just due punishment. A real Dumbrowski, hehehe.

Tomorrow was prequal day. You know, it's funny how the human body reacts to pain. After the first three or four blows from

Erwin, the pain almost completely disappeared, but the mental fear and anguish never did. I'd see his hand coming and hear the sound it made against my head, but the pain didn't register, just the fear of it. As I sat down on my rack thinking about what had just happened and trying to pull things into their proper place, the pain began to register, and my head throbbed, my ears rang, my nose bled, and my whole face was swelling up around my cracked lips.

We went through the normal evening routine and at 9:30 p.m., lights went out and taps was played. The thoughts that ran through my head were always the same after a particularly hard day. I'd think, *Chas, how did you ever get yourself into this mess?* Then I'd remind myself that I'd given up all my rights and privileges because I was obviously not such a bright man. Then I'd say, "Well, old buddy, 190,000 marines can't all be wrong."

That was the approximate size of the active Marine Corps at that time. Then I would think about all the things and people I had left behind and how proud they were going to be of me when I came marching home. That's a real laugh. My mother would end up being disgusted with me and hate the Marine Corps for what they turned me into, and my girl would accuse me of dating movie stars and having too good of a time. Ah, life was at its sweetest, and I was sure it couldn't get any worse, right?

In 2012, as soon as Obama got reelected, one of his first orders of business was to reduce the corps by 20,000 marines. Now their numbers are about 170,000 strong.

Fifty years after I was out of the Marine Corps, I created a decal and the decal said this on the back of it: "The shape of the decal represents the planet we live on. The fire is the turmoil that can erupt at any moment, endangering American citizens and American's interests. The Marine Corps is part of the navy; it is also the only military branch that the president can send anywhere on the planet without congressional approval. The corps is the wedge driven in by the navy to protect our people from the enemy until the other branches are released to help." So why do you think he would reduce his own personal bodyguard by 20,000 when no one that I know of was pushing for it? Marines guard embassies all around the world. They are the inner security; the host country provides the outer perimeter of security.

I got out of my rack and walked into the shower room, ran a cold sink full of water, and soaked my face for as long as I could stand it. I went back to my rack, and I fell asleep despite all the emotions running through my brain. Reveille sounded, and the rush was on. I secured a sink and mirror, and when I looked into that mirror, I was shocked. My eyes were swollen half shut; what little of the eyeball I could see was bloodshot. My bottom lip was cracked down the center and all puffed up. It looked pregnant. I didn't bother shaving or brushing my teeth. I just ran a sink full of cold water and soaked my face in it until everyone left the washroom. I left the washroom, dressed, and went for morning chow.

The section I was in was assigned to the butts for the morning. It was a break for me. It meant I wouldn't fire until after 12:00 p.m. There was usually only one DI in the butt area and the rest were on the firing line kicking butts. This morning, we had two DIs and one PMI. It was prequal day, and they were all over checking this hit and that hit and, for the most part, giving the crew on the firing line the benefit of the doubt on a close shot. Connors was especially lenient, almost desperate, it seemed. I don't know who was firing on my target, but on every firing line, he was just barely qualifying. When he reached the five-hundred-meter line, he seemed to fall completely apart. His first two rounds were Maggie's drawers. I couldn't find a mark anywhere on that target.

Connors got on the radio and wouldn't let me pull the target up until he talked to whoever it was on the firing line. He came over to me mumbling, "Jesus, Jesus, Jesus!" then he mumbled something about Pierson washing out. I pulled the target and waited for the next round. It was on the target at five o'clock in the three ring. He fired six more rounds and needed at least a three on the last round to qualify. I ran the target up and waited for the hit. The next round didn't seem to ever come. Only gravel from above.

I didn't pull the target until Connors yelled, "Mark number 14."

That was my target. I pulled it and looked everywhere for a hit. There was none. I looked it over again, then I looked to see what Connors was doing. He was walking toward me with his head down, shaking it from side to side. I had a pencil in my pocket to mark my score book. I pulled it out and punched a hole in the bull's-eye. I only had to penetrate a piece of paper and a piece of cheesecloth. I returned my pencil and was just about to pull my target up to mark it when I heard a voice from behind me say, "You won't be able to do that tomorrow. There will be a piece of plywood instead of cheese-cloth." I turned around and there stood Corporal Johnson. He was one of the other PMIs. I didn't know what to do. I had egg all over my face.

Just then, Connors came up and said, "Well, Romeo, where did it hit?"

Before I could answer, Corporal Johnson replied, "Bull at two o'clock."

Connors said, "Well, pull and mark it, you big dummy," so I pulled and marked it, and Pierson qualified on prequal day. I believe I could hear him yelling all the way from the five-hundred-meter line.

Corporal Johnson came over and said, "That took balls, Private." I didn't say anything. "I guess if you're going to cheat, go big."

Besides, anyone who knew Pierson would have looked every-where except the bull for his last shot.

We had our noon chow, and everybody was in a pretty good mood. Everyone except Roberts who hadn't qualified, and he wasn't talking. The people who pulled the butts in the morning would fire in the afternoon. By evening, there were three people in our platoon who didn't qualify: Roberts, Beaudrie, and Lee. Roberts, you'll recall, was one of the people in the beginning that wanted to become the guide, but he hurt his back fighting with me. He had sulked pretty badly after I had whupped him, but that was nothing compared to the way he was acting now. He wouldn't talk to anyone. When we returned to our area, everyone, except the above three people, were extremely happy, and everyone, except the three nonquals, were given free time. We all wrestled around with one another, shook hands, patted backs, winked, and made a lot of congratulatory remarks to one another like schoolkids do when they pass a big test, only our big test was tomorrow.

Just because you do something once doesn't guarantee success the next time. Prayers always help. God knows I prayed a lot when I was in the corps. At about 5:30 p.m., we were told to fall outside for evening chow. We fell in, and the squad leaders reported their squad present and accounted for. Private Lee was my squad leader. He had been a squad leader since our second week. He was a good squad leader. He was fair and honest, and he spent a lot of time helping the people in his squad with whatever problem they had. I remember one Sunday we had three whole hours of free time in our platoon area, of course, and he spent the whole three hours of his free time helping Mad Dog learn the proper way to prepare a full field marching pack. The next time we fell out with them for a run, we got about half a mile down the road and straps started coming undone and things started falling out and everyone was grabbing this and catching that, and by the time we got back from the run, all Lawson had on his back was an empty piece of canvas.

He was smiling from ear to ear and walked over to Lee and said, "Thanks a lot for teaching me how to prepare this pack. Hell, the farther we ran, the lighter it got. I really got the straps adjusted right. Even now it feels light as a feather."

Lee said, "Why don't you take it off and we'll check the contents and make sure everything is in it that is supposed to be in it." Lawson undid his harness and pulled the limp piece of canvas off his back. He looked shocked, then he shook his head. Lee informed him that the rest of the squad had his things.

Lawson said, "I packed them all myself."

And Lee said, "Yeah, Mad Dog, and they unpacked themselves, and we all collected them."

That evening, Mad Dog went around asking everybody if they had any of his belongings. Almost everyone teased him a little about the proper way to make up a full field marching pack. By taps, he had all his gear and we all had a good laugh watching Lee teach and demonstrate the proper packing procedure. We knew once he really did figure it out, like with the head calls, he'd probably pack the best full field marching pack in the corps.

That was just one example of the kind of squad leader Private Lee had been and was. I say *was* because, tonight, when he reported our squad present and accounted for, Sergeant Erwin said, "I can't hear you."

Lee repeated his report several more times as loudly as possible, and each time Sergeant Erwin said he couldn't hear him. Finally, he called Lee up front and asked him who he was.

"Sir, I'm Private Lee, sir, serial number 2270188, sir."

Erwin looked at him with all the contempt in the world, like he was a child molester or something, then he grabbed his utility jacket and pulled him nose to nose with himself and said, "You used to be Private Lee. Now you're a nonqual and a maggot. Nonquals and maggots cannot lead squads in my platoon. They follow ten paces to the rear of my platoon so the dogs can eat them. Do you understand, nonqual?"

"Sir, yes, sir."

"Then get to your proper place, maggot."

"Sir, aye, aye, sir."

Lee about-faced and assumed the position ten paces to the rear of our platoon. We were called to attention, and Lee was told to stand at ease. Then he called Roberts and Beaudrie out of the formation and sent them back with Lee. He told them all not to get any closer to his platoon than they were and not to try to stay in step, just straggle along behind. We were all given the command forward march, and we all stepped off together at the proper moment and remained that way until given the order to halt.

The three nonquals straggled along behind us at approximately ten paces. They really looked pathetic back there. When a marine platoon is marching, there are no loose ends or bodies out of alignment. You can look it over from any angle or position; and every arm, leg, hand, foot, or head is on line, all doing the same thing at the same time in the same distance. Those three people to our rear, where the dogs could eat them, were painfully obvious to everyone who saw us. I know they felt like dog food and would have gladly welcomed an attack by a pack of wild wolves rather than go through this humiliation.

When we arrived at the chow hall, we went through our normal procedure of entering and eating. They did not. They had to request permission from the chief mess cook to enter his chow hall as nonquals on prequal day. He refused them entry, and instead, another person prepared three trays and set them on the mess hall steps where they retrieved them and ate outside on milk crates ostracized from their group like pariahs. After chow, the same procedure was followed for returning to our area. We were all given free time, and the nonquals were called into the duty office where they were subjected to further verbal and physical abuse until thirty minutes before taps. At that time, we were all ordered out of the shower room and into the squad bay. It was late October in the foothills of northern California. In the evening, it was necessary to use a sheet and blanket to sleep indoors. We were told to open all the windows in the squad bay, cover up, and go to sleep. We all climbed into our racks and covered up. All the windows were open, and there was a cool breeze blowing through the squad bay. All three nonquals were shoved out of the duty office in a small herd.

The lights were turned off, and they were told to go to their individual racks and pack all their belongings. I didn't know what the hell was going on. Tomorrow was qualification day; they still had another chance, and I couldn't figure out why they were being made to leave, then Erwin's voice came back from almost a week ago: "Don't qualify on prequal day and you won't be around on qualification day."

When they had all their gear packed, Private Lee requested permission to speak. He asked why they were being sent away before they had a chance to qualify, and Sergeant Erwin said, "You're not being sent away. You're just packing your gear now because, in the morning, you won't feel like it."

Lee said, "Well then, are you sending us away in the morning before we have a chance to qualify?"

Erwin said, "That will be up to you, maggots. I don't have the authority to refuse you the right to qualify tomorrow, but I don't think you'll feel like going anywhere but sick bay by the time morning arrives."

Lee said, "Sir, if I have to do PT all night, with no rest or sleep, I'd still want to qualify in the morning and I will qualify, sir."

Erwin laughed and said, "We'll see. Now take off your clothes, everything but your skivvies."

When they were all stripped down to their skivvies, they were marched from the squad bay to the shower room where the hot showers were turned on them. They had to stand under the hot showers for about ten minutes, then when all their pores were wide-open, they were brought back into the squad bay. The air was cold; I was dry and covered, and I was chilly. At one end of the squad bay, there was a linen closet. There were four shelves in it that were about two feet wide and four feet long. Each nonqual was soaking wet. The linen was removed from the shelves, and they each climbed up on one of the shelves and lay down. Erwin walked away.

None of us could figure out what the hell kind of game this was until someone said, "They'll catch pneumonia sleeping in that cold-assed closet all wet."

That was the name of that tune. Every hour on the hour, Erwin would get them all back in the warm shower and then put them back in the closet. You could hear their teeth chattering all night. None of them got any sleep, and when we all fell out for the morning formation and the squad leaders reported, there were three recruits who wanted to be excused from their formation to go to sick bay. We never saw them again, and when we returned from chow and left for the range, their gear was gone.

Erwin had made his promise good, and now we all knew what he meant when he said, "If there are any nonquals on prequal day, they won't be around come qualification day to screw me up because I'll send them to the showers."

He had, indeed, sent them to the showers, and they, indeed, would not be around to screw him up today. We were all hoping none of us screwed up because, if you recall, he also said, "Anyone makes qualification day and then doesn't qualify had better go behind the butts and kill himself because if you didn't, he would."

Sonofabitch, Romeo. You got yourself into an exclusive club this time. That was the thought running through my mind that morning in Pendleton California. I was also wondering if I would qualify and would I kill myself if I didn't, or would Erwin? I decided I wasn't killing myself no matter what, and if he tried, I'd do my best to stop him. I'd had a belly full of Jesus Christ, Erwin. We formed up and marched off to the range.

Corporal Peschke came over the bullhorn with his usual morning cheer and informed us that today was, indeed, the day. I can honestly say that it was the most important day of my young life. I had lettered in varsity baseball my freshman year of high school, and it wasn't shit compared to today. Today was for real—a life-and-death situation. Everyone in the whole world was there: Erwin, Connors, Whaley, Mills, Peschke, and, of course, fifty or sixty of us slimy maggoty civilian rejects. Peschke finished his pep talk by reminding us to remember what we had been taught and we would all do fine.

"Good luck, and keep them in the black."

We fell out, and my group headed for the butts, and the rest of the people headed for the 150-meter line. We pulled our targets and examined them for holes or marks. Corporal Johnson was right; there was a piece of plywood behind each target instead of cheesecloth. I hoped everyone did his best because there was no help coming from the butts today. My pencil was rendered useless after yesterday and what I had gotten caught doing. My little mind was spinning. My main thought was, had I really done Pierson a favor, or had I made it possible for him to be killed? Big question.

Corporal Johnson came over the bullhorn, and we pulled our targets and awaited the hits. I don't know who fired the first round, but he was a real dinger. He put it right in the bull, and that's doing something on the first shot of the day on qualification day from the offhand position. If Ski wasn't two targets away from me pulling targets, I'd have thought for sure it was him. As it turned out, it was Pierson. Yep, old bent barrel Pierson. He probably just got lucky, but it set the standard for everyone shooting that morning, and by twelve thirty, we had 100 percent qualification. Now if the afternoon people could only do as well, everything would be just peachy in paradise tonight. Big if.

We broke for chow, and the atmosphere was like a carnival. We came out of the butts, and they greeted us on the firing line like we were heroes or something. I really don't believe they believed they had done it all on their own. They had, though, believe me. You would have needed an electric drill to cheat that day. We all had lunch, joked, and played around until Peschke cut in on the bullhorn saying, "We're only halfway there, gentlemen."

The carnival atmosphere disappeared, and it was our turn to perform. We collected our rifles and shooting gear and went to the 150-meter line. I put on my shooting jacket, adjusted my sling for the offhand position, checked my windage and elevation with my book, sat down on my shooting box, had a quick thought about back home, said a prayer, and waited for my target to appear. Up it came like a great one-eyed devouring monster. From below its concrete wall, it arose vertically to the top of its carriage and stopped dead still and stared straight at me with its one terrible menacing eye, all black and evil looking. My eyes didn't look very good either.

My time in the duty office was showing all over my face, but my mind was in charge, and as long as I could see my front-sight blade, I was going to qualify. I thought to myself, *I'll put your eye out of business today, darling. Me and my greener don't miss.* I didn't really call it my greener then, but after a tour in Vietnam about a year later, that's when and where it got its name because of all the blood that was spilled with it and thousands of others just like it, and that blood fertilized the earth, ergo it greened shit, the greener.

I fired all ten rounds and only hit the bull twice, but I stayed close enough to it to qualify at the 150-meter line. Next was the timed fire from the 200-meter line. I felt good because I'd done average in the offhand position, and that was my worst position. Learning to shoot standing up never made any sense to me, even at my young age. I mean, if I'm shooting at someone, they are probably shooting at me or are going to start shooting at me. Why would I ever stand there in plain view? I'd be making myself as small as possible and steadying my rifle as much as possible, right? Think about it. Why were we always wearing camouflage clothes?

Later, my theory would be proven by the best teacher in the world—practical application. The rest of the time I served, wherever I was, anytime I had to use my weapon, I was behind something, anything, a tree. The bigger the better; it could be a vehicle, a wall, pile of trash, a grave, a paddy, dike, animals, anything that I would rather have shot than myself. When you're being shot at, the first thing you think of is to cover that ass, boy. Once it was a mud puddle. Why, you ask? Because that puddle was a few inches lower than the ground level, and if you've ever looked under a swing after a rainstorm and seen the puddle of water or after the water in the puddle under the swing has dried, you'll see a depression, and anything is better than nothing. Oh yeah.

I assumed the prone position, the hardest to be hit in, and it just so happens to be the steadiest to shoot from. See how nature and natural instincts seem to coincide with a human's natural instincts? I just remembered that the very last thing I shot in a combat zone was shot from the standing offhand position. I was straggling behind my fire team a couple of hundred meters from our base camp. I think we were in Vietnam, but we could have been anywhere. We were way up north in South Vietnam, I'm sure of that. Anyway, it's hot and I'm itching all over from who knows what. My day is just about over and my mind is on water, hot, cold, or otherwise. I just want it to be wet with something besides my own sweat. My guys are fifteen to thirty feet ahead, and we're on a trail because we are tired and think we own the territory, and it's the shortest route to our base camp. My head is down, looking at the ground for tells, signs of something unusual, but really, I'm daydreaming about home and all the good things waiting for me. I had a girlfriend, loving mother and father, sister, and brother, and lots of friends, or so I thought. Believe me, when you've been gone for three or four years, things don't change back home for you, not in your mind anyhow, but they do for any and everyone else that you left behind. Their life wasn't put on hold. Their lives weren't being threatened and taken every day; they were in a little cocoon while you voluntarily left your soft warm spot to do the right thing to the best of your ability. Yeah, old Susie Q and your buddy would be right where you left them and just like you left them. I can hear Sergeant Dumbrowski then, loud and clear.

One more thing, that old Ford with the fastest six cylinder in town and a sunroof would be waiting too, especially since you'd left it with your friend Art to use as a work car because your dad said it's bad to leave a car undriven for years. All the seals dry up, and everything starts leaking. So your friend Art just landed a job at the Ford Motor Company Rouge Plant and didn't want to park his new car in the lot every day, so he offered you $300 to use it while you were gone and promised to take good care of it, and when you returned, it was yours again. No money, no strings, good deal. I'll take it. Well, more about how everything I left behind turned out later.

I'm back on the trail, about thirty feet behind my fire team, looking down at the ground for tells. Some twelve thousand miles away from all the civilian shit and I feel something land on my bare neck. The first thing I think is leech. My free hand goes to the back of my neck, and my feet keep moving along the trail, and the only thing I'm thinking now is motherfucking, bloodsucking leeches. I touch where it landed and feel something slimy. Leeches are slimy to the touch, but they don't dissolve at your touch. I bring my hand around in front of my face, and I see no leech, only a brown smear on my hand. I bring it to my nose. Damn, it's shit. I stop on the trail, and as I'm turning around, I'm cursing whatever the shit came from.

My fire team pulls up and asks, "What's up, dago?"

A monkey on a low branch over the trail is just sitting there looking at me like I'm a monkey. The smell is in my nostrils, and I'm thinking, *I ain't dirty and smelly enough, but some little monkey has to crap on me. How much lower, Lord?*

Instinctively, I'm looking down the barrel of my M14 rifle with a twenty-round mag loaded with full metal jackets at $.13 apiece in the mid-sixties, and I'm going to use one or however many it takes to get justice. I'll burn the whole area down with a flamethrower. I hear mumbling from my team behind me. It's garbled, but the only thing on Korak's mind is his tormentor. I squeeze one off, and the report brings me back to my senses. For those of you of who have

143

never had the pleasure of reading Edgar Rice Burroughs's series of books on *Tarzan the Ape Man*, Korak was Tarzan's sons name, and it means "killer."

I'm still looking down the barrel; the monkey is right on the end of my front-sight blade, sitting on the branch. I lower my weapon, open my left eye. My team is quiet; everything is quiet, total silence. The monkey's head is down, mine is up. He looks up at me, puts one hand on his chest and the other one over it, takes one more look at me right into my eyes and straight into my heart as if to say, "Why? Why? I was only shitting around."

Then he falls over backward onto the trail. My mind takes me back to 1952. I'm at Stoney Point, Michigan. I have a BB gun, and I'm with my older brother, and I've just shot my first sparrow. I cried then, and my brother laughed at me. I wasn't crying now, but I felt the same sick, sorry feeling in my gut as I did in 1952. I never thought I'd hit that sparrow, but ten years later, I wasn't the same little Christian boy, and I knew, even without thinking, that I would hit my target. I was, by God, a machine programmed to whatever target I viewed instantaneously with no other thought, without a conscience. If it was dead, fuck it; it can't help me, and it can't hurt us. Not on the outside, not in this world.

The guys said, "What's going on?"

And I simply said, "The fucker shit on me. Let's get on back to camp."

They turned and headed down the trail. I picked the dead thing up, used my Ka-Bar to dig a hole, put it in, covered it, and said a quick prayer to my God for it. I caught up with my fire team, and we went into the CP with our rifles over our heads because I'd alerted them, but they didn't know to what.

Back to the sixties and the two-hundred-yard line. I checked my elevation and windage with my book, made the necessary adjustment for the additional fifty meters, and moved back and positioned myself for ten rounds of rapid fire from the sitting position. I was ready for him when he appeared this time. I only had twenty seconds. I was farther away, and his eye was smaller, but I knew today was my day. I lined up, took my breath, and squeezed my better half gently until it erupted again and again and again. I held it to the target until the monster at the end of my front-sight blade disappeared. When it appeared again, I had six white stickers on its eye and four black ones around it. I'd gotten him good this time. Now ten more at the three-hundred-meter line and twenty from the five hundred, and I could go home a winner, brass ring and all.

We moved back to the three-hundred-meter line. I checked my book, made my windage and elevation adjustments, and awaited firing instructions. Corporal Peschke came over the bullhorn and reminded us all to be sure we had our proper windage and elevation for the three-hundred-meter line. We were then told to fire ten more rounds from the kneeling position. It would be timed fire. After we had fired all ten rounds, we would move to the rear of the firing line and await further instructions. He then asked if there were any questions and if anyone needed any help.

There was no reply, and he said, "I want you to remember three things. One, you have plenty of time, so don't rush your shooting. Two, if you know you're hitting at three o'clock in the black, don't be afraid to use a little Kentucky windage. Three, remember Private Pierson just qualified and his gun had a bent barrel. Load and lock, and when the targets appear, commence fire."

We loaded and locked, and up they came one at a time in a steady pattern that, by now, we were familiar with. We'd already gotten our proper body alignment, made all the necessary adjustments, and began our three-hundred-time fire. I knocked the socks off my target in the rapid kneeling, and it was my favorite position, except for the five hundred prone. I think the only reason I liked the five hundred prone so well was because it amazed me to be so far away that an eighteen-inch bull's-eye looked like a black speck on your front-sight blade yet I was still able to hit it regularly. We finished the timed fire at the three hundred meters; we policed our empty casings and retired to the 500-meter line where the proof of the pudding would show.

Our targets were left up, and when we got all the way back there, they looked so very far away and small that I lost all my confidence in myself and my rifle. There just wasn't any way I was going to be able to hit that black eye from here even if I had been doing it consistently all week. The pressure was on, the heat was up. We were given our shooting instructions and, once again, reminded of what Pierson had done and so could all of us. This was our last twenty rounds and our last chance to qualify. Nobody was in real trouble. We all had done fairly well up to this point all we had to do now was stay on target and platoon 189, and Sergeant Erwin would have 100 percent qualification.

Erwin was standing behind us with his usual pleasant personality shining through. I immediately decided that the target was not too far away at all. As a matter of fact, if you had handed me a rock at that very moment, I could have put it in the V-ring. You can't imagine the fear a marine sergeant can instill in an eighteen-year-old recruit with just a look. I'm not going to try to explain it other than to say just imagine meeting your creator, knowing you'd pissed him off. At that particular moment in my young life, there had never been anything more challenging or important. Honest to God. We took our positions on the firing line; our targets disappeared and reappeared one at a time from left to right. We made our adjustments and waited for the command to commence firing. The targets went down and the command was given: "When your targets appear, commence firing."

A few seconds later, they reappeared, and I squeezed off ten rounds as slowly and steadily as time would permit. Targets disappeared and then reappeared. All ten rounds were on the target and inside the scoring rings. No Maggie's drawers. I had two separate five-shot groups. My scores were good, better than I needed to qualify, just ten more shots, keep them on the paper and in the scoring ring and these two weeks would have been a success. Ten minutes later, we were given the command to fire ten more rounds in ten minutes, prone slow fire.

I won't go through every painful shot with you. I'll just say ten minutes later, or approximately thereabout, the targets disappeared, were marked and reappeared, and I wound up with a total of six bulls from the 500 and the other four were in the scoring ring and I qualified as a sharpshooter. We had no nonquals. If you fired above

300 out of a possible 500 points, you were a marksman and you were awarded a marksman medal. It was simply a square piece of chrome-plated metal with what looked like a target engraved on it. It was very blasé.

If you got above 375 points but less than 425, you were a sharpshooter. The medal for this looked similar to the German Iron Cross. It was a four-point star-type thing with a small eagle, globe, and anchor insignia in the center. I thought it was rather fancy. If you fired above 425, you were an expert, the best, and you got two crossed rifles with a lot of lettuce-looking stuff around them. And if you fired 475 to 500, your name was put on a special list, and when you graduated from boot camp, you were eligible to be assigned to sniper school if you wanted to go.

I had a nice talk with a friend of mine whom I grew up with who was in the corps the same time as I was. We were in a bar a year or two after we were discharged, and we were talking about Vietnam and the corps in general. It just so happened that my friend had qualified above 475, and yes, he wanted to go to sniper school. He went and graduated. He got so good with a match rifle and special-loaded bullet that he could almost always make a head shot from about 500 yards on a walking man. He related an experience to me that day that took place while he was in Vietnam that I would like to relate to you, but first let me say sometimes being the best of the best ain't the best.

I believe we were on our fifth beer, and he told me he joined the sniper platoon and was detached to a company that operated around and in the DMZ (demilitarized zone). It simply meant it was no man's land. We didn't own it or control it and neither did the VC. Snipers usually worked in two-man teams. There were several reasons why they worked in two-man teams:

1. One person could be sleeping while the other was scanning so that nothing could get by or through the area they were ordered to watch. There was always a set of eyes on the prize.

2. Four eyes are better than two.

3. Things happen in the boonies; you sprain an ankle, break a leg, and the other man is responsible for getting you back to safety or getting you help.

4. The most important reason, but probably not the last, is if you can't run and you have to hold your position, one man mans a fully automatic M14 while the other man uses his usual sniper tool, a bolt action rifle, so you can hold off a major assault and have a chance at survival. Again, two guns and four eyes are better than one gun and two eyes.

The sniper teams would be given information by the combat intelligence center (CIC) regarding various troop movements, and then they would be assigned an area to work out of, usually watching a road or trail or maybe a small village in a remote area. If the opportunity arose for them to zap a straggler or a high-up military official without jeopardizing their position or their mission, they would do so. They were usually given a particular day and a certain time period to return to their base camp. They pretty much had to return on that day and during that time because of the ever-changing password and the fact that they usually left and returned at night so as not to be seen; in other words, there was a particular password prearranged for their return.

On this particular mission, he was to go out with a Guatemalan. A lot of countries, like Korea and Australia, would send their special forces over to work with us to learn how we operated and allow their people to get combat experience. He had been working with this particular man for about three months. They knew each other fairly well, and Tim said they seemed to enjoy working together. This particular partner was very heavy into the martial arts, and as my friend Tim tells it around our sixth beer, he was bored with killing people form long distances with high-powered rifles. Tim said the guy was always wondering what it would be like to kill someone with his bare hands. They left that morning just before sunup and arrived at their predestined area in time to locate a good hide. They dug in and prepared to do their job. From this hiding place, they were to watch a small open area with crisscrossing trails that were supposed to be used by the Vietcong in the early-morning hours to transport weapons to be hidden in a nearby village. They made themselves as comfortable as possible and began their 50 percent security watch with one man watching and one man resting. They were supposed to return in three days just before sunrise.

It was hot in their hide, and their bodies stunk. It was a stink you become accustomed to after a while. Nothing happened the first day or night. Early the second morning, the Guatemalan was on watch, and Tim was just getting ready to relieve him when his partner suddenly jumped up, jumped out of their hide, and, with a bloodcurdling scream, took off and disappeared from Tim's sight. Tim grabbed his rifle, set up, and leaned forward, and just about that time, he heard a shot go off. He looked in front of his position and saw his partner running at full bore toward a small figure in black about fifty yards away. The Guatemalan was running from left to right directly on line with the other figure, completely blocking Tim's firing area. As he came closer, Tim could see that the Vietcong was having trouble with his rifle and couldn't get another round in his chamber almost at the same time his partner had closed the distance. Upon looking up from his rifle and seeing how close his attacker was, the VC began running backward to extend the distance and give him more time to clear his weapon. Just as the Guatemalan was about to close in on him, he fell over backward, and another round went off. This round caught the Guatemalan in the lower stomach and straightened him up for a second. The VC started to get up but never made it. The Guatemalan caught him square in the face with his boot knocking him flat on his back, and he fell across him, bringing his elbow down across his windpipe.

Tim watched for further movement but didn't see any from either party, so he returned to the cover of his hide because he was sure that all the noise would have attracted attention, and he didn't want his position given away. He still had almost two days before he could return to his base camp. The situation becomes considerably more complicated. They work in two-man teams, and most of the VC knew that. If any of them had heard the gunfire and found Tim's partner, they would probably begin looking for the other bookend. He could leave his hiding place and retreat to the jungle and hide until it was time to return, but then he would be returning alone and marines really don't leave their dead. And if he did return alone, they might not buy his story, and why should they? The Guatemalan had always followed procedure before. There would be an investigation, a hearing, and possibly a court-martial for deserting his partner. Then again, if the Guatemalan wasn't dead and Tim left and returned at the designated time and the Guatemalan managed to get back to the base camp on his own, he would want to kill Tim even though what he had done was foolish and had compromised both the mission and their lives. There didn't seem to be anyone coming, and Tim decided he had only one alternative. He grabbed the M14 full automatic rifle and jumped from his hide, raced to where the two bodies were, pulled his partner off his enemy, and checked for signs of life. He found none. He checked the other man and found none. He picked up his partner and returned with him to their hide.

Now the waiting began. He checked his partner again for life signs. He could find no pulse; there was no movement. He rolled the eyelid back and stuck his finger in the eye; it didn't move. His partner was dead. There was a small hole in the front of his utility jacket and a circle of red around it. He rolled him on his side and looked on his back, and there was nothing. The bullet that entered his body was apparently of a low velocity and bounced around awhile, then fell to rest somewhere deep inside. He watched the open area where the other man was lying. There was no activity for the first hour. He thought about heading out of Dodge with his partner, putting some distance between himself and the dead man, but then the thought crossed his mind that sometimes you can't see what is right under your nose. If there were people in the surrounding area that had heard the shots, they would be coming from all directions, and he was in enemy territory, no man's land. They probably wouldn't be friendlies because he was hours from his base camp, and he certainly didn't want to be discovered lugging his partner and their equipment out in the open. So he decided that he would either sweat it out or fight it out if necessary.

It was one of those decisions that, even if you're a sniper, you don't want to have to face. Their normal tactics are to hit and run. There were three men moving from the elephant grass into the open area. They went directly to the dead man and began examining him.

Then they unrolled what looked like some kind of leather harness. One man put it on, and they hooked the other end of it to the dead man while the third man surveyed the area for danger. The first man took the slack out of the line, and they all jogged away with the dead man bouncing along behind into the elephant grass. The leather harness was what the VC used to evacuate their dead and wounded after a firefight so that we couldn't get an accurate body count. I heard that the other end of the leather harness had two hooks, and if you were dead, they inserted both of the hooks into the top of your diaphragm, above your solar plexus. If you were wounded, but still alive, they put one under each armpit by leaning the upper body forward, raising one arm at a time and wrapping the leather around each armpit. Then the man with the harness would straighten up, taking the slack out of the harness, and the wounded man's head and shoulders would lift off the ground so that only his ass and legs were dragging behind. The VC could run at a good trot, dragging a dead or wounded man behind them for about a mile, far enough to get them out of harm's way.

As the VC disappeared, Tim began to think about his situation more. Had the people who just left really left, or were they waiting for nightfall? If they had figured out that a sniper had killed their comrade, they would certainly want to find that sniper and properly reward him. Nothing was more feared than a sniper on either side because you never heard the bullet coming if it hit you because the bullet traveled faster than the sound. You never had the chance to make your peace because you were already dead. If you get the chance, read a book called *Marine Sniper* written by Charles Henderson that was written about a sniper they called White Feather. His real name was Carlos Hathcock.

If they weren't looking for Tim now, it was only because the area around him was, for the most part, open and void of cover. Their chances of finding his hiding spot and getting to it were next to impossible. He held the high ground. A good sniper, from suitable cover, can hold off an entire platoon. If they were going to look for him, they would do it at night. Even then they would pay a high price because Tim had a starlight scope. The one thing he didn't have was a partner to man the automatic weapon. Suddenly, he felt a little better about his situation until he looked at his partner who would be no help at all. Tim could stay awake all day and all night, but what about tomorrow and tomorrow night until it was time for him to return?

It was hot and getting hotter. It was only a matter of an hour or so as Tim slowly came out of his mild state of shock that he realized another problem existed in the hole with him. His partner was beginning to stink. His bowels had released shortly after he was killed, and the smell was getting worse by the minute. After an hour or two, the flies were coming from all over Asia to enjoy the sweet bouquet from his partner. There was only one thing to do. Tim got his entrenching tool from his pack and dug a small hole about twelve inches wide by twelve inches deep. Then came the really shitty job. He removed his partner's clothes, took out some GI toilet paper, wet it with some water, and washed his partner's ass and legs off. Then he buried the clothes and the garbage in the little hole. That relieved the problem for a while, but by the middle of the next day, there was a new problem. His partner was beginning to deteriorate and stink even worse. There wasn't anything he could do about that stink except breathe through his mouth. That worked for a while until the smell got so bad he began tasting it. His stomach turned over, and he felt better until the smell of his own puke got to him. He buried it like he had his partner's clothes, but the situation got progressively worse until it got to the time he was to return to his base camp.

He hadn't eaten or slept, hardly at all, in more than two days. He was nauseated to the point of desperation, and he had over three miles to cover to get home, not to mention the deadline. He decided to carry his dead comrade back until he grabbed his arm, and it just peeled off down to the wrist. He left alone under the cover of darkness. As he stepped out of that hellhole, he took a breath of fresh air and knew what heaven must smell like. Shit really does bring you closer to your God. They say there are no atheists in foxholes. Believe it.

The entire way back he used his starlight scope to recon the area ahead and around him, not to mention every step had to be checked and treated like there was a booby trap. When he was about six hundred yards from his base camp, he scanned once more between him and the camp perimeter, and he noticed some unusual movement outside the perimeter. As he scanned back and forth with his scope, he detected movement. As he moved closer, he could detect bodies lying all over the ground. He was on a small rise above the area that he had to cover, and every once in a while, one of the bodies would move an inch or two forward, edging closer to the perimeter of his base camp. It was about 4:30 a.m., and in an hour or so, the sun would rise over the surrounding foothills. The situation was easily understandable for the trained observer. This base camp was about to be overrun.

After everything he'd just been through, he felt like turning around and walking away. Thailand sounded pretty good, if he could make it there, but he had a lot of friends that were about to be smoked, but good. The Vietcong would spend the entire night sneaking up on them, and then just before sunrise, they would be right on top of them and they would walk right through them and disappear into the jungle. It looked to Tim like they had another 100–150 yards to cover before they were right on top of their objective. By daylight, they would be there.

Now Tim had another decision to make. He was tired and really didn't care what happened to him, but he knew if he didn't draw some attention pretty soon, it would be too late for his friends. He found some cover beside a small log, dug about an eight-inch trench on the side of it, picked out three good targets, took aim on the first one, and proceeded to do what he did best. The first man merely slumped over where he was lying. The second shot found its mark, and that man rolled over and emitted a shrill scream. That, and the prior shot, brought an almost immediate reaction from the inner perimeter and the whole area surrounding it. Half of the VC attacked the perimeter, and half of them turned and ran away.

As they came Tim's way, he pulled the small log onto him as cover. He could hear footsteps all around him and frightened voices. Suddenly, the lights went out for Tim. When he woke up, he was being carried by his comrades to a jeep. The sun was high in the sky, and they kept telling him he would be all right. And he was all right except for his nose, which was broken and his one eye was cut pretty badly. Apparently, one of the guys running away had jumped on the log and smashed it into his face and knocked him out. He didn't come to for three or four hours because he was so tired, and every time he thought about waking up, he just passed out again, and it took the people from the perimeter that long to secure the area around the perimeter and find him.

The next day, Tim and a half dozen other marines took a chopper to where he left his teammate. They found him where he was left and placed his remains in a bag, and he was eventually returned to his family. The end. PS: I'm sure the government told his family, like all governments do, a feel-good story about how their son died while defending his country, but you know the real story, and they probably never will. It's probably better that way.

Tim would leave Vietnam several months later after several more missions. He saved many fellow marines' lives, like all snipers do, and received several medals and accommodations. He was never wounded, but he contracted malaria and several other infections from cuts he received crawling around in the boonies. He was never again the optimistic young man who loved spending time in the back creeks of his hometown hunting and trapping his youth away, and he never picked up his medals and awards.

He got a job working on the railroad. He married, divorced, remarried, and had his last child. After almost four decades working on the railroad, at the age of fifty-eight, he was the yard safety man, working out of a local yard a few miles from where he grew up and twelve thousand miles from Vietnam. He felt as safe as he ever felt in his mother's arms. It was a cold February day in Michigan, and he had his hood up to cut the cold wind at his back with a coffee in one hand and a radio in the other and his shift just starting. The other crew in the yard was shoving seventeen carloads of sand on an adjacent track. No one, even after an extensive investigation, really knows if it was anyone's fault or just a terrible mishap.

When you work in an industrial area, shit happens. Heavy equipment has no conscience, and you're only allowed one mishap.

Railroad statistics say that the majority of fatal injuries happen to employees with less than one year and employees with more than thirty. You go figure. And so at the ripe old age of fifty-eight, one of this country's finest, one of our beloved corps elite, one of the best of the best, the scrappy Irish lad, the father, husband, friend, the sniper is dragged down like a dog on a cold winter's day just miles from his soft warm spot in the world some forty years after Vietnam. I had spoken to Tim a few months earlier. I was coming from my brother's house on the same street where Tim's family had lived and he'd grown up. He was walking his dog, and as we talked, I asked how long he'd worked for the railroad. He said thirty or forty years, ever since he was a young man. I asked him when he was going to retire, and he said he had a couple more things he wanted to do to his compound up north and get his little girl started in college then he was going to hang it up and enjoy whatever time he had left. A noble idea for a noble man. We had an honor guard for him on the Horse Island bridge in his hometown. The same bridge we all swam off when we were growing up fifty years before. It was a sullen occasion, and we were all sick, sorry, and in disbelief, especially those of us who had grown up with him and served with him in the corps.

Tim's family lives on, and his little girl is grown now. She finished college, and the last time I spoke to her, she was visiting her mom. She'd just returned from South America where she was studying bugs and stuff for a school project. She had received a grant from some college in Ohio to do her masters or doctorate or something like that. Eventually she was going to be a veterinarian. Something special like her dad, not just a regular marine. He was special, and so will she be because the apple doesn't fall far from the tree unless the tree is planted on a hill, and this one was planted on good level ground. She is her dad's best work, and I am as proud to know her as I was to have known and served with Tim Kelly. You just never know, do you?

By 4:15 p.m., platoon 189 had 100 percent qualification, and Sergeant Erwin had a real honest-to-God smile on his usually angry face. Even his most sincere smile had a frightening look about it. If I seem to be talking about Sergeant Erwin like he was some kind of monster, it's only because he really truly was an evil sonofabitch. We had several guys who had fired expert, eight altogether, but only one who fired over 475. Can you guess who it was? If you said Ski, you're right. Old Ski fired 482. The master was about ten feet tall that day.

We formed our platoon up in the parking lot just behind the 500-meter line, and our smoking lamp was lit. As we looked out over all that open space, I recalled how it felt the first time I'd seen it and how it no longer scared or awed me. I had conquered it, and I felt good about it, but there was something sad too. It had cost our platoon three people. I almost felt like I'd been on a patrol into enemy territory, and we had suffered three casualties. We all talked and grab assed until Sergeant Connors called us to attention. We were told to bring our weapons to port arms, open and lock our bolts to the rear, and wait further orders. As we locked our bolts to the rear, Erwin and Mills began checking our weapons one by one to make sure no one had a round left in their chamber or magazine. When they finished, we were told to sling arms, and we marched off into the sun. We only marched a quarter of a mile or so before the order was given to double-time. We all began double-timing and mumbling under our breath. We had a full day, and there had been a great deal of pressure on all of us, and we were tired and didn't feel like running. Not that what you felt like made any difference to them.

We covered about a quarter of a mile, and suddenly Sergeant Mills, in his booming voice, was heard over the patter of our tiny feet, "Platoon 189, stand by."

"Sir, aye, aye, sir."

Then he started his chants. When he finished one verse, we repeated it in sync, then he'd start another as we continued on our way double-timing down the road. We weren't really double-timing anymore though; our feet got lighter, and we weren't tired anymore. We were having fun strutting our qualification strut. We arrived at our barracks in no time. We secured our gear, and we went to chow. There were four platoons in our series, and we had all qualified on the same day. It was like a carnival, noisy and happy, and we were all enjoying ourselves. Then we were called to order, and one at a time, we stood and gave our name, rank, serial number, and our qualifying shooting score. As we did this, one recruit, a house mouse, totaled up the score for the platoon. When we finished, the next platoon did the same. When all four platoons had totaled their combined scores, each platoon commander read off his platoon's score and if there were any nonquals in his platoon. All the other platoons had at least one nonqual. One platoon had four.

Sergeant Erwin called our score off and said, "Zero nonquals."

We were number one with the highest score and no nonquals. One of the other platoon commanders mumbled something. Erwin asked him to repeat himself, and he said, "We don't send our people to the showers on prequal day." You could see that Erwin was furious, but he contained himself. He simply asked if the other platoon commander was going to the NCO club that night.

When he got an affirmative answer, he said, "We'll discuss this there and then in great detail."

We were given the order to eat, and after chow, we returned to our platoon area where we were given free time until taps. There were about six of us sitting in a small group, shooting the shit, when Ski came over.

We all said, "Hey, dinger," and his chest expanded from a forty-two to a forty-six. He asked everyone what their score was and then strutted away. McGowan was just coming over as Ski walked away. He touched Ski on the arm and said, "Did you hear about the guy from 290?"

Ski said, "No, what about him?"

"Well, I just heard he was a late qualifier because his weapon malfunctioned, and by the time they got him a new one and got him squared away, we were already back to our platoon area. He didn't get finished until thirty minutes ago."

Ski said, "Yeah, so what?"

McGowan said, "I just heard he qualified with a 490, and now he's high man in the series."

Ski looked at Mac suspiciously, and Mac stared back at him with an honest-to-God sincere face and said, "Honest. If you don't believe me, go ask Sergeant Connors."

And he walked away. Ski headed for the duty office, knocked three times, requested permission to speak and requested permission to enter, and disappeared through the door. Three or four minutes passed before the door opened. When it did, Sergeant Connors was standing in it. He yelled for McGowan.

"McGowan, you big overgrown gorilla, come here."

Mac ran to where Sergeant Connors was and said, "Sir, Private McGowan reporting as ordered, sir."

Ski was standing behind Connors with a smirk on his face.

Connors said, "Are you trying to give Kowalski a coronary?"

McGowan just looked at him and said, "Sir, the private doesn't understand, sir."

"Yes, you do, oh yes, you do," said Kowalski.

"McGowan, did you tell him there was someone who was a better shot than him?"

Mac got his sincere honest-to-God look again and said, "Sir, no, sir."

Connors said, "Did you also tell him to ask me?"

"Sir, no, sir."

"McGowan, what was your score today?"

"Sir, I fired 370, sir."

"What is 370 from 500?"

"Uh, 130, sir."

"Very good. That's how many push-ups I want from you—130. Now get hot."

Mac dropped down and started pumping them out, and Connors turned to Kowalski and said, "Believe it or not, there are better shots than you. Now get out of here."

Ski left, and Mac was still pumping them out.

Connors said, "Next time, don't send that wacko to me, you big dummy." And he slammed the door. It closed about an inch from where Mac's head was, and we all laughed.

Mac stopped doing push-ups, and Connors jerked the door back open and said, "You still owe me seventy, Mac. Get hot."

Mac started going up and down again with real vigor until the door closed again, and then he collapsed on the floor and began laughing hilariously until he was completely out of breath and doubled over in a ball. The dinger could take no more of this humiliation. He grabbed his shower gear and headed toward the shower. When McGowan finally regained his composure, he joined one of the groups, and we all continued doing our own thing until the lights went out and taps sounded. We all went to bed with the same attitude that night; we had conquered the range. We were number one. Bring on the next challenge.

But remember in the corps, as in the real world, you're only as good as your last move, and there is always another hill, and you never know what's on the other side until you get there. Morning brought reveille, and reveille brought Sergeant Connors and Sergeant Whaley. They, in turn, brought life into our useless bodies. Yes, ladies and gentlemen, we had performed our tasks well. We had won our greatest fight, but if we thought for one moment that we were going to be given a well-deserved rest, we were badly mistaken.

"The parties over girls" was Whaley's opening remark before he commenced to overturn racks and locker boxes and people for all he was worth. Sergeant Connors just followed behind, throwing shower shoes and towels at blurry-eyed stumbling recruit maggots until we all vanished into the shower in a mass of arms and legs.

I knew I should have gotten up ahead of the rest of the herd like I had been doing so I could soak my face to relieve the swelling; now I had to fight with the rest of the animals for water and space. I was eighteen years old and still had my tonsils when I entered the shower room that morning until Pierson came stumbling in and slipped. I was brushing my teeth, and he fell into me, bumping my raised elbow and cramming my toothbrush and half of my forearm down my throat. I panicked and almost swallowed. If I had, I'd have swallowed my toothbrush for sure. Instead, I held on tight and extracted. I learned another good lesson. No brushing your teeth out in the open and keep your elbow down and tucked at your side. You should see the funny look my wife gives me when she comes into the bathroom in the morning and I'm in the corner all tucked in brushing away. I've still got my tonsils though.

We squared our squad bay away, dressed, formed up outside, and double-timed to chow. After chow, we returned, packed our gear, boarded a bus, and started back to MCRD. As we pulled onto the main street, it was like entering Disneyworld. The astounding sights you could behold—cars, bikes, girls; we gawked and stared around at everything that moved. If there hadn't been any identification on the outside of our bus, you would have thought we were a bunch of bald-headed monks who had never been outside their monastery before. What a group. Some of the guys probably still can't get their mouth shut. It all ended abruptly as we pulled up to the main entrance of MCRD and disembarked off our bus.

We were once again lined up on the yellow footprints outside the receiving barracks, standing at attention while Whaley and Connors went inside. We had a new guide again; his name was Carver, or something like that. He wasn't anything special, just another recruit, young and bald. We stood and stood and stood until Sergeants Erwin and Mills appeared. Mills was his usual self—large, imposing, and extremely menacing; but Sergeant Erwin was not his usual self. He had a big piece of white adhesive tape across his nose, a taped ear that didn't look like it was attached to his head by anything but the tape, a black eye, a lip that looked like it had more than a passing acquaintance with a sledgehammer, and one side of his head was all black-and-blue. He didn't say anything; he just looked. I felt a certain feeling of compassion for him because I knew just about how he was feeling since my lip was still swollen, and I had a black eye and plenty of tenderness about my head and shoulders from our last little session.

Mills did all the talking as we got our seabags off the bus and marched to our platoon area. When we arrived, we were given ten minutes to store our gear away and fall in on the Platoon Street. We were in our two columns, standing at attention, and Sergeant Mills began to explain what was ahead of us for the next two weeks until graduation. Ah, graduation, how sweet it would be. While he was laying it all out in front of us, Erwin was laying it all out around us. He was using his favorite hold more effectively and more often than he had when we first met. He even pulled a couple of double gusses off flawlessly. He was really being fancy. In the next thirty minutes, we had all new squad leaders and another new guide. From the sound of Sergeant Mills and the sight of Sergeant Erwin, we were in for a wonderful two weeks at MCRD.

We returned to our respective huts and changed into our PT uniforms. We fell out onto the street and started off on the double for the obstacle courses. For the next two hours, we ran one course after the other as rapidly as possible until we were all completely exhausted. Then we double-timed to chow, ate, and returned to the sandpit for two more hours of PT in the hot California sun. Oh yeah, California—beaches, girls in bikinis, movie stars, and fine cars. We did it all: push-ups, sit-ups, pull-ups, squat thrusts, jumping jacks, running in place, vertically and horizontally. You name it, we did it.

After two hours of solid grunting, groaning, and sweating, we were all just soaked piles of human meat broiling in the sun and sand. Beautiful California. I was absolutely sure my girl was probably sitting at home on her front porch, looking at the canal, imagining me lying on a beach somewhere with a beautiful tanned broad when, in truth, I was lying next to Mad Dog who was spitting sand out of his mouth while, in front of my face, Priebe's big feet were pushing sand in my face as he clawed and strained for that one last push-up before Erwin stepped on his back again. How sweet California is. I love you California. I love your frying sun, I love your soft tasty sand, especially when I'm eating it off someone's boot.

If I had any idea before I enlisted that it would be like this, there is no doubt in my mind that I would have joined the navy, air force, army, or even the coast guard. What can I tell ya? I loved it. I really loved the camaraderie between all of us. There was Mad Dog, gentle Mad Dog, spitting out sand, saliva running from his mouth, snot running from his nose, sand in his teeth, face full of sand, yet he was smiling at me and shaking his head. Pretty soon that smile turned to laughter, and the laughter got louder and louder until it was uncontrollable for him. He rolled over onto his back and burst out like a big bass drum with laughter and yelling over and over.

"I love it. I love it." This, of course, caught the attention of Erwin and Mills, and they both came over to investigate.

The first thing Erwin said was, "What in the hell is wrong with you, Lawson?"

Mad Dog opened his eyes, closed them again, and continued laughing. Sergeant Mills reached down and picked him up off the warm sand and shook him like a little rag doll until he became silent. When Mills let go of him, he was standing at attention and breathing hard and trembling in an effort to stop his laughter.

Mills smiled and said, "What are you laughing about, you little maggot?"

Mad Dog tried to speak but could only manage a "Sir" before he clammed up and shook some more. The platoon was called to attention and we all formed up and returned to our platoon area. By the time we arrived, Mad Dog was completely composed and acting normal, whatever that meant. We went and washed up and everyone knew when we left the washrack and the head that Mad Dog was indeed back to normal. We went to evening chow and returned to our platoon area and spent the rest of the day and early evening sitting on our buckets, studying for a written exam that we were going to take the following day. Everything was peace and quiet again. We were in groups of two and three, asking one another questions.

I remember from where I was sitting I could see the airport runway about six hundred yards away. The big jets kept taking off and landing. In my imagination, I must have departed on about thirty jets that evening; so anxious was I to get home to my family so they could see what a fine person I had become. I was terribly proud of myself. Prouder, I think, than any other time in my life.

Around 7:30 p.m., we secured our study detail and went to the showers. I could hardly wait to write home and tell everyone there that I had qualified as a sharpshooter. It was such a great title, sharpshooter. Yeah, that's me, ole sharpshooter Romeo. I wouldn't bother to tell them that a sharpshooter wasn't as good as expert; they wouldn't have known the difference anyway. Besides, if you just said expert, people would never know expert at what, but sharpshooter, oh yeah, everyone would know you were a gunner. Now if they saw the medal, that would be a different story. The expert medal was two crossed rifles with some kind of floral wreath around them.

I said to myself, "Next time that will be my medal" because you qualify every year, next year for sure.

I'm an old man now, and I'm still a sharpshooter. Yes, I never made expert, but I tried. Every time I see a movie or TV show and I see a marine with his awards showing, the first thing I eyeball are his shooting medals. For me, they are the mark of a marine. Now and for the last thirty-five years, any movie that I saw that had marines in it and they were wearing their uniforms and accommodations, such as *A Few Good Men, Pork Chop Hill, Hacksaw Ridge,* or just about anything on TV, those Hollywood marines always have expert rifle and pistol badges. I cannot remember the last time I saw a Hollywood marine with a sharpshooter or marksman medal, and that's pure bullshit.

I had the opportunity awhile later in my Marine Corps career to qualify with a pistol. I qualified as a marksman. We used old ratty 1911s from who knows what war, and even with a two-handed hold, I could never do any better than marksman. Pistols are inherently more difficult to shoot accurately because they have a much shorter sight radius (the distance between the front and rear sight), which makes aiming much harder.

While I was in the service, I would say about 15 percent of the people I served with were experts with a rifle, and that estimate is probably on the high side because I've always been impressed with the guy wearing them, kind of like you always look up to the judge when you're in court. A long time ago, I found out the only reason you look up to the judge is because they put him on a high perch so you have to look up and it gives him the appearance of superiority, just like your dad was always taller when you were young, to give you the feeling of inferiority and give the impression that he could do no wrong. It kept you in your place.

Any way you look at it, it's all politics, but when I saw a brother with an expert medal, he was special, and I was impressed, and he was the one I most likely wanted to have my six in a firefight. Sharpshooters, probably 40 percent, marksman, 35 percent, there were no nonquals because, unlike Erwin, the corps didn't make them go to the shower; they were just made to do it again until they qualified. You can sprinkle the 10 percent I left out in between all the other categories.

The corps was good, just some of their people were tainted. You have to look up to and appreciate the 15 percenters. Coincidentally, 15 percent is the percentage of qualified people in this country at any one time who serve in its armed forces during a time of war. You and everyone else should always look up to them whether they are the judge, the autoworker, your teammate, neighbor, or that unfortunate wretch you see living from hand to mouth with only other people's discarded possessions as his. Remember, we are the way we are because of that moment in our lives where we cannot help ourselves. Maybe you could help. The point I want to make is that every time I view a theatrical production and I see a marine-enlisted man, E-1 through E-9, the majority of them are wearing an expert medal, not 15 percent but 85 to 90 percent. I know the rifles have changed, the targets have changed, and distances have changed, but really, from 15 percent to 90 percent? I know it's just pretend, but can't Hollywood—the land of fruits and nuts and if it's not a fruit or nut it's a flake—be more real?

Take the shooting scenes for example; in reality, most of the bleeding doesn't occur when the person is hit; it starts on the ground after. Don't get me wrong on this one. I sincerely liked most of the officers I served with, but in the movies, I have never seen an officer with anything but an expert rifle badge. I mean, 100 percent and not just the rifle badge; they will have an expert pistol badge also. Every once in a while, a sharpshooter badge will be the pistol badge, about 5 percent of the time. Now here is my real point, what a platform. You've got the book, you're like two-thirds of the way through it, I know you're hooked, and no matter what I say, you're not going to stop reading, are you? No, I don't think so.

If the corps has improved their teaching techniques so well and if their system of training and teaching such a technically challenging subject to mostly undereducated people, then the educational system in this country should take notice. Now don't get all pissy with me. Some of their recruits are well educated. I don't think they will take you without a high school education or GED equivalent now.

I know a few years ago they wouldn't take you if you were on probation. How silly they are getting? I mean, what better place to serve your probation than boot camp? Today parents send their troubled children, mostly troubled because of their lack of attention to them, to what they call boot camps, which sounds to me like someone doesn't want to do the hard work anymore. But who am I and what do I know? I was only there in the sixties, and we are now in the early part of the twenty-first century.

Back in the sixties, most of the bad boys were sent to the military or jail. Sometimes they were even given a choice. That was always the way it worked, and it didn't just start in the sixties. It was started way before then. What I want to know is, when did it stop and why? The marines did pretty well whenever they were called on. They are still the only military service that the president of the USA can send anywhere in the world without congressional approval. They guard him 24-7 while he is in his own home called the White House. They used to be 190,000 strong until the forty-forth president won his second and last term and cut them by 20,000 troops. Sometimes he forgets to return their salute, but that's not his fault. He probably doesn't know why it's rendered, and he couldn't even pronounce the Marine Corps's name correctly. He called it the Marine Corpse, like a dead guy. It's spelled *corps*, but it's pronounced with the silent *S*, and the commander in chief should certainly know that.

The navy is down to the same strength they were at the time of World War I, so they are getting worked over too. Someone should explain to this president and this Congress why, since the War of Independence, we have never had to fight an enemy on our own soil. I'll bet the Chinese could explain it since they are building four warships for every one of ours that we know of, and the last time I was in China in 1966, their country was surrounded mostly by land, not water, like ours.

Quick quiz: what do you do to your enemy when you are at war with them?

Answer: You cut their communication lines, and haven't we caught China and North Korea messing with our communications and computers? Then you cut their supply lines. To do that to us, you would have to disrupt our imports by sea, and currently we export a majority of our natural resources and import the finished products.

Last question: what does a soldier, marine, military man do when there is no food, no ammo, no supplies, and no communications?

Answer: he takes what supplies he has and his weapon and heads home to his family to protect and save them as best he can.

Good Lord, Mr. President and Congress, wake up. Start doing the hard work of protecting your country's people. The president is supposed to serve the people's best interests, and Congress is ordered to keep a strong-enough military force to fight two wars at the same time on two separate continents, not meddle in the country's citizens' personal affairs. Let the states handle the small lifting. God, wake up, man up, smarten up, and don't let your enemies know what you're doing. Just get it done—yesterday. Okay, I feel somewhat better, scared but better. How about you all? Politicians and people in positions of public trust should have to take a polygraph test every six months.

I'm in South Carolina now, 2015. What a beautiful state. What a "live and let live" state. What a great governor. Keep up the great work. Here's my real point. If the corps has figured out the teaching process so well with rifle and pistol training, then I want them to teach that process to our education system ASAP. If it means cutting out the weak, so be it if the whole is improved. A little common sense in our educational system from grade one through the rest of them would be a start. Common sense would tell you that everyone isn't cut out to be a scholar. Teach them the basics—reading, writing, general math—and after about eight years, give them aptitude tests, and when you find out what their strengths are, send them in that direction. I don't care what their parents want them to be. Quit making them learn things that are nonsensical to them and make them feel inferior. Get off your high horse, educators. You're a great thing for the right person.

I finished my letters and taps sounded. Hurry up tomorrow I'm getting better and better every day. That is how we all felt now. We didn't dread tomorrow coming anymore. We looked forward to it. We were over the hump, so to speak, way past the halfway mark, and there wasn't really much they could do to us that they hadn't already done. In less than two weeks, we'd be on our way to Camp Pendleton California for ITR (infantry training regiment). Four weeks of that then home. Being back at MCRD was easier now. It was even fun from time to time. We were like the seniors are in high school. Our boots were bloused, our bodies were hard, our marching skills were at a level where other platoons watched us admiringly as we marched by. There really weren't too many platoons that were ahead of us in their training now. Whenever we were near another platoon, we stood taller, straighter, and stiller than ever before, not because we were in fear of the DIs, not anymore, but because we were an eleventh-week platoon and we were proud. It was our turn to set the example for our younger brothers. I remember seeing those older platoons when I first arrived. They were so squared away. There were no fatties in their ranks; nobody milled around, and they all looked like they belonged together. Now finally, it was our turn to look like we belonged together.

I could remember how we all used to hate the grinder and COD, but now we were glad when they formed us up and we headed for that large flat empty area of asphalt. There were new platoons, and when we entered the grinder and saw them all stumbling around, we would lean back and strut like peacocks. By now, everyone had at least one good friend he could talk to and get what was bothering him off his chest. We weren't like a bunch of zombies anymore. When we were in our platoon formation, wherever we were, we were like a well-oiled machine, like one big group of manly masculinity moving across the area. No more individuals, one large deadly machine.

My good friend was a guy named Bear. He bunked below me ever since we formed our platoon. We had talked before though we only recently became real buddies. Everyone in the platoon is required to do one week of mess duty at some point during the first three months.

For some reason, we were supposed to have been excused from this usually looked-forward-to experience. Most platoons had a ball during the week they were on mess duty because their platoon commander and DIs weren't around most of the day. They were watched and instructed by regular marines who were cooks and dieticians. Usually you could get away with murder while on mess duty. Your day started at 4:30 a.m. and ended at 8:00 p.m., which only left an hour and a half for your regular DIs to play with you. Most of that was spent showering and getting ready for tomorrow. I had heard of marines who gained as much as ten pounds in one week of mess duty, so it had to be pretty damn soft. We were all looking forward to it.

One day, we were told we wouldn't have to pull mess duty and waste a whole week getting fat and sloppy. We were all pretty depressed about this turn of events. The next morning, things changed and we were marched to the mess hall at 4:00 a.m. and were informed we would have to pull three days of mess duty because of some mess up. We all became undepressed. We were assigned various jobs. Some of us served the food while some of us wiped tables, scrubbed floors, emptied shit cans, peeled spuds. We all had our particular duties before, during, and after each meal. We were allowed to smoke anytime we had free time, and we could eat anything at any time that we had free time.

There was one job they gave to the guide; it was a skating job, which required no real work. He just wandered around with the head mess cook, checking on what everyone else was doing. Our guide didn't get this job. Pierson did. That's right, old bent barrel Pierson was allowed to skate for three whole days. You see, Pierson knew the chief mess cook. They came from the same hometown, and as soon as they saw each other, they became inseparable. At the end of the three-day tour, Pierson would decide he wanted to become a mess cook after leaving boot camp. We all agreed with and encouraged his decision. We decided the mess hall was the safest place in the crotch for old Pierson. His name changed from bent barrel Pierson to Pick Pick because he ran around like an old mother hen picking over her chicks. He was constantly giving instructions to someone about something because they could never do it the right way. He'd grab the stirring spoon from your hand, push you aside, and stir it himself because you weren't doing it right. He'd take your knife away and peel your potatoes because you were peeling way too much of the potato. Didn't you know how much potatoes cost these days?

If you were serving on the line, all you had to do was let him catch you giving out too big a portion, and he'd grab your spoon away and push you aside and do it himself, which would then allow you to go outside and have a smoke. Pick Pick relieved four guys at one time from the serving line at one meal and did it all himself. I believe he had found his place in the corps. Pots and pans may get a little bent and dented, but they are still operable, not like those stupid rifles.

Bear and I were assigned to the scullery. We washed and steamed all the large cooking utensils and trays. One day, he did the wrong thing at the wrong time, and he cooked his hand really good. A steam burn is probably the worst kind of burn you can get. He was sent to sick bay where they treated his hand. He returned to the mess hall with his hand all wrapped in gauze bandages and tape. When we returned to our platoon area and Sergeant Erwin saw him, he asked him what was going on.

Bear explained what had happened, and Erwin said, "Well, what the hell did they send you back here to me for?" You can't keep up with the platoon like that. Go pack your shit and report back here. You'll be going to sick bay for a while."

Bear returned to our hut and informed me about what was going on. At first, he was happy that all he had to do was lie around for a week or two and then it would be time for graduation. How lucky could he get? News flash, that wasn't lucky. Remember, if you get set back for any reason, you have to make up the time with a new platoon. That would mean he'd have to spend four or even six more weeks in boot camp and he wouldn't go to ITR with us or home with me. We were both from Michigan. Something had to be done, but what? Orders were orders.

I said, "How bad is your hand, and really, what can you do?" His hand was all bandaged up. We unwrapped about half the bandage and left his fingertips exposed. He already looked better.

I told Bear, "You're going to have to show Erwin you can do whatever he tells you to do. You will have to go back to the duty hut and request permission to stay with your platoon. If you can just force yourself to do what he tells you to do, me and the rest of the guys will carry you for the next couple of weeks." He never even thought about it twice. He turned around and headed toward the duty hut and Sergeant Erwin.

Bear assumed the position to the right of the door and knocked three times, not real hard but hard enough to hurt pretty good and to certainly be heard. There was no response from inside. He knocked again, harder this time with his elbow.

Erwin said, "Do I hear someone at my door?"

"Sir, Private Weeks requests to speak to the platoon commander."

"I didn't hear you knock, turd."

This time, Bear kicked the side of the duty hut hard. We were all out on the platoon street watching. We knew Erwin had heard that, but there was no response from inside. We all encouraged Bear to do it again. Bear really lay into the side of that hut, and there was still no response. He didn't know why Sergeant Erwin hadn't replied, but we did. He had left the duty hut by the rear door and was standing on the platoon street with us watching Bear kick the side of the hut. Bear turned to look at us with a confused expression on his face and saw Erwin standing there.

All the color drained out of his face and he said, "Sir, Private Weeks requests permission to stay with his platoon sir."

Erwin's look changed from one of anger to one of confusion. He had thought the Bear was ready to go to sick bay and leave his platoon without even trying to stick it out. He had come around from the rear because he knew Bear was kicking the door instead of hitting it, and I believe he was going to rough him up a little before he left for being a quitter.

"What did you say, Private?"

"Sir, the private doesn't want to leave his platoon, sir. The private can do whatever he has to do to keep up, sir."

"Bullshit, you can't do anything. You can't even do a push-up, you maggot."

"Sir, the private can, sir." As an answer to this, Bear dropped down to the front, leaning rest position, and began to pump them out.

"Sir, one, sir, two, sir, three, sir, four, sir."

Pretty soon we were all counting with him. After about thirty push-ups, Erwin gave us the signal to be quiet. All we could hear was Bear as he counted off. We were all staring and listening, and you could hear pain in his voice and you could see his wrapped hands trembling. We waited for Erwin to stop him; his bandages began to become spotted, and his hand was bleeding, and it was soaking through the bandages. Bear was up to fifty before Erwin ordered him to stop. He jumped to his feet and assumed the position of attention.

Erwin said, "You'll have to do sixty-five to get the maximum on the PT test, Private."

"Sir, the private can do sixty-six, sir."

Erwin said, "What did you want to speak to me about in the first place?"

"Sir, the private requests permission to stay with his platoon, sir."

"Permission granted."

We all cheered aloud, and Erwin turned toward us, and with what was as close as he'd ever come to a smile on his face, he yelled that we were becoming a really loose platoon and we still couldn't make as much noise as a bunch of girls. He then turned and walked away as we all crowded around Bear to congratulate him. Marines are such a strange breed. Years later, I would begin, because of my experiences within the corps and life in general, to understand what a delicate balancing act it was to make people fear, respect, emulate, and love you as a leader and always answer your call to duty. Not just to support and work with them even when it wasn't their desired choice but to die for and with them at any given moment. No complaining, no excuses, no bitching, just do it. I never led more than a few men at a time, but after a time, I loved them more than myself. Their safety was more important than mine, and to me that is what a leader is.

Unconditionally, good or bad, what a job our first general had. What a job our first president had. What a man he was. Shouldn't we all still be trying to emulate him? I know I am. I think sometimes when life's confusion has quieted down to a dull roar that men like Washington were able to keep their edge over their men because of traits like Mills and Erwin and Connors and, yes, even Whaley had—the strength of Sergeant Mills, the fearless relentlessness of Sergeant Erwin, eye on the prize, the quiet, subtle, open warm nature of Sergeant Connors, and yes, yes, yes, the ruthless viciousness of the heart and body of a Sergeant Whaley—because in the bitter bloody end of a conflict, that is what usually decided that conflicts outcome. Sergeant Erwin, like Washington before him, had to balance all the characteristics of all those individuals to produce a fine platoon of United States Marines with all of it done, for his part, as platoon sergeant in three short months. His raw material at the start was about sixty-five slimy civilian misfits all individuals.

For the next two weeks, we all took turns helping Bear get dressed and carrying him over the obstacle courses. We were a really tightly knit team now. We were becoming what they wanted now. We were no longer self-centered, slimy civilians; we were becoming a platoon pulling together. It was amazing to see McGowan looking so military all the time, and the rest of the guys all had an unmistakable military bearing.

We finished our last day of mess duty and spent most of our final days going to and from one place or another. There were final shots to receive, final tests to take, final fittings to be made; and a lot of our time was spent preparing for our final inspection. They would line us up in our proper formations with our proper uniforms, and we would always have dry runs before the real McCoy. It wasn't much fun when Mills, Whaley, or Erwin would inspect us because they were extremely stern and hard on us. There was always something wrong with someone's uniform or gear.

After the inspections, we would retire and repair whatever was wrong. A few hours later, we would have to do it all over again. There were shoes to polish, rifles to clean, haircuts for some, showers and shaves, dirty ears to clean, fingernails to cut and clean, bad breath to be cleared up, you name it, they corrected it. Before long, we were ready. When they inspected us now, they were looking and asking questions. What's your fifth general order? What kind of rifle is this? Who are you? What are you? Who's your favorite person?

To that one we always answered, "Sir, Chesty Puller, sir (the epitome of a marine, the Babe Ruth of the Marine Corps)."

Whenever Connors asked that question to Pierson, he would say, "Sir, you are, sir."

To which Connors would get all red faced and frown at him real hard and say, "You from California, boy? You look like one of those California queers. Now who's your favorite person, Pierson?"

Pierson would get real serious and say, "Sir, John Wayne, sir."

We would all snicker, and Connors would move to the next person muttering, "Jesus, Jesus, Jesus."

He'd snatch McGowan's rifle away and say, "Who are you?"

And McGowan would reply, "Sir, Private McGowan, sir."

And Connors would mumble and say, "Yeah, Private McGowan, probably forever, so what is this private?" while holding Mac's rifle in front of him.

And Mac would say, "Sir, that is a 7.62 by 52-millimeter semi-automatic air-cooled shoulder weapon, sir."

Connors would say, "What make is it, Private?"

Mac would look confused and say, "Sir, the private doesn't understand, sir."

And Connors would tap McGowan on his crotch and say, "What is that?"

Mac would flinch and say, "Sir, my gun, sir."

"And what is this dummy?" as he shook Mac's rifle in his face.

"Sir, my rifle, sir."

We'd all laugh and remember the day at the range when Mac had to run up and down holding his stuff and yelling about his rifle and his gun and which was for shooting and which was for fun.

Whenever Connors had the duty, we were all so relaxed. I remember one night, when he had the duty, it was about 11:00 p.m., we were all tucked in and I was sound asleep when I felt somebody shaking me. It was Priebe who told me to get up and come to the back of the hut. I just lay there for a few minutes, wondering what time it was and what was going on. I could hear faint noises coming from the back area. I rolled out, walked back, and waited for my eyes to focus properly due to the lack of light, and when they did, all I could see was asses and legs sticking out from under blankets. I lifted one blanket and was immediately jerked under it. What I saw

I didn't believe. They had blankets draped from the top rack down over the sides and ends of the bottom rack. There were about eight guys around the bottom rack on their knees with the blankets over their head and backs. There was a small flashlight hanging down from the top rack, and money was all over the blanket. People were talking in whispers. The bastards had a set of dice made out of soap. It was a crap game.

I never learned how to play craps, but McGowan had, and he was running the game. He had his utility cover on his head with the brim turned up; it gave him an almost childlike appearance under the dim light provided by the flashlight. He was shuffling money from one person to another, collecting the dice and passing them to the proper person and calling the points. You're faded, roll, and the man with the dice would roll them into the locker box at the end of the rack. This was proof positive boys would be boys, and it was a new world for me. I jumped on in. McGowan would say your points six, and people would start putting money down all over the rack. I just watched for fifteen or twenty minutes, trying to figure out what was going on. We never had any real money until about three days ago when we had gotten paid. We had all received about $350 bucks. I had already sent most of mine home. I went to my locker box and got $10 out and returned. I listened and watched, and I finally decided what was logical.

I put my money down and Mac asked, "Are you with the shooter or not?"

I didn't know what it meant, but I said, "I'm with him."

The shooter rolled the dice and made a ten, then more people started putting money on other people's money and saying strange things like, "C'mon, big Ben," "Sixty-four, fifty-five, what's six and four? What's five and five?"

"What's seven right?" someone would say, and before long, the shooter rolled the seven right. I just watched as my ten was pulled away. I returned to my locker box and grabbed ten more dollars. I watched for a long time before I put it down again. People had stacks of money in front of them, but nobody had more in front of him than a guy named Thomas. He had three stacks of ones, fives, and tens, and the twenties were stuck in his boxer shorts. I figured he knew what he was doing, so I watched him and listened to him. Pretty soon, Mac was telling me to put my money down or leave so somebody else could take my place who was a gambler. I got a little mad at him for talking to me that way and gave him a hurt look.

He said, "Well, Romeo, you ain't betting, and that's what this is all about. C'mon now. A scared man can't gamble, and a jealous man can't leave home."

I almost blurted out, "I was trying to learn the game."

But that wouldn't have been too hep, so I said, "I'm coming. Keep your shirt on."

And he said, "Well, put your money down then."

I laid my money down without even realizing it, and Murphy let the dice roll. He came up on seven, and I still didn't know what happened.

Mac placed a ten on top of my ten and said, "Pick up your money, or are you letting it all ride?"

I figured I'd won, so I gave him a hard look and said, "Yeah, let it ride, motherfucker."

Murphy threw the dice again. This time, it came up on a four.

Everyone said, "Little Joe from Kokomo." I just watched.

Someone had put twenty dollars on top of my two tens, and Mac gave him his money back and said, "I've got Romeo covered."

Murphy rolled again. A six, then an eight, then a five, then a twelve. Everyone was yelling for a seven, except a couple of people, and Murphy.

They were yelling, "C'mon, Joe 31, 22, a row of rabbit shit, and a pimple."

The next thing Murphy threw was a pair of twos. Everyone started picking up money.

I started picking up mine, and Mac said, "What's the matter? No guts?"

I left my money, and Mac put his money on top and said, "Shoot, Murphy."

If you haven't already put two and two together, Private Murphy did qualify. He took the splint off his finger after the first shot and finished the day. Focus, young man, focus.

Murphy said, "Are you covering Romeo's forty?"

And McGowan said, "I just did."

"No, you didn't you just paid him for his twenty for the four."

Mac was becoming irritated and told Murphy to roll and shut up.

Murphy said, "Pick up your money, Romeo. You're not faded."

I started to say that Mac had just put that twenty down when Mac dropped forty more on top of the forty already down. Murphy grinned at me now and threw the dice. They stopped with a six and a five showing. Someone started calling Murphy a lucky SOB. I just sat there looking at all that money and wonderings whose it was.

Murphy said, "Pick up your money, Romeo. I'll probably throw snake eyes next."

I didn't know what he meant, but I picked up my money. McGowan wasn't looking too happy, and I figured I was about sixty dollars ahead. I didn't put any money down until someone else got the dice. I watched Thomas bet, and after a while when he put his money down, I put my money down and bet the same way he did. If he picked up money, I picked up money. If he didn't, I didn't.

It went on like that for about thirty more minutes, and then Mac handed me the dice and said, "It's your roll, Romeo."

I had them in my hand, but I wasn't sure what to do. Humphrey Bogart would have turned green with envy with the way I handled it. I had about 120 dollars in my hand. I was about 100 to the good. I looked right at old McGowan, shook the dice, and said, "I never shoot." and threw the dice across the rack into the locker box and walked away with my money. Don't ask me because I don't know what I rolled. I put my money away after counting it a couple of times and crawled into my rack. I was in that place between sleep and consciousness when I became aware of the hut door opening ever so quietly and a bent over figure slinking past my rack. The first thing I thought about was my money being stolen. I rolled over and watched as the bent figure slowly and quietly sneaked down the center of the squad bay toward the crap game. I slipped out of my rack onto the floor and began sneaking up on this intruder. I was right behind him and ready to jump all over him when I realized it was Sergeant Connors. He was right next to all the guys shooting craps. I almost shit myself. I'd almost grabbed him. I started back to my rack, and when I got to it, I could see he was feeling around for the light switch on the far wall.

I guess in my excitement I had picked up someone's boot to beat the intruder with. I was ready to get in my top rack with the boot still in my hand. Connors was still fiddling for the light switch. I decided to fling the boot at the guys on the floor around the rack, hoping that some of them would make it to their racks in the ensuing confusion before Connors found the lights and identified them all. I let that boot fly. As soon as it left my hand, I knew it was on target. Not my original target, but Connors and I yelled, "Look out."

Some things never change. Connors ducked down just as the boot smashed him in his bare shin. He never saw it coming, and when it hit him, he was shocked. Back in the early days right up until I joined the marines, I was a pitcher. I lettered my freshman year in high school, and I could let it fly pretty good, not like an ordinary guy off the street. I just wanted you to know I had an arm, and the corps had only strengthened it in the last three months. I went from Nolan Ryan to Goose Gossage, only I didn't know it until I let that boot fly, but as soon as I did, I knew, just like when I was pitching and let a wild one fly from the mound. Back then, I'd yell look out and cringe, thinking I was, or had, beaned the batter. It happened more in practice than in the games. The guys got to know me and were always ready to duck.

I went to my first high school reunion, my fiftieth. And two guys I had played baseball with approached me. One guy said, "You know, you ended my baseball career."

And I said, "Say what?"

And he said, "Yeah, you proved to me I couldn't hit a good curveball."

Yep, I had a good one, boy. I'd start behind the batter about head high, and it would curve around to his front and drop down about waist high on the middle inside of the plate.

The batter would usually be sitting on his butt, breathing a sigh of relief and disgust. On certain days, it was my best pitch, on other days, not so much.

The second guy said, "Hey, I remember you. You ended my baseball career."

I was ready for the accolades to come, but they were a bit different than the first guys.

"I quit because you hit me three times in one week, and I could never hit your fast ball."

Oh yeah, I was good.

Then he said, "I couldn't hit it because I was too afraid you'd hit me."

We all laughed and had a beer.

Back to the intruder. I was going to jump the intruder because a few weeks before, when we went to the range, we were told if there was anyone we couldn't identify entering our platoon area we were supposed to jump them and bring them to the duty hut. There had been an incident at the other Marine Corps boot camp in Parris Island. A platoon commander came back in the morning hours from the EM Club drunk. He formed up his platoon in full field marching gear and took them out for a run. It ended up in a swampy area where a few of them drowned, so the powers that be were having young officers take off their rank insignia and wander into recruit areas, looking for abuse like our series lieutenant had done at the rifle range when he found our bitch sheets.

Back to the errant boot. As I said earlier, I let it fly, and as soon as I let it go, I knew it wasn't going where it was supposed to go. I hit Connors in the shin, and he yelled like a stuck pig, and all hell broke loose. There was shouting and screaming and white skivvies flying all over that hut. All of a sudden, the lights came on, and there were only two people out of their racks. They were on the floor in a tangle of arms and legs. It was McGowan and Connors. They had ahold of each other's legs and arms and were all tangled up. When Mac saw who had hold of him, he almost shit a load right then and there. He had this great wad of money in one hand and a real distasteful look on his face. Connors let go of him and staggered to his feet. When he got to his feet, he yanked Mac to his feet. The lights were on, and everyone was pretending to be asleep. How stupid. Connors screeched for everyone to get on the deck in front of their racks. His shin was bleeding, and he was furious.

He said, "Everyone of youse motherfuckers is going to jail! Who threw that fucking boot?"

No one said shit. We all looked around real stupidly at one another and then at Sergeant Connors. I'll be damned if I was going to admit I did it. I was only trying to help out my fellow marines. Besides, if I had saved them by doing it, I would have been a hero. Now they could all suffer with me. Connors was really smoking now. He looked down at his shin, then back at McGowan. He had him by the neck with both hands, and Mac was foaming at the mouth. Connors must have thought he was choking him to death because he let go of his neck and told him to sit down and catch his breath. Then Connors started interrogating everyone individually. The blankets were still hanging from the end rack, and there were six guys without blankets on their racks. These six guys were obviously guilty, and they would pay for everyone. Sergeant Connors still wanted to know who threw the boot, and he was becoming increasingly agitated that the coward sonofabitch wouldn't fess up. What kind of a puke was he? I knew what kind. A scared kind.

I had had the dog piss kicked out of me quite a few times since entering boot camp, and I wasn't really looking forward to another ass kicking and then jail and maybe an undesirable discharge. Oh no, Mr. Bill.

After twenty minutes of slapping one guy and choking another, mostly the guys without blankets, and then any turd who looked at him, Connors returned to where McGowan was sitting. He looked at McGowan and then at the boot, and everyone thought the same thought as he picked it up. Da da da daaaaaaaaaa, whose name would be in the boot? Connors was shaking the boot and promising to incarcerate the low life sonofabitch when he caught him, and he would catch him. He grabbed McGowan by the arm and pulled him to his feet next to him.

Mac had a chance during the last twenty minutes to dispose of the wad of money he had in his hand and the dice he had jammed into his mouth when all this commotion started. That's why he was foaming; the dice were made out of soap. He was looking considerably more confident. Connors continued making his threats. He really was a funny little guy standing there in white boxer shorts with his name stenciled on them, his scrawny white legs sticking out of them into a rather large pair of combat boots with his shin partially covered with dry blood. He may have looked silly, but there wasn't one swinging dick in that hut that night that had even the slightest hint of a smile on his face.

Connors shoved McGowan forward and told him to get in front of his rack. Then he began jerking the blankets from around the dice table. As he did, a large bundle of bills fell to the floor.

Everyone stared, and Connors asked, "Whose money is this?"

No one spoke up, but McGowan was dying. There had to be two or three hundred dollars there, and he had the dirty scraped knees to prove he had worked for it.

Connors asked again, "Whose money is this?"

Again, no answer. He picked up the bills and noticed something else—two wet white pieces of soap almost the same size lying against the wall where McGowan had thrown them when he removed them from his mouth. He walked over and picked them up. He was holding the boot in one hand and money and dice in the other. He yelled for everyone to get in their racks, shut the light off, and just stood there. The hut became unbelievably quiet.

"Well, if it doesn't belong to anybody, then it's found money and will be turned over to the widow and orphans fund. Thanks, Mr. Anonymous."

Then he threw the boot across the room and hit the trash can, knocking it over, and it slowly rolled across the floor. He must have ducked out the back door. No one was sure if he had left or not, and no one was willing to find out. We all just lay there thinking our own thoughts until we fell asleep, and the next thing we heard was reveille sounding over the loudspeaker.

Witski was the first one to hit the floor that morning, and he walked directly over to where the boot was lying and picked it up and looked inside. His face got red, and he started to yell something and then thought better of it. Lawson asked, "Whose name was in it?"

Witski said, "I knew it. I fucking well knew it was mine. I laid awake all night wanting to get out of my rack to be sure, but I wasn't sure where that sneaky little bastard was, but I knew as sure as I'm in this green sonofabitch. Who the hell threw my boot? I could have been killed last night—crippled, maimed, and incarcerated. You guys just don't care who you get in trouble. All you want to do is go home, and you fuckers are trying to get me arrested and busted up. From this day on, I don't want anyone of you motherfuckers to ever touch another thing of mine as long as I live."

There was a lot of talk in the washroom that morning about the mysterious flying boot and who had propelled it. I wasn't sure if anyone had seen me throw it or not, but after everything was said and my name wasn't mentioned, I figured I was in the clear. McGowan kept bitching about running the whole game and losing all his money to Connors.

Parker said, "You should have spoken right up and said it was your money."

Murphy said, "He couldn't because he'd just had his mouth washed out with soap. Besides, he got it by cheating anyhow."

McGowan called him a liar, and Murphy called him a cheater, and we all expected a fight to arise, but Connors and Wheeler came in and ran us all out. We went to a few classes that morning; one of them was on how to wear our uniform properly. The instructor asked who the sloppiest person in the platoon was, and there was a unanimous reply of Pierson. He asked us to point Pierson out, and all eyes turned toward that prime example of the Marine Corps 10 percent. He started to object, but Whaley was already in his face, shaking his head negatively. He was told to go up on the stage with the instructor. The instructor began pointing out various things that were proper and improper.

Out of a possible twelve things, Pierson only had one right. His boots were on the right feet. We went to chow, and Pierson gave all the recruits who were passing out chow a disgusted look for passing out too much. He was really too much. A cook's life it would be for Mr. Pierson. I could see him twenty years down the road older, much fatter, and just as happy as a pig in slop.

We had some free time after chow because it was too hot to do any physical bullshit, and that was what was scheduled. They had some rule that if the temperature was above a certain number—I think it was probably 150, ha ha—the recruits weren't supposed to be put through any physical torture. Today it was hot just sitting still. We were told to go into our huts and study for our final test in two days. We sat around asking one another questions.

Murphy came over to me, asking about McGowan. In essence, what he wanted was for me to watch his back for him because he knew McGowan was out to get him after what he'd said in the washroom. He explained to me how half the guys in the game were just like me and didn't know the first thing about shooting craps. McGowan had talked them into it, and they just went along because they didn't want him mad at them. I could understand that. Remember, McGowan was much older and much tougher than all of us. I had only gotten the best of him in our first encounter out of luck, but the other people didn't know that, and it was convenient for me not to tell them.

You'd be surprised how many guys would have liked to have gotten a piece of me in those first few weeks at MCRD but didn't want to chance it because they remembered I was the one who had put McGowan away in the first place. A reputation can be a very helpful thing at certain times. I told Murphy I was a friend of Mac's, and I would have a talk with him on Murphy's behalf.

I found McGowan, who was still quietly complaining to anybody who would listen about Connor's getting all his money.

"The somabitch knew it was my money. He saw it in my hand when he got the lights on. That's the only reason he was able to get ahold of my neck. I had one hand full of money and a mouth full of soap, and I couldn't hardly do anything. He's pretty strong for a little guy though."

I said, "Look, Mac, that's all over with. You're lucky you're not in jail."

"Might as well be. Ain't got no money, can't do anything I want to do."

If you were guilty of having done a dirty deed, assault on a DI, stealing, or some other heinous crime, you were sent to CCU (correctional custody unit). It was for the hard-core recruit who couldn't adjust or thought in his dull little brain that he could beat the system. We'd see ten or fifteen of them double-timing wherever they went. They had white helmets and always a pick ax or sledgehammer over their shoulder or at port arms. Someone said they were going to or coming from a rock pile where they broke up big rocks into little ones. I don't know. I never saw the pile or where they went, only them coming and going, and they never looked happy.

I said to Mac, "Look, Murphy is all upset because he thinks you're going to jump his ass over the washroom incident this morning. He wants me to watch his back for him."

"He's right to be scared because I am going to kick his ass and take his money too if I can get it."

I said, "Why, Mac? You were cheating, weren't you?"

He said, "No, hell no. If a dummy wants to play a game and don't know how, you can make up the rules and win. That ain't cheating. That's being smart. Shit, man, I grew up in Chicago, and I had to lose a lot to learn how to play. Then I had to lose a lot more before I learned how to win. You have to pay for everything you get."

I looked at McGowan and said, "You're something else, Mac. You really are," then I walked away.

He yelled at me, "Are you gonna help him, Romeo?"

I yelled back, "Maybe yes, maybe no. I like him, and he still has a bad finger."

Mac shook his head and smiled.

I found Murphy and told him not to worry because everything would be all right. Erwin came in and called us all to attention. He began explaining how gambling was illegal and how he wasn't running no floating crap game. He said he had a very good idea who was behind it all, and his eyes never left McGowan and McGowan never flinched. He then said that what was more important was who had assaulted a DI. Everyone, with the exception of a few heavy sleepers, knew what he was referring to.

"Youse people haven't been worth a shit since we returned from the range. You think you're marines because your platoon took the range with 100 percent qualification. Well, you're not marines. You're pukes. Just gutless civilian pukes. There ain't one of you motherfuckers I couldn't whip with one hand, not one. You wouldn't make a pimple on a marine's ass. Assaulting a DI is a court-martial offense, but to do it from behind in the dark by throwing things takes a real coward. If I find out who this gutless wonder is, I will personally see to it that he gets sent to the hospital, then to the brig. They say we can't exercise you faggots today because it's too hot. You all think you're going to get to sit around, giggling like a bunch of girls. Wrong, wrong, wrong. I don't fucking care what they say. You fucking pukes belong to me, and now you're going to realize that. I've been too easy with you. Assume the front leaning rest position." We all dropped down.

"I'll do the counting so that if some snitch comes by, he won't hear all you girls crying. The only sound I want to hear is your sweat hitting the deck. Ready, exercise. One, two, three."

I won't bore you with all the details. Suffice to say we continued to do PT until evening chow. There were plenty of kicks and slaps passed around for good measure for those caught malingering as Sergeant Erwin liked to call it. Every few minutes, Erwin would get next to one of us pukes and ask if it was him that threw the boot and tell the puke it will be all over if you come clean.

I said, "Sir, no, sir" when it was my turn. Connors and Whaley were playing the same game in the other two huts in the hopes that someone had heard something and would snitch. Mass punishment was rampant back then, and why not? Whatever happened, we were all in it together. I always hated mass punishment. It was usually unfair to about 99 percent of the people, but it worked for the corps. To this day, I never accuse anyone of anything unless I can prove it. Due process.

Pierson was too exhausted at the chow hall to complain about the amount of chow being dished out, and the guys handing it out could sense this. It was so hot nobody really felt like eating. The guys giving the food out cut their normal amount in half for everyone, except Pierson. They really loaded him up. His tray must have weighed five pounds. We were all picking away like birds, just trying to empty our trays, and Pierson was gorging himself. He knew if Erwin saw how much was left when we went to dump our trays, he'd get killed. He couldn't eat anymore and began asking the guys around him for help. Nobody helped, mostly because they couldn't eat what they had themselves. You could see the desperation in his eyes. He was going to die. Erwin was going to kill him.

Suddenly, he began grabbing handfuls of food off his tray and disappearing under the table with them, then his hand would return above the table empty. He was crazy if he was dropping it on the floor because we policed our own eating area, and he'd just have to put it back on his tray dirty and eat it. He continued to do this until all his excess food had disappeared. We were told to stand and leave the mess hall. We formed our lines and began moving out of the mess hall one by one to scrape our trays. Suddenly there came a loud yell from the rear of the mess hall. It was the mess sergeant, and he was yelling at some skinheaded recruit to stop. We all stopped, and Erwin came back to see what the commotion was. The mess cook stopped right behind Pierson. Erwin stopped right in front of Pierson. The mess sergeant started yelling about his floor and pointed to a line of potatoes, peas, and corn all over the floor and under the table we had just left.

After a few insulting remarks, he bent down and pulled Pierson's pant leg away from his boot, causing the remainder of the food that was stuffed there to drop onto the floor. Pierson looked down, and the mess cook looked up, and for the first time, he realized who the recruit was. Erwin grabbed Pierson in his favorite hold, around the old gus, and began dragging him from the mess hall. Pierson began going into convulsions all over Erwin's arm. Erwin let go of his throat, and Pierson let go of his dinner all over the table, the floor, and Erwin's arm. Erwin called Sergeant Mills in from outside. When Mills came in and saw the mess, he started getting sick.

Erwin said, "Take him outside and kill him."

Mills said, "I can't and tried to cover his own mouth."

The smell of that puke in that horrific heat really curdled your stomach. I remember trying to breathe through my mouth, but you could taste the smell. Sergeant Mills turned and retreated out the door, and Erwin grabbed Pierson and threw him outside. We all rushed the door at once and half-killed one another trying to get up wind of Pierson and Sergeant Erwin. There were trays all over the floor of the mess hall, along with other shit. That mess sergeant had really made a mess. We were finally formed up.

Sergeant Mills had disappeared somewhere, and Erwin had rinsed his arm off in one of the shit cans used to rinse off the trays. Pierson marched about ten yards to the rear of our platoon as we marched back to our platoon area. Pierson stayed to the rear of our platoon for the next ten days until we graduated. There never was any further disciplinary action against Pierson other than making him march behind the rest of the platoon for the remainder of time. Everyone called him by his new nickname now—Pierson the Puke. Everyone, that is, but Sergeant Mills. He called him asshole, shit-bird, fuckup, 10-percenter, maggot, slimeball, faggot, and numerous other endearing things, always cleverly avoiding the term *puke*. I think Sergeant Mills, for all his manly appearances, had a weak stomach. I saw Pierson, or Puke, chatting with the head mess cook in the chow line a few days later. They were mending fences. Hell, all of us recruits looked the same from behind. Puke was smiling, so everything must have been okay.

We were rapidly approaching our graduation day; after which, we would be given four full hours of base liberty. They only gave us that because so many of the recruits' parents came down from wherever they lived to see their son graduate. Had we been marched back to our area without them having the chance to embrace us and chitchat, there would have been a big stink raised.

Twelve weeks of unbelievable shit we had gone through for four hours of base liberty. Then there were four more weeks of ITR (infantry training regiment) and then home for thirty beautiful days, or twenty. I really don't remember, but it seemed like ten, especially after the incident between Curtis and his mom. I could never really relax after that. I guess I was worried about some incident setting me off and how I would react. Not really. I mean, you have to really be some kind of wacko to shoot at your own mom. I might have said something like, "Pass the fucking salt" at the dinner table, but that's as bad as it would ever get.

Everywhere we went, we were rushed. So many things to do and so little time—final tests, final fittings, final haircuts; everything was final. We were all looking forward to finally getting out of MCRD and away from our tormentors. We had no real idea what our next stop would be like. We knew it couldn't be worse than this. We had heard we got a weekend liberty. We could go to LA or anywhere as long as we were back by 0630 Monday morning. The only good thing about those final days was the absence of PT. The only time anyone did any push-ups was when someone screwed up. We would spend our days studying different subjects and going to different places as a platoon.

Occasionally, one person would be sent by himself to tailoring to be refitted or some other place. This was a rare occasion, and everyone would immediately gather around this individual upon his return to listen to him tell about his adventurous excursion away from the platoon by himself. Once, Murphy brought back two candy bars using the old Pierson camouflage trick in his bloused pant cuffs.

Our time was really getting short now. We only had eight more days until graduation, and tomorrow morning we had our final written exam. I hadn't done very well on our first two written exams, and I was determined to do well on this one. If I could only find some extra study time. There never was any real time when you could be by yourself, except after taps, and everyone else was asleep, and then there was no light to read by. I recalled a small light hanging from the rack during the dice game. If I could locate the person who owned it, I could borrow it, and after taps, when everyone else was asleep, I could cover my head turn the light on and study.

I spent most of that morning trying to find out who owned the flashlight. Most of the guys acted suspicious of me, as if I was planning on trying to get another crap game going. They all let me know they weren't interested. I finally located the owner, but he assured me that he no longer had it as it had been confiscated during the raid, and since he hadn't been back to the PX (post exchange), he didn't have another one. I pursued this a little further because the only things we were allowed to purchase were toilet articles and cigarettes. He finally confessed that he had stolen the light. I was shocked because I couldn't imagine anyone trying something like that. It would have been sure death if he were caught. This little guy obviously had big balls or a very small brain or both. He'd never drawn any attention to himself the entire time we had been in boot camp. That was obviously his MO (modus operandi as the police would say). Don't draw attention, be inconspicuous, strike quickly and swiftly. I could see right away where this guy was going to fit in once he was in the regular corps, and his talent was discovered. He would become his platoon's cumshaw expert. If they needed or wanted anything that another company had, he would locate it, steal it, or, in military lingo, cumshaw it and return it to his company. There is usually one of these talented individuals somewhere in every company.

I realized my efforts were futile, and I was doomed to another low test score the following day. I didn't like getting low test scores, but I really hated the badgering that came afterward from Erwin. Nobody, but nobody, could make you feel less human than Sergeant Erwin. I was sitting on my locker box, anticipating my chewing out, when McGowan came over and squatted next to me.

"What are you thinking about, Romeo?"

"Nothing, Mac."

"You sure look like you were out of it, somewhere deep in thought."

"Yeah, I guess I was. I was seeing Erwin working me over tomorrow after I screw up this last written exam."

"Shit, Romeo, you and Erwin have been around so many times I would think you'd be completely comfortable with your esophagus encircled by his big sandwich grabber. In fact, you know how it only takes three pounds of direct pressure at this point for you to find breathing difficult?"

"Yeah, Mac, I can hear him saying it now, but it isn't breathing that would become difficult. It only takes three pounds of direct pressure to crush your esophagus."

"Well, the guys and me have been discussing, and we think that the number of times he's held yours, which is almost twice the amount he's bothered anyone else, you must have built up some kind of tolerance, and we wanted to bet you could take five pounds before yours cracked."

"Gee, thanks, Mac, and how much of what you all win would go to my family?"

"Oh, Romeo, you shithead, you ain't got no sense of humor."

"It's not that I don't have a sense of humor, Mac. It's just the fact you are telling the joke and your face could kill any joke. I heard they aren't giving you a rifle for combat, but instead, they are going to make you wear a big blow up of your face with your teeth out."

"That's not funny, Romeo."

"You're right."

"Why the hell did you say it then?"

"I don't know. I guess I'm becoming morbid like the rest of you assholes. Look, Mac, I'm sorry. I'm just uptight about this bullshit test."

McGowan stood up and sauntered off looking like he was really hurt, then he spun around, fell on his knees in front of me, and popped his lower plate halfway out of his mouth. I couldn't help but smile. He was really an all right guy, and he had been a good friend for quite a while, and I had been partially responsible for his teeth problems. Sometimes I wonder what would have happened if I hadn't gotten that lucky punch in. He would have, at the very least, put me in the hospital.

He stood up and put his teeth back in place, and I beckoned for him to come sit next to me. We talked about home and our families and friends, and it helped to relieve my anxieties and pass a little time. Sometimes we were better off in the beginning of boot camp when we didn't have any free time at all. It was hard to adjust to all this freedom and personal responsibility, but it was all part of the corps program, and I would learn to adjust like I had to everything else. The corps was truly well-thought-out, mostly through trial and error, which meant pain and suffering and blood and death. What a battle machine it was, and if you're going to fight, it's best to be with the best.

Mac left, and I studied as best I could. I was always a screw off in high school, and my study habits proved themselves to be extremely poor now. I finally threw everything into my locker box and went to see Sergeant Connors.

After gaining admittance to the duty hut and being asked what I wanted, I said, "Sir, the private requests permission to run the obstacle courses, sir."

Connors looked at me like I was totally insane. "You what? Are you going nutsy on me, Romeo?"

"Sir, no, sir. The private is restless, sir, and he needs some physical activity in order to maintain his composure and put things into perspective."

"You are going nutsy on me, Romeo. I've heard all the crazy bullshit in the world. I thought there wasn't anything I hadn't heard, but I never heard anything like this. What's bothering you, wacko?"

"Sir, I just need to run and jump and climb and burn some anxiety off."

"Anxiety over what?"

"Sir, the exam tomorrow, sir."

"Romeo, if you think running the obstacle course will help you pass the exam, you really are going wacko on me, boy. As a matter of fact, I don't think you've got any lead left in your pencil at all. You're running on empty, boy, but if running obstacle courses will keep you from totally going crazy on me, then go run the obstacle course."

"Sir, aye, aye, sir."

I about-faced and headed out the door. I opened the locker box, pulled out my yellow sweatshirt, and was putting it on when Bear came over to see what was up. When I explained, he asked if he could come along. I waited while he went to ask permission. When he came back, Sergeant Connors was with him, and he ordered everyone out of the huts and onto the Platoon Street. He called us to attention and explained how I had come to him with an unusual request. There was a certain amount of laughter and sarcastic remarks before he restored quiet, then he told everyone to put on their sweatshirts and prepare for the obstacle course.

Some people broke ranks, mumbling my name, but on the whole, I think most of them were also ready for a good workout. Of course, I could be prejudiced. We got to the first course, and we were told we wouldn't run the course in the usual way, but instead it would be a free-for-all. We would all take off at once. Anything was fair, short of murder, and we would run all three courses consecutively, and the first three turds to finish would have their smoking lamp lit for the rest of the day. I can only compare the reward for the three winners with one other thing that we all looked forward to and would have to wait until we got back to our girls before we got that. No matter who tells you differently, no one, but no one, gets his nuts off in the Marine Corps boot camp while he is in a regular platoon and on saltpeter.

Anyhow, we were ready to kill to be one of the first people. Cigarettes ain't nowhere near as good as getting laid, but in boot camp, it was the best pleasure we could look forward to. Sitting here now at sixty or seventy and having given up cigarettes over thirty years ago, that last statement sounds so stupid, but back then and there, it was absolutely true. We were put in one long line facing the first obstacle on the first course.

Connors said, "I will say go. When you wackos take off, stay in the boundaries of the obstacle course you are running. Nobody will skip an obstacle and nobody will cheat. Anyone caught cheating will be reprimanded firmly. Gooooooo!"

Some of us just stood there waiting to hear how he was going to kill, cripple, and maim the cheaters because we weren't used to hearing words like *reprimand*, and we were kind of expecting a one, two, three count before the go. Connors was always kind of a joker with us. Only two guys took off immediately. One of them was Witski. If you don't remember Witski, he was the one back in the beginning of the book who gave Erwin such a hard time about getting up. Remember, he wasn't going to school?

Well, he was off like a shot, and as soon as we all saw that Connors wasn't calling him back but was smiling like a shit-eating dog, we realized the joke was on us, and we all took off like jackrabbits. There was a lot of yelling and screaming, punching and clawing, kicking, biting, but no hair pulling. We hit the first obstacle in a huge wave of bodies. I believe I cleared that obstacle without touching it because there were so many bodies covering it. People were falling from it onto other people and then being thrown to the sandy ground below only to attempt to climb it again.

The first obstacle was an eight-foot wall about ten feet wide and twelve inches thick. When you got to the top without being pulled back down, you just fell over to the other side, onto clawing, kicking bodies in a pile on the ground. You fought your way clear to the next obstacle. It was like that at about the first three obstacles, then the bodies began to thin out like in a long-distance race. The obstacle courses were lined up side by side so you could finish one and immediately start the next one. One of the obstacles on the second course was a large pool of water that you swung across on ropes from above the pool. All the fatties used to fall in the pool and have to crawl out soaking wet only to attempt it again with the added water weight.

We were all moving along in small groups of twos and threes. There was very little mauling, except when you were lucky enough to catch up with someone in front of you who was at a delicate spot on a certain obstacle and then you could push or pull him out of your way and take a position in front of him.

Witski was still a good two obstacles ahead of everyone else because of his quick start and the massive body buildup at the first two or three obstacles. I was moving along quite well and was about halfway through the second course. There were four guys ahead of me by one obstacle, and Wtiski was three obstacles ahead. The guys ahead of me were pushing and shoving one another when they got close enough to touch. I decided to lie back just out of reach until they expended most of their energy fighting one another.

The last course was the hardest with the highest walls and most difficult challenges. I figured I could wait just behind these four guys until we had only three obstacles left, then I would close the remaining gap, knock two or more of them off from behind, and be one of the winners. I was enjoying being the quiet pursuer. I would occasionally check my rear for any possible over takers, then turn my concentration on my front. I felt great. I was completely in control, breathing hard and working hard. My confidence steadily increasing with my closing pace. I was having a great time in boot camp. And this was just what I needed. I was eighteen years old, and in the last two months I had increased my body strength unbelievably. I could feel this terrific strength surging through my body now as I pulled myself from one obstacle to another.

I remember watching a hockey game back in the mid-fifties. The Detroit Red Wings had just finished a game with the Toronto Maple Leafs. I don't remember who won, but a news reporter and cameraman were going to be allowed in the locker room to interview some of the Red Wings. I looked up, and they were interviewing Mr. Hockey himself, freaking Gordie Howe. He had his shirt off, and he looked like a real-life Popeye. His muscles were huge. The camera man couldn't take the camera off him. The sportscaster had to tug on his arm to give him some camera time while he asked Gordie questions.

Gordie used to check guys right over the boards into the stands, and he never had anybody protecting him or fighting his battles for him, like some of the players that came after him.

Finally, the sportscaster said, "Gordie, how'd you get so strong?"

"I was a farmer all my young life in Canada, baling and stacking hay. Those bales weigh about 70 to 75 pounds dry and 120 wet. You do that from the time you're big enough to lift them until you're a grown man, and you'll be strong too."

Then the sportscaster said, "Do you think being so strong makes you a better player?"

Gordie said something then that I never forgot. He said, "There is no compensating for strength. As good as you are, as much talent as you have, if you are 20 percent stronger, you will be 10 percent better. There is no compensating for strength." And he walked away with the cameraman right behind him until the sportscaster got the cameraman by the arm and pulled him over to another player. Mr. Hockey, what a player, what a man. I heard he is having some health problems and staying with his daughter in Texas. Good luck, Mr. Howe, and thanks for the advice and the memories.

I started to close the gap between me and the four ahead of me. I was working my way across the first obstacle on the third and last course. This obstacle consisted of pieces of logs that were about six inches around at their ends. They were buried in the ground at different heights, and you had to step or jump from one to the other without falling off. They simulated sunken pilings sticking out of the water, and they covered about fifteen- to twenty-yard area.

My four adversaries were at the next obstacle, the tunnel. The tunnel was just that, and it was only wide enough for one man to crawl through at a time. It stretched for about ten yards with a little hook in the middle. It went underground and came out. These four recruits had apparently come to an unsurmountable pass. There was no way they could agree on what order they would enter, and I couldn't wait any longer because the herd was approaching rapidly from the rear.

I decided against brute force, and instead I said, "Hey, you guys look behind you."

They were startled because they didn't know I was behind them, and when they looked behind them, I dove into the tunnel and was gone like a flash. I was on my way now. Only one guy ahead of me now but I couldn't see Witski anywhere. I could see the end of the course about sixty yards away. He must be behind one of the obstacles out of my vision. I continued on. There were only about five more obstacles. I approached another wall. I cleared the wall and looked ahead. I could see Sergeant Connors standing at the far end of the last course but still no Witski.

I figured, the hell with him. He disappeared like the other guy who took off in front of all of us. He probably had fallen out somewhere along the way or maybe the four Dumbrowskis had caught up with him and waylaid him. It was irrelevant I was ahead and running free. Free like the wind. I didn't really care about winning when we started. I had just wanted to run and jump and climb and expel some energy. We had been so inactive since returning from the range, and I was turning into a nervous wreck, especially after the boot-throwing incident. Every day I waited to be called into the duty hut and be accused of being the dirty low-down coward that assaulted a drill instructor from behind. I needed to do something physical, and I always enjoyed the obstacle courses. But now that I was in the lead and they had been training us to be winners since we arrived here, it was only natural for me to want to be a winner now that I had that chance. I cleared the obstacle, and there was Witski sitting with his back against the pole, panting.

I began to pass him, and he yelled out. "Romeo, how far back are the rest of them?"

I looked over the last obstacle, and I could see they were beginning to pile up two obstacles behind, clawing at one another like madmen. Remember, being able to smoke was the greatest pleasure we were allowed.

I looked at Witski and said, "They are about three minutes away."

He got up, and we continued on our way over the remaining obstacles together. Witski laughed every time we crossed another obstacle, and he would look back at the others scrambling to catch up. He laughed louder the closer we got to the finish line and Sergeant Connors. We both started laughing and yelling crazy stupid things.

Witski kept saying, "It's the first time in ten weeks that I did anything right, and I get to smoke all day. Hot damn, I'm a winner. A winner! Come on, you bunch of maggots, catch me if you can. This Pollack is too smart for all you dummies."

We finished together, and Witski pulled a cigarette and match from his pant cuff. He lit the cigarette and almost coughed himself to death. We sat there, and Connors stood there watching the rest of the platoon finish. When they had all finished, we regrouped and returned to our platoon area where the smoking lamp was lit for the whole platoon for the rest of the day. Witski bitched for the rest of the day because he had worked so hard for nothing special. His last remark that night as he put out his umpteenth cigarette was that he still hadn't done anything right. Boot camp sucks, school sucks, life sucks and probably always will.

Bear realized after the small battle at the first obstacle that his hand needed a little more time to heal, and Connors let him jog around the courses while we ran. We were awakened at the normal time and went through the normal routine. After morning chow, we were taken to the classroom for our final written exam. These tests weren't really hard; they were all about things we had been covering for the last few months, but I had such a mental block about written tests that it was impossible for me to do well on any kind of written test no matter how simple. After the testing was over, we returned to the platoon area. I had strong feelings about the test we had just taken. They were positive feelings. As a matter of fact, I was absolutely sure that I had passed that third and final test.

I was standing by my rack when Erwin came in. Someone called attention on deck and everyone faced the center of the hut. He walked around looking from one person to another, and every once in a while, he would stop in front of someone who always had trouble with the tests, and he would ask them how they thought they had done.

Usually that person would say, "Sir, the private thinks he did well, sir."

When he got in front of me, he didn't stop. He walked right past me and straight to the door. He never passed up the opportunity to harass somebody about their failings, and he had walked right by me without saying a word. I was sure he must be getting old and his memory was failing. People had begun comparing remarks he had made and deciding for themselves whether they had passed or failed. I had done my best and wasn't going to worry. It wouldn't change anything anyway. We'd all know after our evening shower. We were told to fall out with our rifles for some COD (close order drill)—the grinder. We formed our platoon and headed toward the grinder at port arms and on the double. I was just any old recruit now, not the platoon guide or squad leader or anything special, and life was uncomplicated and leisurely even if I was at MCRD as a recruit in his eleventh week.

As we drilled on the grinder, I couldn't help but notice the improvement in everyone around me. Hardly anyone made mistakes anymore, and as a unit, we really looked sharp. It was difficult to believe that three months ago we were all herded off in shower shoes to our new platoon area with Sergeants Erwin and Mills poking us along like a bunch of cattle. The other thing I noticed were the hills surrounding MCRD. Before I had always been too focused on what we were trying to do to notice anything else, but now I could see houses scattered all over the hills, and I couldn't help but feel curious about what kind of people lived in them. I'd been in California for three months and never been off the base, except to go to the rifle range. As I looked up on the hills, I could see laundry hanging on the line and cars parked alongside the houses and in the streets, but it seemed no matter how hard I looked, I could never see any people moving around outside. It was like looking at a painting of a hill-side—nothing ever moved. I decided then and there that I didn't like California.

We finished the drilling on the grinder, cleaned up, and went to evening chow. They had some really good spaghetti. Someone had obviously dripped enough sweat from their brow into the sauce or something because it really tasted great, and everyone totally gorged themselves. Pierson was trying to figure a way to carry some back to the platoon area on the sly for a late-evening snack. You see, when they sounded taps, we weren't really tired anymore because we weren't doing anything physical anymore, so we would wait awhile, then sit around in little groups and bullshit about home and what we were going to do when we got there.

McGowan was going to get three broads and a case of bourbon whiskey and lock himself up for two weeks. Mad Dog was going to kick ass and take names until it was time to come back from leave. I was going to spend most of my time with my girlfriend, but before any of us did that, we had ten more days of MCRD and four more weeks of ITR at Pendleton. That was all right though because at least we wouldn't be where we were and anyplace was better than MCRD.

We formed up outside and, for some reason, double-timed back to our platoon area where we were to try on our new tropical uniforms to make sure everything fit before graduation.

Everyone was helping everyone else get squared away. Connors and Mills had the duty, and they would move from one recruit to another making adjustments that were needed. If you could have been a silent observer and didn't have to participate in any of this, it would have been one of the funniest shows on earth. Great big Sergeant Mills and little Sergeant Connors making adjustments like someone's mother dressing her young son. They finally got everyone straightened out and called us to attention. We were lined up beside our racks. Connors took one side and Mills the other. As they stepped in front of you, you were to bring your rifle to port arms, snap the bolt to the rear, lock it, and wait for the inspecting officer to snatch it from your hands and inspect it. We had been through this a few times before at other less formal inspections, and it was really a tricky procedure.

Sometimes the person handling the inspection would slowly reach out and place his hand on your weapon, and you just released your grip and let it go. But sometimes the inspecting officer would snatch it from you. You were always at attention, looking straight ahead; you just had to develop a feel for what was happening. McGowan could never get along with the snatchers. He was terrified they would drop his weapon and his sights would never be the same. We all tried to assure him that he would be receiving another weapon as soon as we graduated, but he insisted on holding his weapon until he was absolutely sure the inspecting officer had it securely in his grasp.

McGowan screwed up a lot of inspection officer's technique, and Sergeant Mills knew it, so when Sergeant Mills stopped in front of Private McGowan, he leaned real close and got nose to nose with Mac and said, "You fucking gorilla. If I reach for your weapon, you'd better open those dick skinners of yours and drop your piece, or I'm going to rip your head off and shit in it. Do you understand?"

McGowan said, "Sir, yes, sir."

Sergeant Mills checked Mac's shoes, his cover, his military alignment, his fingernails, behind his ears, and in his ears, and he even made Mac breathe in his face so he could check his breath. He never made an attempt to snatch his rifle. He asked McGowan some questions about his general orders and military history. He even asked him his rifle's serial number and his serial number, but he still didn't reach for his piece. He was standing directly in front of McGowan, looking right into his brain, and McGowan was looking straight ahead, not flinching or moving a muscle. Sergeant Mills moved his right hand from his side, and just as suddenly, McGowan released his grip. Sergeant Mills's hand went to his face to wipe some perspiration away, but McGowan's rifle dropped onto Sergeant Mills's dress shoes and clanged to the cement deck. Sergeant Mills never flinched; he merely looked down at his shoes, then at the rifle, then at McGowan, and then he started yelling.

"You mother this! You big dummy! You maggot, you sorry-assed fuck!"

McGowan just kept staring straight ahead, and Sergeant Mills kept screaming names at him until Sergeant Connors came over and relieved him. Sergeant Connors pushed McGowan all over the squad bay, asking why he'd thrown his rifle at Sergeant Mills and telling him he was going to court-martial him for assaulting a drill instructor.

"If you weren't standing right next to me the other night, I would have sworn you were the fucking boot thrower."

The pushing stopped, and we were told to put our uniforms away. The ones who were told they needed alterations were to fall out in twenty minutes with their uniforms under their arms. The rest of us could use our free time to square away our gear while they were at the tailors.

We started doing as we were told, and McGowan pulled his locker box over near mine and brought his dress shoes and some polish. He was just about to say something when one of the house mice rushed up and yelled for him to report to the duty hut. The house mouse turned to leave, and McGowan grabbed him by the collar and turned him around.

"What the fuck do you mean report to the duty hut? For what?"

Peters, the house mouse, said, "Hell, I don't know."

"Well, who the hell wants me?"

"Sergeant Mills."

McGowan let go of the house mouse and uttered one defeated "Shit. I knew I got off too easy with Mills."

The duty hut was next to ours, and you could hear what was going on if things heated up. We knew things were going to heat up, so we lined the wall and listened at the windows. There is no need to describe it blow-by-blow. McGowan went right in. He never even got to knock once. As soon as he approached the doorway, a tree trunk reached out and jerked him inside. The rest took about thirty minutes. After he'd gotten severely beaten around the head and shoulders, they put him in a wall locker and beat on it with ax handles. When McGowan came back to our hut, he looked dazed and was carrying a pair of dress shoes. He sat down on his locker box. I figured I'd let him recover before asking him how he was.

The first thing he said was, "He didn't have to call me a nigger. I ain't no nigger. I was a nigger, but I ain't no more."

I looked at him, wondering what he was talking about. I couldn't figure out what he meant, so I asked him, "What the hell are you talking about?"

"Sergeant Mills, he didn't have to call me that. I ain't no nigger. Hell, I used to steal and rob people and pimp and push weed and be a regular jitterbug motherfucker, but I've been really trying since I came here, and I thought I was doing okay, and this guy whom I look up to the most and am trying my hardest to be like calls me that. Shit, man, I quit."

"Aw hell, Mac, it's just a word, a name. Don't let it define you. Your actions define you, not what anyone says you are. He just got a little excited when you dropped that nine pounds on his toes. I see you have another pair of shoes."

"Yeah, I've got to square these away by taps or spend the night in the wall locker."

"How was that wall locker?"

"Shit, you'd go crazy in the thing after a couple of hours. Sounds like a bomb going off when they hit it with those axe handles. Connors said it was just another test a marine recruit has to go through before he graduates. He said it simulated battle conditions. Man, they got names for all their games, don't they?"

"Yeah, I guess so. I guess you could say they've got their shit together, Mac."

"Yeah, and if I don't get these shoes together, I'll be going back into combat, and I'm still shell-shocked from the last time." He looked down at the shoes and said, "How the hell am I going to get that squared away?"

One of the shoes had a gouge in it that was about one-sixteenth of an inch deep and ran all the way across the toe. No amount of shining would remove it. The leather was cut right away.

Priebe walked over to where we were and said, "Let me see the shoe, Mac."

McGowan gave it to him. Priebe stuck his finger in a can of shoe polish and dabbed it into the groove, then he took out his lighter and turned the shoe over so the toe was facing down. He lit the lighter and held the flame up to the shoe. McGowan grabbed the shoe away from Priebe, shoved him to the ground, and accused him of trying to get him killed.

Priebe said, "Look, I ain't going to burn the damn shoe. I'm just going to melt the polish on the toe so it fills in the tear in the leather and let it harden. I've done it before in civilian life. You've just got to trust me. I used to be a shoe repairman. Now give me the shoe and stand back, boy."

McGowan said, "Nigger, boy, what's next?"

Priebe said, "Shine."

Then Priebe put more shoe polish in the tear and heated it with his lighter. As it melted, you could see it filing in the tear in the leather, and as he took the flame away, it would harden. He repeated the process several times and handed the shoe back to Mac.

"Now you can get to polishing this sucker."

Mac smiled like a little boy who had just found an old toy that he hadn't seen in a couple of years and had thought was gone forever.

He brought the shoe over to his locker box, sat down, showed it to me, and said, "Ain't that Priebe something?"

I said, "Yeah, but don't tell me. Tell Priebe."

He just looked at me questioningly, and the light came on, and he yelled across the squad bay, "Hey, Priebe, you're something else! Yes, you are!"

Priebe's whole face lit up, and he smiled and said, "Yeah, I ain't bad for an old nigger, am I?"

The guys came back from the tailors, and we all took our inspection uniforms to the base cleaners and returned on the double to our area. Sergeant Mills informed us that in three days we would be running the CMC. That was the big one. The commandant of the Marine Corps physical fitness test. No platoon could graduate without passing it 100 percent. It was supposed to be a grueling endurance test with full field marching packs, helmets, and rifles. The packs weighed about forty pounds. All in all, you lugged just under sixty pounds of equipment over a course that covered a little over four miles. You ran, jumped, climbed, crawled, carried wounded comrades, you name it we did it. You had to do it all together. Everyone in the platoon had to finish. The best time got the CMC pennant, and that was the one that really counted. You could have four or five pennants, but if you didn't have the one that said CMC, you weren't shit on graduation day. Well, not really. You were some kind of shit, but not hot shit like you were if you won the CMC pennant.

I guess, thinking back now and reading over this material, it's safe to say in the corps you're only as good as your last move, and if you aren't the lead dog, the scenery never changes. Think about that one for a while. Constant pressure. Sergeant Mills let us know, in no uncertain terms, that he wanted it bad. He also let us know that for the next two days we were going to practice. We were told to get our packs and fall out. It had been about three weeks since I'd felt the familiar bite of pack straps over my chest and shoulders, and I wasn't' cherishing the thought of the next two days at all.

It was 6:15 p.m. A warm dreamy California evening. We formed up on the Platoon Street with all of us in our proper place in the formation. All of us wearing yellow sweatshirts with a large red Marine Corps eagle, globe, and anchor on the front. We had utility trousers, boots, utility covers, and, of course, our field marching packs and rifles.

Sergeant Mills said, "I don't know how far we're going to run tonight, but I know were' going to run until the first maggot falls out or until it gets dark, whichever happens first."

Sunset was about three hours away. I was praying for the first maggot who would fall out as long as it wasn't me. We ran down the Platoon Street and out to the main avenue. Down the main avenue to the grinder. Once around the grinder, approximately three miles, and back to where we had entered it. Sergeant Mills began chanting, which always made the running easier. We turned from the grinder and ran down another street past the PX, around the PX, a mile or two down another avenue, and out to the San Diego Airport fence. The very fence that two and one-half months ago, I was sure I'd be climbing before I ever graduated. We ran another mile along the fence, watching planes land and take off, knowing in a very short time we would be on one heading home. Home sweet home. *Casa dulce casa*. Along the fence and back down it. Six miles. We circled the sandpit and were brought to a halt.

Sergeant Connors asked if anyone had fallen out yet, and we all answered, "Sir, no, sir."

Then he said, "Does anybody want to quit?"

We all answered, "Sir, no, sir."

Connors said, "Fuck you! You're all liars. Assume the position."

We all dropped to the front leaning rest position and started doing push-ups until no one could do anymore, then we formed up and marched back to our platoon area. We showered and had mail call. We had about thirty minutes before taps, and McGowan returned Sergeant Mills's shoes. They were really squared away. Mills just looked at them and grunted.

McGowan returned to the squad bay and said, "He took them and never said nuthin'. I don't believe that nigger."

We all laughed and had a little grab-ass session with one another until taps sounded.

Sleep came fast. We were all worn-out and pleased with ourselves. Reveille came too soon, as always, and we went about our normal morning routine. I was working on my pack straps because they kept telling us that if our packs were adjusted properly, you couldn't even feel the weight. I believed them because they almost never lied before. Well, only that one time at the range about the bitch sheets. I could definitely feel my pack's weight. The straps practically cut me apart. To this day, I can't wear coveralls because the straps remind me of my old pack straps and how they started hurting like a sonofabitch after an hour.

Peters, the house mouse, came in and yelled for Private Romeo to report to the duty hut. It didn't compute right away because I hadn't done anything wrong. I was still standing by my rack when Bear patted me on the shoulder and asked me why I wasn't reporting. I turned, surprised, then ran next door to the duty hut. I knocked and I knocked, and no one answered my knock. I wasn't disgusted at all because I knew if you were told to report to the duty hut and you knocked more than once you were all right. They were not going to kill you; they just wanted to play with your knuckles for a while. Finally, Sergeant Whaley said to come inside. I followed the proper procedure to the letter because I knew Whaley still wanted to kill me, and I wasn't going to give him a legitimate reason. He asked me who I knew in California, and I said that I didn't know anyone.

He said, "Bullshit, shitbird. Someone is here to see you."

I told him I didn't understand, and he informed me that someone was waiting to see me in the visitor's area. I knew what the visitor's area was because we had a few guys from California in our platoon, and about once a week, after our eighth week, their families would come to see them. Sergeant Whaley told me it was 9:30 a.m., and I had better be back by 11:00 a.m. I went through the proper procedure and left the hut. When I entered my squad bay, I located Peterson. He was a California fag, or so we called him, and I asked him where the visitor's area was. He gave me directions and asked who had come to see me. I told him I didn't know and took off for the visitor's area.

I ran in the direction Peterson had given me until I saw someone coming toward me. It wasn't another recruit, so I slowed down to a walk, and when he was about five yards from me, I saluted and said, "Sir, good morning, sir."

He saluted and returned my verbal greeting, just like I was a regular marine. I walked another ten yards and began running again. I wondered what was going on, and I hoped this wasn't some kind of trick that would get me in trouble right before graduation. It would be just like Whaley to tell me I had a visitor and then report me missing after I'd left the area. I'd be picked up, brought back, and court-martialed for trying to desert. Me with only eight or nine days to go. I immediately stopped running and started walking at a normal pace. At least if they picked me up they wouldn't be able to say I was running. I only had two thoughts in my mind: what an asshole Whaley was and who had come to see me. I turned a corner and saw a small brick building with a sign that read MCRD Visitor Area.

I entered the door and saw a sergeant sitting behind a counter reading, and I approached him and requested permission to speak. He granted permission, and I told him I was reporting as ordered. He didn't give me any shit at all. He told me to go right through the door marked Visitor's Area. I opened the door, and there was a picnic area in a regular garden setting. It was like Alice in Wonderland. No sand, just real grass and picnic tables and benches and lawn chairs and shade trees. Hell, they even had candy machines. I didn't have any money because we weren't allowed to carry any, but the machines were there. It wasn't a mirage. I looked around for someone I knew, but I didn't see anyone. There were recruits sitting and walking with their families. There wasn't one drill instructor anywhere. There also wasn't anyone I recognized, so I figured Whaley had set me up.

All of a sudden, this little man with black gray hair, wearing a gray suit, caught my eye. He stared at me, and a small smile crept over his face, and I started my way toward him. I wasn't used to seeing him in a suit and never expected to see him in California because he was a factory worker from Michigan. He was also my father. I took off my utility cover and walked toward him. He looked at my head, and his smile broadened. We shook hands and embraced.

He said, "I see you've got a haircut like I gave you when you got in trouble with the police when you were fourteen. Have you been bad again?"

I laughed and said, "No, Dad, I've been really good since I left home."

We embraced again, and I turned and saw my mother standing next to me with tears in her eyes and a smile on her face. I hugged her, and neither one of us could say anything because of all the feelings swelling up inside of us.

My dad said, "Let's have a seat over there."

We turned toward a picnic table, and there was my baby sister. I swear she looked three years older than when I left home three months before. We all sat and talked and touched to be sure it was real. They couldn't get over how much I had grown and changed. I couldn't get over them coming all the way across the country to see me and not even letting me know about it. I guess they really did love and miss me. Boy, what a surprise. Before you could say shit, it was 11:00 a.m. and I was late.

I jumped up and said, "I have to leave. My DI said to be back at eleven, and I'm late."

I started off, and my dad said, "Don't go. You only got here an hour ago. Surely you can stay longer. What's he going to do? Beat you or something?"

I smiled and said, "Probably. I've got to leave. Please come again tomorrow."

When I returned to the platoon area, they were gone, and it was the first time I'd ever been there alone, and it was eerie, and I didn't like it at all. It was 11:15 a.m., and I figured they were at chow. I decided to wait in the area until they returned because I wasn't given any orders to do anything else, and a good marine obeys his last order. Whaley had merely said be back by eleven. I sat on my locker box and decided to have a cigarette. I finished, and the smoke hung in the hut forever. I just knew one of the DIs would come in and kill me for sneaking a smoke, but none of them did. At about twelve, I could hear my platoon coming into the area. They stopped on the

Platoon Street outside, and I heard Whaley tell the mouse to see if I was back.

Peters popped his head into the hut, smiled real sinister, closed the door, and said, "Sir, the private is here, sir."

Whaley dismissed the platoon, and they all came scrambling in. They looked at me like I had some kind of disease. My buddy Bear came over and asked me why I hadn't come back at eleven. I explained who my visitors were and that I had just lost track of time. He said Whaley formed them up at about ten minutes before eleven and waited until eleven, and when I didn't show, he marched them to chow thirty minutes early.

Before they left, Whaley said, "Well, people, that's one shitbird down."

"You'd better prepare yourself, Romeo. He's going to can your ass if it's the last thing he does."

I thanked him for letting me know how it went down. I couldn't help but hate Whaley for this. A wonderful thing had just taken place for me, and old Whaley was going to screw me while I was still smiling. Oh well, maybe if they court-martialed me really quick, I could ride home with my parents.

I have to say this here and now. The USMC is a fine organization with many fine leaders doing a fine job of training our marines. They always have, and we'd better hope they always will. If I made Sergeant Whaley sound like a real turd, it's only because he really was, and I'm not apologizing. I was expecting to be called to the duty hut at any minute, but the entire day passed and the house mouse never showed his ugly little face. We were given free time, taps sounded, and still Whaley hadn't called for me. I was in my rack thinking about seeing my parents again tomorrow, and the squad bay door opened quietly, and a harsh light shined directly into my face.

I heard Whaley say, "C'mon, shitbird, let's do it."

I climbed out of my rack and walked over to where he was standing. He never took the light out of my face, and I was completely blind. When I got close to him, I requested permission to speak.

"Granted, shitbird."

I said, "Sir, may I get dressed, sir?"

"No, shitbird."

At least now I knew there wasn't going to be a court-martial. Sergeant Whaley had his own way of having someone ejected. Besides, this was so much more personal, and Whaley liked to keep things on a personal level. We walked to the duty hut, and he steered me inside by placing his hand on my neck and shoving me down onto the deck. My hands hit the concrete floor as I caught myself. I managed to keep my head form cracking against the concrete, but my knees skidded across the floor, and the hide peeled off as I skidded to a stop. I didn't wait to estimate the damages. I got to my feet as quickly as possible before he could get over me. Whaley loved it when you were down.

"What happened, shitbird? You trip?"

"Sir, yes, sir."

"Clumsy, shitbird, very, very clumsy. Assume the position."

I dropped down into the front leaning rest position and prepared to pump them out.

Whaley said, "No counting required, shitbird. We'll keep this little workout nice and quiet between you and me, all right?"

"Sir, yes, sir."

I began doing push-ups until I couldn't do anymore, then I rolled over and did sit-ups until I couldn't do them anymore, then I rolled over and did more push-ups, then more sit-ups, then I did my squat thrusts until I was dragging my feet over the concrete because I couldn't lift them anymore. Every once in a while, he'd give me a good kick in the ass with his boot to help me up or a boot in the shoulder to help me back down. The sweat was dripping off me. He had closed the doors and windows because he didn't want anyone to hear me grunt like a little pig. It must have been ninety degrees in that duty hut, and he kept asking me why I had disobeyed a direct order, and I kept saying, "Sir, the private has no excuse, sir."

The blood was running from my hands, knees, and my feet pretty freely now. My heart was doing Mach 2, and I kept thinking, *C'mon, Whaley, get the gun and put the poor shitbird out of his misery. You want to. I know you do.* I kept thinking it, but I never said it. I just kept doing what he wanted me to do. Now he wanted me to duckwalk like a good shitbird, so I duckwalked up and down the aisle. I was doing pretty well, but every eight or ten steps, he'd put his boot on my back and kick me forward onto my face. The first time this happened, I let go of my ankles and caught myself with my bloody hands.

He didn't like that and said, "No, shitbird. No fair using your hands."

So the next time, I turned my face to the side and landed on my shoulder. First one shoulder, then the other. After a while, my shoulders became black-and-blue, and I was aching from head to toe.

My legs never really got too tired from the duck walk because he never let me walk very far before he kicked me over onto my face. I was feeling like shit. I'd just showered after being shitty all day, and here I was at twelve midnight, sweating and bleeding like a pig, crawling around on a concrete floor, being molested by a sadistic psycho DI while wearing nothing more than my underwear. Marine boot camp was a real holiday.

I hope all the Suzy Qs who were ever left at home while their boyfriends went to boot camp read this and realize that we weren't really running around with Hollywood beauties. It was all only in their minds. Whaley kept asking me stupid questions as I crawled around and picked myself up. There was no real pain anymore because my body was numb from the pain. The mind is a wonderful thing. Whaley kept asking me these questions, and I kept answering them as best I could. He asked me if I wanted to leave the duty hut.

Naturally, I said, "Sir, yes, sir."

And he said, "Why?"

Now this is the truth, so help me God. I said, "Sir, because I have to get up early and have a very busy day planned for myself tomorrow, sir."

I said it just like that, honest, just like a civilian explaining to the host of a party why he or she had to leave the party early. I figured, fuck it. He's got me so tired and worn-out that if he tried to kill me, I wouldn't be able to fight back and it would be over very quickly.

I was kneeling on the concrete, and he was standing behind me. I was expecting to have my testicles kicked up around my ears when he said, "Go ahead then, leave."

I did my best to stand, staggered to the door, waited for my good night kiss, but it never came. I returned to my hut, went in as quietly as possible, crawled into my rack, and fell asleep. It had been a hell of a day. Every time I think about this particular incident, I realize that I was the one who allowed Whaley to do this because I played right into his hands by coming back late. I also realized that it takes a particularly cold-blooded person to inflict that kind of pain on someone intentionally.

I am considerably older now, and I realize I made the first mistake. I realize in war that your first mistake can very often be your last, and I have since then suffered more pain, but I have never suffered more humiliation. Sergeant Whaley was a special case. He was the exception rather than the rule. I wouldn't want anyone to reject the Marine Corps as a possible vocation because of what I said about Whaley. I'm not recruiting for the corps. If I was, I would have excluded Whaley and created a more likable character. I mention him because he was the truth. This whole book has been a truth. I would like to say that your chances of finding an asshole like Whaley in the air force, army, or navy are just as good as finding one in the police department or teaching profession. They might not be able to kick the shit out of you in civilian life, but they could ruin careers. I can only emphasize this so that any responsible person who reads this material will pay closer attention and investigate more closely when someone tells them that they are being mistreated. Whaleys really do exist.

Reveille sounded over the bullhorn outside our hut at 5:30 a.m. as usual. I rolled from my rack, like always, but when I hit the deck, I still had my sheet tangled around me, and my legs collapsed. I fell to my knees, and I rolled to my side because they hurt so badly. I tried rolling to my other side, and it hurt so badly that I put my hands down to get up, and they started cracking and bleeding, so I just lay there, watching everybody scrambling around until Bear grabbed my arm and helped me to my feet.

I didn't know what a mess I was until I looked in the mirror. There were a few small scuffs on my face, some dirt and sweat lines, and my white underwear were gray, yellow, brown, and bloodstained. My hands were covered with dry blood and dirt, and my knees were swollen considerably, and my shoulders hurt so badly that I could hardly move them. I didn't bother washing up I just stepped into the shower and let the water rinse everything away. I dried and put on the dirty underwear so I wouldn't get in trouble for returning to the hut nude. I changed into the utilities and boots and carefully fell out. Bear tied my boots for me. His hand were doing a lot better now. Sometimes that old saying about one hand washing the other or you scratch my back and I'll scratch yours or covering each other's back really do take place, especially in the corps.

We were seated in the mess hall, eating breakfast. I was doing my best to manipulate my silverware with my swollen hands when I noticed the house mouse grinning at me like the coldhearted toad he was. I gave him a really hard look that normally would have made him cringe and turn away, but he didn't. Instead, he gave me an even bigger grin and flashed me the finger. I couldn't figure out what had brought about this big change in the guy who had been licking the DIs boots for three months and taking abusive remarks from the whole platoon because he was a suck ass. Maybe he sensed my soreness and figured in my condition he could kick my ass. That's all I needed, the house mouse beating my ass in front of the platoon. I ignored his gestures and finished my meal. There really are times when discretion is the better part of valor. Is this hill worth dying for?

We formed up outside and marched back to our platoon area. Whaley was being relieved by Erwin and Mills. As he walked by, he snatched Peters out of the formation and began chewing his ear. When he finished saying whatever it was he was saying, Peters said, "Sir, yes, sir."

I don't want you all to think the platoon house mice were suck-ups, like in school or civilian life. They didn't choose to be house mice; they were chosen. But in our platoon, it seemed the DIs knew who to choose after a week or so because, after a little while, they assumed the role to a T and became the snitches and suck-ups they were meant to be. Whaley walked away, whistling. Peters was one of the house mice. There were two of them. I don't know how they are picked, but sometime around the second week, two recruits are told that when they hear one of the DIs call for a house mouse they are supposed to come running. Curtis was the other house mouse. You remember old pleasant Curtis. We went out one night when we were on leave. He was the one who took the pan away from his mom and knocked her down the steps, went and got a rifle, walked her out the back door, and lied to her about counting to ten. She knew he was a liar though, because at eight, she ducked behind a tree and old Curtis opened up on that tree.

Yeah, Curtis and Peters, two normal guys, average in every way, except Peters was on the small side and older. Basically, the house mice spent a lot of time in the duty hut, cleaning it and taking care of the DIs gear. They were like maids and secretaries, and along with the chores came benefits. They heard a lot of stuff that the DIs discussed, and it gave them an edge on us other recruits. They almost always knew what we were going to do the next day, so they were always able to psyche themselves up for it. They never got thumped on by the DIs or us either because picking on one of the mice was like hurting the son of a mayor in a little town. Retribution was harsh.

They were special, and keeping one close to you could be helpful. That's pretty much why Curtis and I were tight. When I was a guide for those few weeks, I needed all the inside info I could get. Curtis was from my state, so he would let me know what he knew. It made it a little easier for me. The house mice got out of any dirty detail too. They just hung around, waiting on the DIs and running for and after anything the DIs needed or wanted. Those of us who weren't house mice were glad we weren't because they were looked upon as the teacher's pet and the suck-ups and like they really didn't belong with the rest of us.

We were to spend some time in our huts, working on our gear until about 10 a.m., then we were going to go for some final shots and do a few other small things that needed taking care of. I was applying some Vaseline to my hands and knees and talking to Bear about my little session with Whaley when Peters came to the door, walked over to me, and said, "You're wanted in the duty hut again, shitbird."

I looked at him standing there, looking defiant and cocky. I couldn't figure out his new attitude. It was like he'd already kicked my ass once and was sure he could do it again. I said, "Peters, I have to take that shit from the DIs, but I don't have to take it from you. You'd better leave before I kill your scrawny little ass."

He looked up at me and said, "Try it, shitbird."

I was about to jump to my feet when I realized I was wounded and nothing worked right. That's why he was challenging me; it was like battling a one-armed man who couldn't move. I realized then that's what he and Whaley had contrived for me—to have the smallest, slimiest little weasel of a house mouse kick my ass in front of the whole platoon. Peters saw my feeble attempt to stand up and knew positively then that I was a severely wounded animal and lunged for me. Peters was reaching for my neck, and Bear got his neck instead and was literally slapping the dog shit out of him with his other hand. When he let go of him, Peters fell to the floor and started crawling for the door. All the way to the door, he was yelling about telling Whaley on Bear for interfering and Bear was booting him in the ass.

I got up, put on my clothes, and thanked Bear for handling that little matter for me, and I reported to the duty hut and Sergeant Erwin. He informed me that I had visitors and that I had to get my shots before I went to see them. I had completely forgotten about my family. I felt bad about keeping my family waiting, but without the shots, there would be no graduation. At that time in my life, there was nothing more important than graduating, not even seeing my family. I received my shots and went directly to the visitor's area. I was allowed to spend two full hours with my parents before returning to the platoon area. I felt like a civilian again, and that wasn't good because I forgot to say sir to Sergeant Mills, and he worked me over for it.

On top of what Whaley had dished out the night before, I was feeling pretty ragged. To be truthful, I wished that night that my parents would have stayed in Michigan. They never had any idea what I'd gone through. I kept my palms hidden through the visit so they wouldn't ask questions, but when my dad shook my hands to leave, he noticed the cracks, and I said they were from a rope burn I received from a tug-of-war contest we had the day before.

He said, "There's nothing else? What's wrong?"

I wanted to say something like, "I hate it here. These men are really mean, and they beat me. I'm going home with you guys." But I knew I couldn't, not legally, and I knew my wonderful father who had never been in the service and had only three friends in the neighborhood that had gone off in World War II and only one had returned and he didn't talk about it. My dad would never understand the trials a marine recruit has to go through to become a United States Marine. I also knew he would have gone looking for Sergeant Whaley, and that wouldn't have done any of us any good. Nothing would have changed Whaley. I was hard to the treatment, and my dad would have been turned over to the police, but I would have put everything I owned, or earned in the future, on the fact that if my dad and Whaley ever did lock up that the only thing that would have beaten Whaley to the hospital would have been the lights on the ambulance he was in. And after they got my dad's shoe out of his ass, everything he ate for a long time would have tasted like shoe polish.

I met some pretty impressive marines in the last three months, but my dad was still my only hero on this planet. What a guy. I assured him everything was good, and in four or five more weeks, I would be home and we'd all talk about everything. He accepted what I said and let go of my hand and gave me a great big hug. Then it was time to face my mom. She looked at me, and I can never ever explain what her face and eyes said. I was such a mother's boy. Even now, as I stood hovering over her, I couldn't find one word. I bent down and laid my head on her shoulder, and we wrapped our arms around each other and just held on. Dad patted my back and hers until we separated a moment later.

My little sister was smiling at me and crying, and I picked her up, hugged her, and said, "You be a good girl."

My dad said, "They might be able to come and see me tomorrow, but they had to get on the road early because he could only get ten days of vacation, and it was a three- or four-day drive home."

I obviously couldn't go through this again, so I said, "Well, Dad, we're so busy getting ready. I probably can't even get a pass tomorrow, so you guys head on back, and I'll see you in a month."

I turned and walked to the exit. Sometimes the shortest walk seems like the longest walk ever. I took the walk.

There really wasn't much for us to do the last week, but they managed to keep our young minds and bodies occupied most of the time with cleaning our living quarters and completing unfinished things, like getting our final dentist appointments and minor chores. Our days were mostly spent in or near our own platoon area, and once again, boot camp took on a college campus lifestyle. The DIs would pass among us and question us about one thing or another. They would even make little jokes about things that happened earlier in our training, and it was all right if we smiled a little bit in front of them.

Sergeant Erwin called us to attention on the afternoon before we were to run the CMC. He was holding a large stack of manila envelopes in his hands, and he called the house mouse front and center to hold them while he passed them out. They were our orders telling us where we would be reporting to after we completed ITR. As he called your name off, you would follow the same procedure you followed for receiving your mail. When everyone had received their envelope, he permitted us to open them. He said that if anyone had any questions about where they were going or what they would be doing, they should ask him and he would explain. People were going all over—some to the fleet marine force, some to radio school, some to mechanic school, some to electronic school; it all depended on your test scores and if Erwin had made any particular evaluations or recommendations.

I was to report to sea school after returning from my twenty-day leave. I had no idea what sea school was, but I could see where it was. It was in San Diego, California, at MCRD. *Holy shit*, I thought, *I'll be coming right back to this hellhole twenty days after my twenty-day leave.* I could hear Sergeant Dumbrowski laughing again, and I didn't like it.

Once again, Sergeant Erwin, in his own subtle way, had done me a favor. You had to be recommended for sea school. Each platoon commander picked three or four of his most squared-away marines for this rather plush duty. Exactly why he picked me I'll never know. Vietnam was just starting to go hot and heavy in the mid-sixties. Anything could happen to you on the ground in Vietnam, but sitting on a naval ship in the Tonkin Gulf was about as safe as being in your mother's arms if she didn't drop you. The sea duty tour lasted two years so for at least two years I was assured of staying alive, pretty much. I'd like to think Sergeant Erwin knew what he was doing and wanted to spare me any unnecessary pain that could possibly end in my death. You have to remember, in the early sixties everyone who knew anything figured we'd go over there and square old Ho Chi Minh away and come home most ricky-ticky-die.

Most of the recruits were requesting permission to speak and were asking questions about their orders. I decided not to. Just knowing I had to return to MCRD was depressing enough for me. I was depressed until I realized my orders meant they had a place for me in the corps which, of course, meant I was going to graduate, which, of course, made me very, very happy. Now we were ready for the CMC (commandant of the Marine Corps physical fitness test). It was a grueling physical endurance test, and some of us almost didn't make it. What we didn't do was take the CMC streamer, and that didn't make Erwin very happy. He left us to straggle back to our area alone. We all knew he was mad, but we had no idea how mad until that evening when he started calling people to the duty hut one at a time to work them over. There were only twenty-two of us he didn't send for. I was grateful I was one of the twenty-two. He hadn't bothered me since that last written test. I guess he figured Whaley was giving me all I could handle. Everyone was grumbling because he had roughed them up, and they had all made it. So what if he wouldn't be carrying the CMC streamer on graduation day? We had three of the other six that were awarded, and that wasn't half bad.

Someone said, "Yeah, but it's only half good too."

We went through our final dress inspection by the series CO with flying colors, and graduation day was finally upon us. We awoke on that wonderful morning of mornings, dressed in our usual uniform, and went to chow. The graduation ceremony was scheduled for two that afternoon, so we had about seven hours to go. Most of us spent the time packing our seabags with everything we owned and writing our last letters from MCRD. After the graduation ceremony, we would be given a few hours of base liberty, and then the following morning, we would board a bus for Camp Pendleton.

I want to elaborate on how I felt that morning. There was a great deal of anxiety mixed with a strong feeling of accomplishment. I had done everything with a group, but on that morning, I was feeling everything as an individual. I knew that at any time in the last three months I could have quit, like so many did, and regardless of how large or tightly knit the group was, I would have still gone down in flames by myself. I was, at that moment, my own person for the first time in my entire life. There were still plenty of worlds to conquer, but I had as good a start as anyone could have.

When a platoon graduates from boot camp, five of its members are awarded PFC stripes. That makes them a private first class, which makes them one step higher than a private. This award is supposed to be given to the five most squared-away people. Usually, if you are the guide or squad leader, you receive the PFC stripe. We had changed guides and squad leaders regularly for the entire three months, and no one had been told who was going to be awarded the PFC stripe that I knew of anyhow.

I was absolutely sure that because of all the shit I had been put through that first month and all the ass kickings I'd taken and given to square everyone away that I was going to be called to the duty hut any minute and Sergeant Erwin was going to award me with a set of blues and PFC stripes. You see, there was also what they called the platoon honor man, and he received a promotion to PFC and a set of blues. It was twelve noon, and we had just returned from noon chow, and we were told to dress for the graduation ceremony. We unwrapped our freshly laundered tropicals and began dressing. They hadn't called anyone yet. They were probably waiting until the last moment. They always kept you waiting until the last moment. We were all dressed and ready to go when we heard Erwin holler for us to fall out. We formed up on the Platoon Street in two columns, and we were told to form our platoon and stand at ease.

Our smoking lamp was lit, and Erwin said, "I wish that I could have awarded you all with PFC stripes, but they only allow us to promote five people from each platoon. At the beginning of training, I agreed to let Sergeant Whaley choose the honor man and the other four PFCs. Everyone who was ever a squad leader or a guide has contributed to this platoon's success. Then Sergeant Whaley stepped forward and called off the PFC's names and they came out of the duty hut wearing their new stripes, which automatically made them outrank the rest of us.

I don't need to name names because all the people who were picked as PFCs were regular recruits. None of them had excelled at anything. As they came out, they took their position at the head of the platoon as squad leaders. The honor man was the last to be named.

Sergeant Whaley said, "This platoons honor man is…"

We were all waiting and looking around for whoever was missing. Who was in the duty hut with a set of blues and PFC stripes? Sergeant Erwin called Sergeant Whaley front and center. He mumbled something to Whaley and walked away.

Sergeant Whaley said, "The honor man for platoon 189 is PFC Peters."

The entire platoon broke up. We knew it was a joke. It had to be a joke, but it wasn't. Peters came out of that duty hut with a set of blues on, strutting like a little peacock. I've rarely seen a marine in his dress blues who didn't look good, but honest to God, these blues didn't improve his looks one bit. He was still a short, skinny little house mouse. He always resembled a little troll but never more than at that very moment. I took it very personally. I mean, what had he ever done to make this platoon better? He'd gotten out of all the shit details. Nobody, except the DIs, even knew anything about him except he was short and ugly with big ears, none of which he could help, but any contact any of us had with him it certainly seemed like his personality matched his appearance. He was extremely antisocial and always seemed to have a smirk on his face whenever he was sent to tell one of us to report to the duty hut. We knew that he had heard the DIs talking about whoever it was, but he never gave anyone a heads-up. He'd just tell them and smirk and return to whatever he was doing. He was like a shadow person.

Suddenly I didn't dislike him anymore. I hated him. I was eighteen, and I'd never really hated anything or anyone before, but I'm being honest. I hated that little rat shit bastard, and I felt like he was wearing my blues. Peters took his place in front of the platoon as its guide. Whaley placed the guidon in his hands, and we were called to attention. Sergeants Mills, Connors, and Erwin joined us as we marched off to the parade grounds.

As we marched out of our platoon area and onto the main street, the sun shone brightly on our freshly shaved faces. We marched past old well-kept buildings with spotless yards surrounding them and under large trees that offered us a small moment of relief from the harsh sun.

As we marched along to our final event at MCRD, my mind went slowly back to where all this began. I could see myself standing in the front yard of my home in Michigan with my arm around my father, smiling while my mother snapped a picture for posterity. Then I saw myself boarding a plane and Bear offering me an air sickness pill. I saw myself standing on yellow footprints in front of the receiving barracks while Sergeant Erwin and Sergeant Mills introduced themselves. We shuffled off as a platoon for the first time with our yellow sweat shirts, utility trousers, shower shoes, and a bucketful of personal hygiene items all paid for by Uncle Sam and free to anyone willing to pay the price.

As I look now, I see tall straight clean lines, no stragglers, no one out of sync. It was all so precise and military, but I knew it wasn't always that way. I remember how it was before we all learned to stand tall alone and as a platoon. I remember the special instructions that were given to Parker, McGowan, and me. I remember Witski not wanting to go to school and being thrown on the floor from the top rack by Sergeant Erwin and being roughed up until he realized where he was that first morning.

I remember it all so well. Please tell me I'm not the only one who remembers all these things. I can't be the only one affected so profoundly by these things. Surely more people than I remember the futility of trying to teach sixty-five slimy civilians how to walk along in harmony. It's called close order drill. Although some who were there are now gone, surely the ones who remain can still remember. I can still see the Dionne-Dewey comedy team, and I know somewhere, somehow, they got back together again. I know Murphy related all his experiences to the other half of that inseparable team and thereby enabled Dewey to live through him all the experiences that Sergeant Erwin's bitch sheet caused him to miss.

I like to think he has forgotten that day in a small bathroom at the rifle range. I pray that he realizes now that he was but a mere child then, and children crack and cry and feel ashamed. So do grown men when given the right stimuli. Be well, brother. I don't know what eventually happened to you. Whether you were sent back to another platoon or hospitalized or discharged or what, but whatever happened, wherever you ended up, I want you to know two things.

One: For the entire time that you were a member of our platoon, you were a real leader. We all liked you and respected you, especially me. Because my fine friend that day in that small shitter I was only just a few more seconds away from cracking myself. Our eyes met for those few seconds as I crawled out of that torture chamber. You had witnessed my beatdown and knew what was in store for you. Your eyes said help. I could see the terror that was behind them, and my mind said stay, help, fight for him, he's your brother, and he didn't do anything wrong. They said nothing would be held against us, but my heart failed me, and I didn't stay and fight for you, and to this very day, more than fifty years later, I am ashamed to my very core.

Two: If you did wash out and become a civilian again, I hope that you and Murphy are back together being best buds, sharing your lives and raising your families together.

Three: It seems like there is always one more thing. Walt Disney, a man who has brought more joy and excitement than anyone else I can think of, was undesirably discharged from the Marine Corps way back decades ago before you ever came in because he couldn't adjust to military life. His discharge was framed and hung on the back wall of his office right behind his chair with all his other awards. Don't be ashamed. You tried and he tried. God decides, brother man, not the almighty corps, not the drill instructors, only God.

I'm sure McGowan watches for uppercuts like a bitch and is smiling in remembrance wherever he is. I write this for all of them and all of you, but mostly for myself. I'm afraid to forget. I know that as long as I'm able to get it all down on paper before I become old and forgetful, I'll always just have to read it to myself and some of my fondest memories will come back to life again. So you see, it is really a selfish writing I have done. Selfish and, perhaps to some, foolish, but to me and for me, it's been most gratifying. You see, I have three small sons who, someday, will say to me, "Dad, what was the Marine Corps like?" And I will slyly smile and say, "Have you got a few hours?" Then I'll hand them my manuscript, and they will know what their dad went through those first few months and hopefully why.

We graduated, and those who had relatives in attendance went off with them, and those that didn't went off in small groups to explore the main PX see a movie or go to the EM club and drink if you were twenty-one. I wasn't twenty-one and neither was Bear, but we had a friend who was. Bear, McGowan, Priebe, and I went to the EM club. Mac ordered four beers and got two beers, plus a couple of cokes, and we returned to the table. We finished our drinks and took a walk.

Every time one of us looked at the other one, we laughed and said, "Is that all there is, my friend?"

The next morning, we boarded the bus for camp Pendleton. Sergeant Erwin was the only one there to say goodbye.

He shook each of our hands and said, "Good luck, Marine."

Barretta would have said, "And that's the name of that tune."

Kojak would have said, "Who loves ya, baby?"

And Sergeant Erwin would have told you, "You're not guaranteed anything but one hour sleep a day and one meal."

Sergeant Erwin told me, "I was hard on you, Romeo, because when I first saw you, you reminded me of myself, and I decided you were going to be my kind of marine or nothing."

Staff Sergeant B. J. Erwin participated in operation Black Ferret on July 14, 1965, and died in a rain-soaked jungle in Southeast Asia twelve thousand miles away from his soft warm spot on this planet with his rifle in his hand, killing his country's enemies.

Sergeant Major B. T. Mills is presently a series master gunnery sergeant at Camp Lejeune, North Carolina, and will retire honorably in 1985.

First Sergeant S. S. Connors is the head enlisted man in charge of security for the marine guard detachment at the naval shipyard in Bremerton, Washington, and will retire in 1982.

Sergeant B. Whaley was not recommended for reenlistment in 1963 after pumping twenty rounds through the ceiling of the upstairs apartment and hitting his neighbor in the television, refrigerator, sofa, coffee table, and right kneecap. I have no idea where he is or what he is doing or even if he is alive. He served his time at hard labor and was discharged undesirably. I assume he was the way he was during my tour in boot camp because he was having marital problems. His wife ran off with the upstairs neighbor after he was released from the hospital and before Private Whaley was released from the brig. Whaley's wife is proof that everyone doesn't like the Marine Corps.

My mother was another one. She wrote several letters to the commandant of the Marine Corps after I was discharged, thank God, telling him what a terrible thing his organization had done to her once-sensitive boy. His only reply was he'd taken her boy and made a man and a marine out of him.

I'm forty now, and my mom is sixty-plus, and you know what, I'm my mom's favorite man now. There are three kinds of people in the world: marines, former marines, and people who wish they had been marines. Ask any marine. *Semper Fi.*

CPSIA information can be obtained
at www.ICGtesting.com
Printed in the USA
LVHW082348050619
620330LV00030B/808/P

9 781644 249024